Practical Real-Time Data Processing and Analytics

Distributed Computing and Event Processing using Apache Spark, Flink, Storm, and Kafka

Shilpi Saxena
Saurabh Gupta

BIRMINGHAM - MUMBAI

Practical Real-Time Data Processing and Analytics

First published: September 2017

Production reference: 1250917

Published by Packt Publishing Ltd.
Livery Place
35 Livery Street
Birmingham
B3 2PB, UK.
ISBN 978-1-78728-120-2

www.packtpub.com

Credits

Author
Shilpi Saxena
Saurabh Gupta

Copy Editor
Safis Editing

Reviewers
Ruben Oliva Ramos
Tomas Oliva
Prateek Bha

Project Coordinator
Nidhi Joshi

Commissioning Editor
Amey Varangaonkar

Proofreader
Safis Editing

Acquisition Editor
Tushar Gupta

Indexer
Tejal Daruwale Soni

Content Development Editor
Mayur Pawanikar

Graphics
Tania Dutta

Technical Editor
Karan Thakkar

Production Coordinator
Arvindkumar Gupta

About the Authors

Shilpi Saxena is an IT professional and also a technology evangelist. She is an engineer who has had exposure to various domains (machine to machine space, healthcare, telecom, hiring, and manufacturing). She has experience in all the aspects of conception and execution of enterprise solutions. She has been architecting, managing, and delivering solutions in the big data space for the last 3 years. She also handles a high-performance and geographically-distributed team of elite engineers.

Shilpi has more than 12 years (3 years in the big data space) of experience in the development and execution of various facets of enterprise solutions both in the products and services dimensions of the software industry. An engineer by degree and profession, she has worn varied hats, such as developer, technical leader, product owner, tech manager, and so on, and she has seen all the flavors that the industry has to offer. She has architected and worked through some of the pioneers' production implementations in Big Data on Storm and Impala with auto-scaling in AWS.

Shilpi also authored Real-time Analytics with Storm and Cassandra with Packt Publishing.

Saurabh Gupta is an software engineer who has worked aspects of software requirements, designing, execution, and delivery. Saurabh has more than 3 years of experience working in Big Data domain. Saurabh is handling and designing real time as well as batch processing projects running in production including technologies like Impala, Storm, NiFi, Kafka and deployment on AWS using Docker. Saurabh also worked in product development and delivery.

Saurabh has total 10 years (3+ years in big data) rich experience in IT industry. Saurabh has exposure in various IOT use-cases including Telecom, HealthCare, Smart city, Smart cars and so on.

About the Reviewers

Ruben Oliva Ramos is a computer systems engineer from Tecnologico de Leon Institute, with a master's degree in computer and electronic systems engineering, teleinformatics, and networking specialization from the University of Salle Bajio in Leon, Guanajuato, Mexico. He has more than 5 years of experience in developing web applications to control and monitor devices connected with Arduino and Raspberry Pi using web frameworks and cloud services to build the Internet of Things applications.

He is a mechatronics teacher at the University of Salle Bajio and teaches students of the master's degree in design and engineering of mechatronics systems. Ruben also works at Centro de Bachillerato Tecnologico Industrial 225 in Leon, Guanajuato, Mexico, teaching subjects such as electronics, robotics and control, automation, and microcontrollers at Mechatronics Technician Career; he is a consultant and developer for projects in areas such as monitoring systems and datalogger data using technologies (such as Android, iOS, Windows Phone, HTML5, PHP, CSS, Ajax, JavaScript, Angular, and ASP.NET), databases (such as SQlite, MongoDB, and MySQL), web servers (such as Node.js and IIS), hardware programming (such as Arduino, Raspberry pi, Ethernet Shield, GPS, and GSM/GPRS, ESP8266), and control and monitor systems for data acquisition and programming.

He has authored the book *Internet of Things Programming with JavaScript* by Packt Publishing. He is also involved in monitoring, controlling, and the acquisition of data with Arduino and Visual Basic .NET for Alfaomega.

I would like to thank my savior and lord, Jesus Christ, for giving me the strength and courage to pursue this project; my dearest wife, Mayte; our two lovely sons, Ruben and Dario; my dear father, Ruben; my dearest mom, Rosalia; my brother, Juan Tomas; and my sister, Rosalia, whom I love, for all their support while reviewing this book, for allowing me to pursue my dream, and tolerating not being with them after my busy day job.

Juan Tomás Oliva Ramos is an environmental engineer from the university of Guanajuato, Mexico, with a master's degree in administrative engineering and quality. He has more than 5 years of experience in management and development of patents, technological innovation projects, and development of technological solutions through the statistical control of processes. He has been a teacher of statistics, entrepreneurship, and technological development of projects since 2011. He became an entrepreneur mentor, and started a new department of technology management and entrepreneurship at instituto Tecnologico Superior de Purisima del Rincon.

Juan is a *Alfaomega*reviewer and has worked on the book *Wearable designs for Smart watches, Smart TVs and Android mobile devices.*

He has developed prototypes through programming and automation technologies for the improvement of operations, which have been registered for patents.

I want to thank God for giving me the wisdom and humility to review this book. I thank Packt for giving me the opportunity to review this amazing book and to collaborate with a group of committed people. I want to thank my beautiful wife, Brenda; our two magic princesses, Regina and Renata; and our next member, Angel Tadeo; all of you give me the strength, happiness, and joy to start a new day. Thanks for being my family

Prateek Bhati is currently working in Accenture. He has total experience of 4 years in real-time data processing and currently living in New Delhi. He completed his graduation from Amity University.

www.PacktPub.com

For support files and downloads related to your book, please visit www.PacktPub.com.

Did you know that Packt offers eBook versions of every book published, with PDF and ePub files available? You can upgrade to the eBook version at www.PacktPub.com and as a print book customer, you are entitled to a discount on the eBook copy. Get in touch with us at service@packtpub.com for more details.

At www.PacktPub.com, you can also read a collection of free technical articles, sign up for a range of free newsletters and receive exclusive discounts and offers on Packt books and eBooks.

https://www.packtpub.com/mapt

Get the most in-demand software skills with Mapt. Mapt gives you full access to all Packt books and video courses, as well as industry-leading tools to help you plan your personal development and advance your career.

Why subscribe?

- Fully searchable across every book published by Packt
- Copy and paste, print, and bookmark content
- On demand and accessible via a web browser

Customer Feedback

Thanks for purchasing this Packt book. At Packt, quality is at the heart of our editorial process. To help us improve, please leave us an honest review on this book's Amazon page at `https://www.amazon.com/dp/1787281205`.

If you'd like to join our team of regular reviewers, you can e-mail us at `customerreviews@packtpub.com`. We award our regular reviewers with free eBooks and videos in exchange for their valuable feedback. Help us be relentless in improving our products!

Table of Contents

Preface

This book will have basic to advanced recipes on real-time computing. We will cover technologies such as Flink, Spark and Storm. The book includes practical recipes to help you to process unbounded streams of data, thus doing for real-time processing what Hadoop did for batch processing. You will begin with setting up the development environment and proceed to implement stream processing. This will be followed by recipes on real-time problems using Rabbit-MQ, Kafka, and Nifi along with Storm, Spark, Flink, Beam, and more. By the end of this book, you will have gained a thorough understanding of the fundamentals of NRT and its applications, and be able to identify and apply those fundamentals to any suitable problem.

This book is written in a cookbook style, with plenty of practical recipes, well-explained code examples, and relevant screenshots and diagrams.

What this book covers

Section – A: Introduction – Getting Familiar

This section gives the readers basic familiarity with the real-time analytics spectra and domains. We talk about the basic components and their building blocks. This sections consist of the following chapters:

- Chapter 1: Introducing Real-Time Analytics
- Chapter 2: Real-Time Application – The Basic Ingredients

Section – B: Setup and Infrastructure

This section is predominantly setup-oriented, where we have the basic components set up. This sections consist of the following chapters:

- Chapter 3: Understanding and Tailing Data Streams
- Chapter 4: Setting Up the infrastructure for Storm
- Chapter 5: Configuring Apache Spark and Flink

Section – C: Storm Computations

This section predominantly focuses on exploring Storm, its compute capabilities, and its various features. This sections consist of the following chapters:

- Chapter 6: Integration of Source with Storm
- Chapter 7: From Storm to Sink
- Chapter 8: Storm Trident

Section – D: Using Spark Compute In Real Time

This section predominantly focuses on exploring Spark, its compute capabilities, and its various features. This sections consist of the following chapters:

- Chapter 9: Working with Spark
- Chapter 10: Working with Spark Operations
- Chapter 11: Spark Streaming

Section – E: Flink for Real-Time Analytics
This section focuses on exploring Flink, its compute capabilities, and its various features.

- Chapter 12: Working with Apache Flink

Section – F: Let's Have It Stringed Together

This sections consist of the following chapters:

- Chapter 13: Case Study 1

What you need for this book

The book is intended to graduate our readers into real-time streaming technologies. We expect the readers to have fundamental knowledge of Java and Scala. In terms of setup, we expect readers to have basic maven, Java, and Eclipse set up to run the examples.

Who this book is for

If you are a Java developer who would like to be equipped with all the tools required to devise an end-to-end practical solution on real-time data streaming, then this book is for you. Basic knowledge of real-time processing will be helpful, and knowing the fundamentals of Maven, Shell, and Eclipse would be great.

Conventions

In this book, you will find a number of text styles that distinguish between different kinds of information. Here are some examples of these styles and an explanation of their meaning. Code words in text, database table names, folder names, filenames, file extensions, path names, dummy URLs, user input, and Twitter handles are shown as follows: "Once the `kafka_2.11-0.10.1.1.tgz` file is downloaded, extract the files."

A block of code is set as follows:

```
cp kafka_2.11-0.10.1.1.tgz /home/ubuntu/demo/kafka
cd /home/ubuntu/demo/kafka
tar -xvf kafka_2.11-0.10.1.1.tgz
```

New terms and **important words** are shown in bold. Words that you see on the screen, for example, in menus or dialog boxes, appear in the text like this: "In order to download new modules, we will go to **Files** | **Settings** | **Project Name** | **Project Interpreter**."

Warnings or important notes appear like this.

Tips and tricks appear like this.

Reader feedback

Feedback from our readers is always welcome. Let us know what you think about this book-what you liked or disliked. Reader feedback is important for us as it helps us develop titles that you will really get the most out of. To send us general feedback, simply email feedback@packtpub.com, and mention the book's title in the subject of your message. If there is a topic that you have expertise in and you are interested in either writing or contributing to a book, see our author guide at www.packtpub.com/authors.

Customer support

Now that you are the proud owner of a Packt book, we have a number of things to help you to get the most from your purchase.

Downloading the example code

You can download the example code files for this book from your account at http://www.packtpub.com. If you purchased this book elsewhere, you can visit http://www.packtpub.com/support and register to have the files emailed directly to you. You can download the code files by following these steps:

1. Log in or register to our website using your email address and password.
2. Hover the mouse pointer on the **SUPPORT** tab at the top.
3. Click on **Code Downloads & Errata**.
4. Enter the name of the book in the **Search** box.
5. Select the book for which you're looking to download the code files.
6. Choose from the drop-down menu where you purchased this book from.
7. Click on **Code Download**.

Once the file is downloaded, please make sure that you unzip or extract the folder using the latest version of:

- WinRAR / 7-Zip for Windows
- Zipeg / iZip / UnRarX for Mac
- 7-Zip / PeaZip for Linux

The code bundle for the book is also hosted on GitHub at
`https://github.com/PacktPublishing/Practical-Real-time-Processing-and-Analytics`. We also have other code bundles from our rich catalog of books and videos available at `https://github.com/PacktPublishing/`. Check them out!

Errata

Although we have taken every care to ensure the accuracy of our content, mistakes do happen. If you find a mistake in one of our books-maybe a mistake in the text or the code-we would be grateful if you could report this to us. By doing so, you can save other readers from frustration and help us improve subsequent versions of this book. If you find any errata, please report them by visiting `http://www.packtpub.com/submit-errata`, selecting your book, clicking on the **Errata Submission Form** link, and entering the details of your errata. Once your errata are verified, your submission will be accepted and the errata will be uploaded to our website or added to any list of existing errata under the Errata section of that title. To view the previously submitted errata, go to
`https://www.packtpub.com/books/content/support` and enter the name of the book in the search field. The required information will appear under the **Errata** section.

Piracy

Piracy of copyrighted material on the internet is an ongoing problem across all media. At Packt, we take the protection of our copyright and licenses very seriously. If you come across any illegal copies of our works in any form on the internet, please provide us with the location address or website name immediately so that we can pursue a remedy. Please contact us at `copyright@packtpub.com` with a link to the suspected pirated material. We appreciate your help in protecting our authors and our ability to bring you valuable content.

Questions

If you have a problem with any aspect of this book, you can contact us at `questions@packtpub.com`, and we will do our best to address the problem.

1
Introducing Real-Time Analytics

This chapter sets the context for the reader by providing an overview of the big data technology landscape in general and real–time analytics in particular. This provides an outline for the book conceptually, with an attempt to ignite the spark for inquisitiveness that will encourage readers to undertake the rest of the journey through the book.

The following topics will be covered:

- What is big data?
- Big data infrastructure
- Real–time analytics – the myth and the reality
- Near real–time solution – an architecture that works
- Analytics – a plethora of possibilities
- IOT – thoughts and possibilities
- Cloud – considerations for NRT and IOT

What is big data?

Well to begin with, in simple terms, big data helps us deal with three V's – volume, velocity, and variety. Recently, two more V's were added to it, making it a five–dimensional paradigm; they are *veracity* and *value*

- **Volume**: This dimension refers to the amount of data; look around you, huge amounts of data are being generated every second – it may be the email you send, Twitter, Facebook, or other social media, or it can just be all the videos, pictures, SMS messages, call records, and data from varied devices and sensors. We have scaled up the data–measuring metrics to terabytes, zettabytes and Yottabytes – they are all humongous figures. Look at Facebook alone; it's like ~10 billion messages on a day, consolidated across all users. We have ~5 billion likes a day and around ~400 million photographs are uploaded each day. Data statistics in terms of volume are startling; all of the data generated from the beginning of time to 2008 is kind of equivalent to what we generate in a day today, and I am sure soon it will be an hour. This volume aspect alone is making the traditional database dwarf to store and process this amount of data in reasonable and useful time frames, though a big data stack can be employed to store process and compute on amazingly large data sets in a cost–effective, distributed, and reliably efficient manner.

- **Velocity**: This refers to the data generation speed, or the rate at which data is being generated. In today's world, where we mentioned that the volume of data has undergone a tremendous surge, this aspect is not lagging behind. We have loads of data because we are able to generate it so fast. Look at social media; things are circulated in seconds and they become viral, and the insight from social media is analysed in milliseconds by stock traders, and that can trigger lots of activity in terms of buying or selling. At a target point of sale counter it takes a few seconds for a credit card swipe, and within that fraudulent transaction processing, payment, bookkeeping, and acknowledgement is all done. Big data gives us the power to analyse the data at tremendous speed.

- **Variety**: This dimension tackles the fact that the data can be unstructured. In the traditional database world, and even before that, we were used to having a very structured form of data that fitted neatly into tables. Today, more than 80% of data is unstructured – quotable examples are photos, video clips, social media updates, data from variety of sensors, voice recordings, and chat conversations. Big data lets you store and process this unstructured data in a very structured manner; in fact, it effaces the variety.

- **Veracity**: It's all about validity and correctness of data. How accurate and usable is the data? Not everything out of millions and zillions of data records is corrected, accurate, and referable. That's what actual veracity is: how trustworthy the data is and what the quality of the data is. Examples of data with veracity include Facebook and Twitter posts with nonstandard acronyms or typos. Big data has brought the ability to run analytics on this kind of data to the table. One of the strong reasons for the volume of data is veracity.

- **Value**: This is what the name suggests: the value that the data actually holds. It is unarguably the most important V or dimension of big data. The only motivation for going towards big data for processing super large data sets is to derive some valuable insight from it. In the end, it's all about cost and benefits.

Big data is a much talked about technology across businesses and the technical world today. There are myriad domains and industries that are convinced of its usefulness, but the implementation focus is primarily application-oriented, rather than infrastructure-oriented. The next section predominantly walks you through the same.

Big data infrastructure

Before delving further into big data infrastructure, let's have a look at the big data high–level landscape.

The following figure captures high–level segments that demarcate the big data space:

Segments	Example
Vertical Apps	Predictive policing, BloomReach, Myrrix
Ad/Media Apps	Media Science, Turn, Recorded Future
Data as a service	Factual, Gnip, Kaggle
Business Intelligence	Oracle, SAP, IBM
Log Data Apps	Splunk, Loggly, Sumo Logic
Analytics Infrastructure	Hortonworks, Cloudera, DataStax
Operational Infrastructure	Couchbase, Teradata, Hadapt
IaaS	Amazon web services, Microsoft Windows Azure, Google Cloud Platform
Technologies	Apache Hadoop, Apache HBase, Apache Cassandra
Structured Databases	Microsoft SQL Server, MySQL, PostgreSQL

It clearly depicts the various segments and verticals within the big data technology canvas (bottom up).

The key is the bottom layer that holds the data in scalable and distributed mode:

- **Technologies**: Hadoop, MapReduce, Mahout, Hbase, Cassandra, and so on
- Then, the next level is the infrastructure framework layer that enables the developers to choose from myriad infrastructural offerings depending upon the use case and its solution design
- **Analytical Infrastructure**: EMC, Netezza, Vertica, Cloudera, Hortonworks
- **Operational Infrastructure**: Couchbase, Teradata, Informatica and many more
- **Infrastructure as a service (IAAS)**: AWS, Google cloud and many more
- **Structured Databases**: Oracle, SQLServer, MySQL, Sybase and many more
- The next level specializes in catering to very specific needs in terms of
- **Data As A Service (DaaS)**: Kaggale, Azure, Factual and many more
- **Business Intelligence (BI)**: Qlikview, Cognos, SAP BO and many more
- **Analytics and Visualizations**: Pentaho, Tableau, Tibco and many more

Today, we see traditional robust RDBMS struggling to survive in a cost–effective manner as a tool for data storage and processing. The scaling of traditional RDBMS, at the compute power expected to process huge amount of data with low latency came at a very high price. This led to the emergence of new technologies, which were low cost, low latency, highly scalable at low cost/open source. To our rescue comes *The Yellow Elephant—Hadoop* that took the data storage and computation arena by surprise. It's designed and developed as a distributed framework for data storage and computation on commodity hardware in a highly reliable and scalable manner. The key computational methodology Hadoop works on involves distributing the data in chunks over all the nodes in a cluster, and then processing the data concurrently on all the nodes.

Now that you are acquainted with the basics of big data and the key segments of the big data technology landscape, let's take a deeper look at the big data concept with the Hadoop framework as an example. Then, we will move on to take a look at the architecture and methods of implementing a Hadoop cluster; this will be a close analogy to high–level infrastructure and the typical storage requirements for a big data cluster. One of the key and critical aspect that we will delve into is information security in the context of big data.

A couple of key aspects that drive and dictate the move to big data infraspace are highlighted in the following figure:

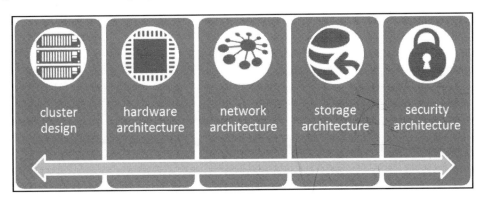

- **Cluster design**: This is the most significant and deciding aspect for infrastructural planning. The cluster design strategy of the infrastructure is basically the backbone of the solution; the key deciding elements for the same are the application use cases and requirements, workload, resource computation (depending upon memory intensive and compute intensive computations), and security considerations.

  Apart from compute, memory, and network utilization, another very important aspect to be considered is storage which will be either cloud–based or on the premises. In terms of the cloud, the option could be public, private, or hybrid, depending upon the consideration and requirements of use case and the organization

- **Hardware architecture**: A lot on the storage cost aspect is driven by the volume of the data to be stored, archival policy, and the longevity of the data. The decisive factors are as follows:
    - The computational needs of the implementations (whether the commodity components would suffice, or if the need is for high–performance GPUs).
    - What are the memory needs? Are they low, moderate, or high? This depends upon the in–memory computation needs of the application implementations.

- **Network architecture**: This may not sound important, but it is a significant driver in big data computational space. The reason is that the key aspect for big data is distributed computation, and thus, network utilization is much higher than what would have been in the case of a single–server, monolithic implementation. In distributed computation, loads of data and intermediate compute results travel over the network; thus, the network bandwidth becomes the throttling agent for the overall solution and depending on key aspect for selection of infrastructure strategy. Bad design approaches sometimes lead to network chokes, where data spends less time in processing but more in shuttling across the network or waiting to be transferred over the wire for the next step in execution.

- **Security architecture**: Security is a very important aspect of any application space, in big data, it becomes all the more significant due to the volume and diversity of the data, and due to network traversal of the data owing to the compute methodologies. The aspect of the cloud computing and storage options adds further needs to the complexity of being a critical and strategic aspect of big data infraspace.

Real–time analytics – the myth and the reality

One of the biggest truths about the real–time analytics is that nothing is actually real–time; it's a myth. In reality, it's close to real–time. Depending upon the performance and ability of a solution and the reduction of operational latencies, the analytics could be close to real–time, but, while day-by-day we are bridging the gap between real–time and near–real–time, it's practically impossible to eliminate the gap due to computational, operational, and network latencies.

Before we go further, let's have a quick overview of what the high–level expectations from these so called real–time analytics solutions are. The following figure captures the high–level intercept of the same, where, in terms of data we are looking for a system that could process millions of transactions with a variety of structured and unstructured data sets. My processing engine should be ultra–fast and capable of handling very complex joined-up and diverse business logic, and at the end, it is also expected to generate astonishingly accurate reports, revert to my ad–hoc queries in a split–second, and render my visualizations and dashboards with no latency:

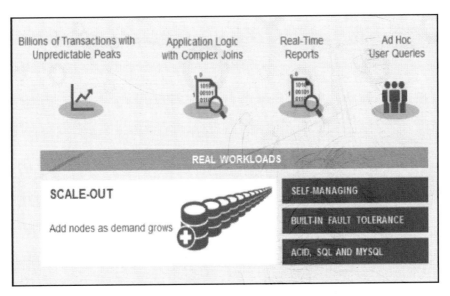

As if the previous aspects of the expectations from the real–time solutions were not sufficient, to have them rolling out to production, one of the basic expectations in today's data generating and zero downtime era, is that the system should be self–managed/managed with minimalistic efforts and it should be inherently built in a fault tolerant and auto–recovery manner for handling most if not all scenarios. It should also be able to provide my known basic SQL kind of interface in similar/close format.

However outrageously ridiculous the previous expectations sound, they are perfectly normal and minimalistic expectation from any big data solution of today. Nevertheless, coming back to our topic of real–time analytics, now that we have touched briefly upon the system level expectations in terms of data, processing and output, the systems are being devised and designed to process zillions of transactions and apply complex data science and machine learning algorithms on the fly, to compute the results as close to real time as possible. The new term being used is close to real–time/near real–time or human real–time. Let's dedicate a moment to having a look at the following figure that captures the concept of computation time and the context and significance of the final insight:

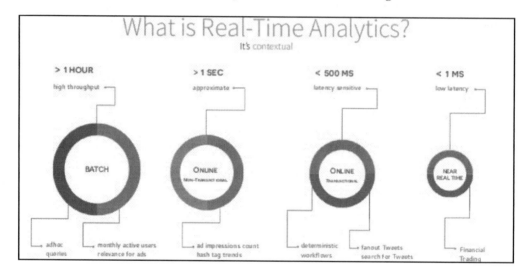

As evident in the previous figure, in the context of time:

- Ad–hoc queries over zeta bytes of data take up computation time in the order of hour(s) and are thus typically described as batch. The noteworthy aspect being depicted in the previous figure with respect to the size of the circle is that it is an analogy to capture the size of the data being processed in diagrammatic form.
- **Ad impressions/Hashtag trends/deterministic workflows/tweets**: These use cases are predominantly termed as online and the compute time is generally in the order of 500ms/1 second. Though the compute time is considerably reduced as compared to previous use cases, the data volume being processed is also significantly reduced. It would be very rapidly arriving data stream of a few GBs in magnitude.
- **Financial tracking/mission critical applications**: Here, the data volume is low, the data arrival rate is extremely high, the processing is extremely high, and low latency compute results are yielded in time windows of a few milliseconds.

Apart from the computation time, there are other significant differences between batch and real–time processing and solution designing:

Batch processing	Real–time processing
Data is at rest	Data is in motion
Batch size is bounded	Data is essentially coming in as a stream and is un–bounded
Access to entire data	Access to data in current transaction/sliding window
Data processed in batches	Processing is done at event, window, or at the most at micro batch level
Efficient, easier administration	Real–time insights, but systems are fragile as compared to batch

Towards the end of this section, all I would like to emphasis is that a **near real–time** (**NRT**) solution is as close to true real–time as it is practically possible attain. So, as said, RT is actually a myth (or hypothetical) while NRT is a reality. We deal with and see NRT applications on a daily basis in terms of connected vehicles, prediction and recommendation engines, health care, and wearable appliances.

There are some critical aspects that actually introduce latency to total turnaround time, or TAT as we call it. It's actually the time lapse between occurrences of an event to the time actionable insight is generated out of it.

- The data/events generally travel from diverse geographical locations over the wire (internet/telecom channels) to the processing hub. There is some time lapsed in this activity.
- Processing:
    - **Data landing**: Due to security aspects, data generally lands on an edge node and is then ingested into the cluster
    - **Data cleansing**: The data veracity aspect needs to be catered for, to eliminate bad/incorrect data before processing
    - **Data massaging and enriching**: Binding and enriching transnational data with dimensional data

- Actual processing
- Storing the results
    - All previous aspects of processing incur:
        - CPU cycles
        - Disk I/O
        - Network I/O
        - Active marshaling and un–marshalling of data serialization aspects.

So, now that we understand the reality of real–time analytics, let's look a little deeper into the architectural segments of such solutions.

Near real–time solution – an architecture that works

In this section, we will learn about what all architectural patterns are possible to build a scalable, sustainable, and robust real–time solution.

A high–level NRT solution recipe looks very straight and simple, with a data collection funnel, a distributed processing engine, and a few other ingredients like in–memory cache, stable storage, and dashboard plugins.

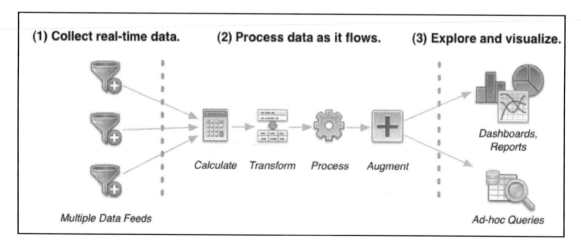

(1) Collect real-time data.   **(2) Process data as it flows.**   **(3) Explore and visualize.**

Calculate Transform Process Augment

Multiple Data Feeds

Dashboards, Reports

Ad-hoc Queries

At a high level, the basic analytics process can be segmented into three shards, which are depicted well in previous figure:

- Real–time data collection of the streaming data
- Distributed high–performance computation on flowing data
- Exploring and visualizing the generated insights in the form of query–able consumable layer/dashboards

If we delve a level deeper, there are two contending proven streaming computation technologies on the market, which are Storm and Spark. In the coming section we will take a deeper look at a high–level NRT solution that's derived from these stacks.

NRT – The Storm solution

This solution captures the high–level streaming data in real–time and routes it through some Queue/broker: Kafka or **RabbitMQ.** Then, the distributed processing part is handled through Storm topology, and once the insights are computed, they can be written to a fast write data store like Cassandra or some other queue like Kafka for further real–time downstream processing:

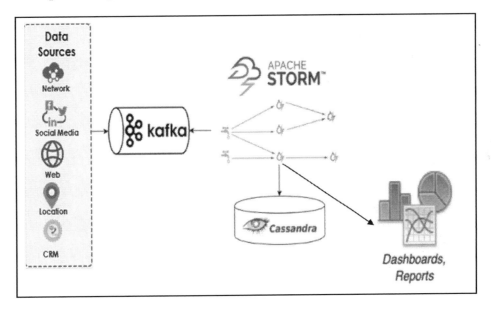

As per the figure, we collect real–time streaming data from diverse data sources, through push/pull collection agents like Flume, Logstash, FluentD, or Kafka adapters. Then, the data is written to Kafka partitions, Storm topologies pull/read the streaming data from Kafka and processes this flowing data in its topology, and writes the insights/results to Cassandra or some other real–time dashboards.

NRT – The Spark solution

At a very high–level, the data flow pipeline with Spark is very similar to the Storm architecture depicted in the previous figure, but one the most critical aspects of this flow is that Spark leverages HDFS as a distributed storage layer. Here, have a look before we get into further dissection of the overall flow and its nitty–gritty:

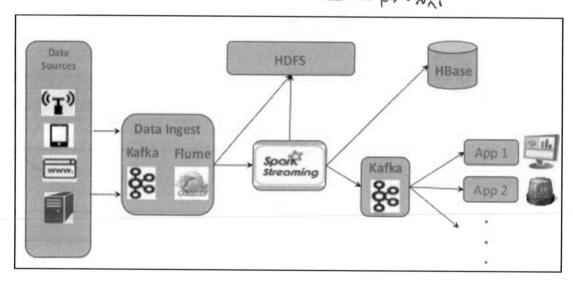

As with a typical real–time analytic pipeline, we ingest the data using one of the streaming data grabbing agents like Flume or Logstash. We introduce Kafka to ensure decoupling into the system between the sources agents. Then, we have the Spark streaming component that provides a distributed computing platform for processing the data, before we dump the results to some stable storage unit, dashboard, or Kafka queue.

One essential difference between previous two architectural paradigms is that, while Storm is essentially a real–time transactional processing engine that is, by default, good at processing the incoming data event by event, Spark works on the concept of micro–batching. It's essentially a pseudo real–time compute engine, where close to real–time compute expectations can be met by reducing the micro batch size. Storm is essentially designed for lightning fast processing, thus all transformations are in memory because any disk operation generates latency; this feature is a boon and bane for Storm (because memory is volatile if things break, everything has to be reworked and intermediate results are lost). On the other hand, Spark is essentially backed up by HDFS and is robust and more fault tolerant, as intermediaries are backed up in HDFS.

Over the last couple of years, big data applications have seen a brilliant shift as per the following sequence:

1. Batch only applications (early Hadoop implementations)
2. Streaming only (early Storm implementations)
3. Could be both (custom made combinations of the previous two)
4. Should be both (Lambda architecture)

Now, the question is: *why did the above evolution take place?* Well, the answer is that, when folks were first acquainted with the power of Hadoop, they really liked building the applications which could process virtually any amount of data and could scale up to any level in a seamless, fault tolerant, non–disruptive way. Then we moved to an era where people realized the power of now and ambitious processing became the need, with the advent of scalable, distributed processing engines like Storm. Storm was scalable and came with lighting–fast processing power and guaranteed processing. But then, something changed; we realized the limitations and strengths of both Hadoop batch systems and Storm real–time systems: the former were catering to my appetite for volume and the latter was excellent at velocity. My real–time applications were perfect, but they were performing over a small window of the entire data set and did not have any mechanism for correction of data/results at some later time. Conversely, while my Hadoop implementations were accurate and robust, they took a long time to arrive at any conclusive insight. We reached a point where we replicated complete/part solutions to arrive at a solution involving the combination of both batch and real–time implementations. One of the very recent NRT architectural patterns is Lambda architecture, which is a most sought after solution that combines the best of both batch and real–time implementations, without having any need to replicate and maintain two solutions. It gives me volume and velocity, which is an edge over earlier architecture, and it can cater to a wider set of use cases.

Lambda architecture – analytics possibilities

Now that we have introduced this wonderful architectural pattern, let's take a closer look at it before delving into the possible analytic use cases that can be implemented with this new pattern.

We all know that, at base level, Hadoop gives me vast storage, and has HDFS and a very robust processing engine in the form of MapReduce, which can handle a humongous amount of data and can perform myriad computations. However, it has a long **turnaround time (TAT)** and it's a batch system that helps us cope with the volume aspect of big data. If we need speed and velocity for processing and are looking for a low–latency solution, we have to resort to a real–time processing engine that could quickly process the latest or the recent data and derive quick insights that are actionable in the current time frame. But along with velocity and quick TAT, we also need newer data to be progressively integrated into the batch system for deep batch analytics that are required to execute on entire data sets. So, essentially we land in a situation where I need both batch and real–time systems, the optimal architectural combination of this pattern is called Lambda architecture (λ).

The following figure captures the high–level design of this pattern:

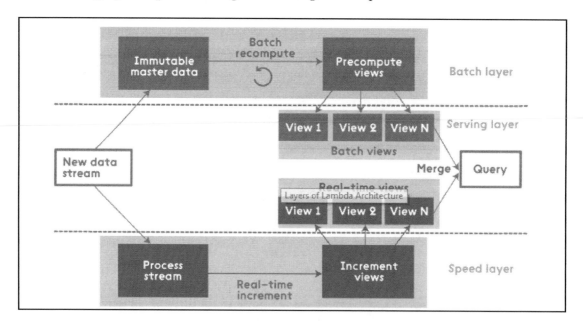

The solution is both technology and language agnostic; at a high–level it has the following three layers:

- The batch layer
- The speed layer
- The serving layer

The input data is fed to both the batch and speed layers, where the batch layer works at creating the precomputed views of the entire immutable master data. This layer is predominately an immutable data store with write once and many bulk reads.

The speed layer handles the recent data and maintains only incremental views over the recent set of the data. This layer has both random reads and writes in terms of data accessibility.

The crux of the puzzle lies in the intelligence of the serving layer, where the data from both the batch and speed layers is merged and the queries are catered for, so we get the best of both the worlds seamlessly. The close to real–time requests are handled from the data from the incremental views (they have low retention policy) from the speed layer while the queries referencing the older data are catered to by the master data views generated in the batch layer. This layer caters only to random reads and no random writes, though it does handle batch computations in the form of queries and joins and bulk writes.

However, Lambda architecture is not a one-stop solution for all hybrid use cases; there are some key aspects that need to be taken care of:

- Always think distributed
- Account and plan for failures
- Rule of thumb: data is immutable
- Finally, plan for failures

Now that we have acquainted ourselves well with the prevalent architectural patterns in real–time analytics, let us talk about the use cases that are possible in this segment:

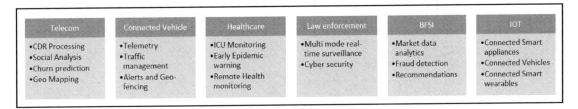

The preceding figure highlights the high–level domains and various key use cases that may be executed.

IOT – thoughts and possibilities

The Internet of Things: the term that was coined in 1999 by *Kevin Ashton,* has become one of the most promising door openers of the decade. Although we had an IoT precursor in the form of M2M and instrumentation control for industrial automation, the way IoT and the era of connected smart devices has arrived, is something that has never happened before. The following figure will give you a birds–eye view of the vastness and variety of the reach of IoT applications:

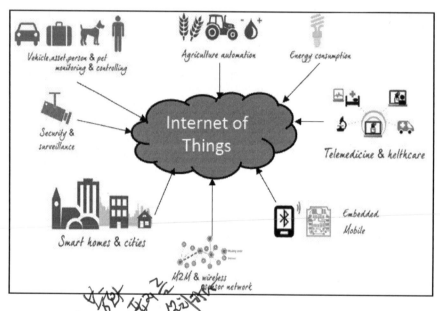

We are all surrounded by devices that are smart and connected; they have the ability to sense, process, transmit, and even act, based on their processing. The age of machines that was a science fiction a few years ago has become reality. I have connected vehicles that can sense and get un–locked/locked if I walk to them or away from them with keys. I have proximity sensing beacons in my supermarkets which sense my proximity to shelf and flash the offers to my cell phone. I have smart ACs that regulate the temperature based on the number of people in the room. My smart offices save electricity by switching the lights and ACs off in empty conference rooms. The list seems to be endless and growing every second.

At the heart of it IoT, is nothing but an ecosystem of connected devices which have the ability to communicate over the internet. Here, devices/things could be anything, like a sensor device, a person with a wearable, a place, a plant, an animal, a machine – well, virtually any physical item you could think of on this planet can be connected today. There are predominantly seven layers to any IoT platform; these are depicted and described in the following figure:

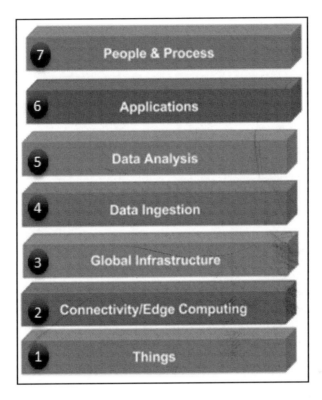

Following is quick description of all the 7 IoT application layers:

- **Layer 1**: Devices, sensors, controllers and so on
- **Layer 2**: Communication channels, network protocols and network elements, the communication, and routing hardware — telecom, Wi–Fi, and satellite
- **Layer 3**: Infrastructure — it could be in-house or on the cloud (public, private, or hybrid)

- **Layer 4**: Here comes the big data ingestion layer, the landing platform where the data from things/devices is collected for the next steps
- **Layer 5**: The processing engine that does the cleansing, parsing, massaging, and analysis of the data using complex processing, machine learning, artificial intelligence, and so on, to generate insights in form of reports, alerts, and notifications
- **Layer 6**: Custom apps, the pluggable secondary interfaces like visualization dashboards, downstream applications, and so on form part of this layer
- **Layer 7**: This is the layer that has the people and processes that actually act on the insights and recommendations generated from the following systems

At an architectural level, a basic reference architecture of an IOT application is depicted in the following image:

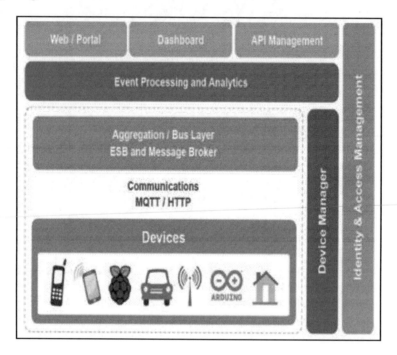

In the previous figure, if we start with a bottom up approach, the lowest layers are devices that are sensors or sensors powered by computational units like RaspberryPi or Ardunio. The communication and data transference is generally, at this point, governed by lightweight options like **Messaging Queue Telemetry Transport (MQTT)** and **Constrained Application protocol (CoAP)** which are fast replacing the legacy options like HTTP. This layer is actually in conjunction to the aggregation or bus layer, which is essentially a Mosquitto broker and forms the event transference layer from source, that is, from the device to the processing hub. Once we reach the processing hub, we have all the data at the compute engine ready to be swamped into action and we can analyse and process the data to generate useful actionable insights. These insights are further integrated to web service API consumable layers for downstream applications. Apart from these horizontal layers, there are cross–cutting layers which handle the device provisioning and device management, identity and access management layer.

Now that we understand the high–level architecture and layers for standard IoT application, the next step is to understand the key aspects where an IoT solution is constrained and what the implications are on overall solution design:

- **Security**: This is a key concern area for the entire data-driven solution segment, but the concept of big data and devices connected to the internet makes the entire system more susceptible to hacking and vulnerable in terms of security, thus making it a strategic concern area to be addressed while designing the solution at all layers for data at rest and in motion.
- **Power consumption/battery life**: We are devising solutions for devices and not human beings; thus, the solutions we design for them should be of very low power consumption overall without taxing or draining battery life.
- **Connectivity and communication**: The devices, unlike humans, are always connected and can be very chatty. Here again, we need a lightweight protocol for overall communication aspects for low latency data transfer.
- **Recovery from failures**: These solutions are designed to run for billions of data process and in a self–sustaining 24/7 mode. The solution should be built with the capability to diagnose the failures, apply back pressure and then self–recover from the situation with minimal data loss. Today, IoT solutions are being designed to handle sudden spikes of data, by detecting a latency/bottle neck and having the ability to auto–scale–up and down elastically.
- **Scalability**: The solutions need to be designed in a mode that its linearly scalable without the need to re–architect the base framework or design, the reason being that this domain is exploding with an unprecedented and un–predictable number of devices being connected with a whole plethora of future use cases which are just waiting to happen.

Next are the implications of the previous constraints of the IoT application framework, which surface in the form of communication channels, communication protocols, and processing adapters.

In terms of communication channel providers, the IoT ecosystem is evolving from telecom channels and LTEs to options like:

- Direct Ethernet/WiFi/3G
- **LoRA**
- **Bluetooth Low Energy (BLE)**
- **RFID/Near Field communication (NFC)**
- Medium range radio mesh networks like Zigbee

For communication protocols, the de–facto standard that is on the board as of now is MQTT, and the reasons for its wide usage are evident:

- It is extremely light weight
- It has very low footprint in terms of network utilization, thus making the communication very fast and less taxing
- It comes with a guaranteed delivery mechanism, ensuing that the data will eventually be delivered, even over fragile networks
- It has low power consumption
- It optimizes the flow of data packets over the wire to achieve low latency and lower footprints
- It is a bi–directional protocol, and thus is suited both for transferring data from the device as well as transferring the data to the device
- Its better suited for a situation in which we have to transmit a high volume of short messages over the wire

Edge analytics

Post evolution and IOT revolution, edge analytics are another significant game changer. If you look at IOT applications, the data from the sensors and devices needs to be collated and travels all the way to the distributed processing unit, which is either on the premises or on the cloud. This lift and shift of data leads to significant network utilization; it makes the overall solution latent to transmission delays.

These considerations led to the development of a new kind of solution and in turn a new arena of IOT computations — the term is edge analytics and, as the name suggests, it's all about pushing the processing to the edge, so that the data is processed at its source.

The following figure shows the bifurcation of IOT into:

- Edge analytics
- Core analytics

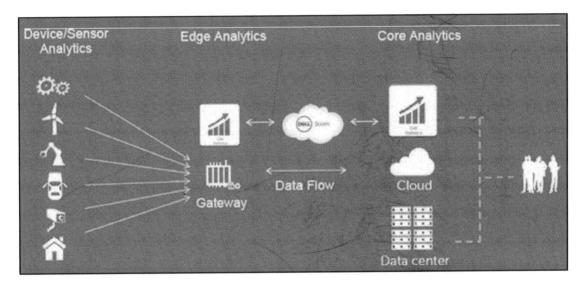

As depicted in the previous figure, the IOT computation is now divided into segments, as follows:

- **Sensor–level edge analytics**: Wherein data is processed and some insights are derived at the device level itself
- **Edge analytics**: These are the analytics wherein the data is processed and insights are derived at the gateway level
- **Core analytics**: This flavour of analytics requires all data to arrive at a common compute engine (distributed storage and distributed computation) and then the high–complexity processing is done to derive actionable insights for people and processes

Some of the typical use cases for sensor/edge analytics are:

- **Industrial IOT (IIOT)**: The sensors are embedded in various pieces of equipment, machinery, and sometimes even shop floors. The sensors generate data and the devices have the innate capability to process the data and generate alerts/recommendations to improve the performance or yield.

- **IoT in health care**: Smart devices can participate in edge processing and can contribute to detection of early warning signs and raise alerts for appropriate medical situations

- In the world of wearable devices, edge processing can make tracking and safety very easy

Today, If I look around, my world is surrounded by connected devices—like my smart AC, my smart refrigerator, and smart TV; they all send out the data to a central hub or my mobile phone and are easily controllable from there. Now, the things are actually getting smart; they are evolving from being connected, to being smart enough to compute, process, and predict. For instance, my coffee maker is smart enough to be connected to my car traffic, my office timing, so that it predicts my daily routine and my arrival time and has hot fresh coffee ready the moment I need it.

Cloud – considerations for NRT and IOT

Cloud is nothing but a term used to identify a capability where computational capability is available over internet. We have all been acquainted with physical machines, servers, and data centres. The advent of the cloud has taken us to a world of virtualization where we are moving out to virtual nodes, virtualized clusters, and even virtual data centers. Now, I can have virtualization of hardware to play with and have my clusters built using VMs spawned over a few actual machines. So, it's like having software at play over physical hardware. The next step was the cloud, where we have all virtual compute capability hosted and available over the net.

The services that are part of the cloud bouquet are:

- **Infrastructure as a Service (IaaS)**: It's basically a cloud variant of fundamental physical computers. It actually replaces the actual machines, the servers and hardware storage and the networking by a virtualization layer operating over the net. The IaaS lets you build this entire virtual infrastructure, where it's actually software that's imitating actual hardware.

- **Platform as a Service (PaaS)**: Once we have sorted out the hardware virtualization part, the next obvious step is to think about the next layer that operates over the raw computer hardware. This is the one that gels the programs with components like databases, servers, file storage, and so on. Here, for instance, if a database is exposed as PaaS then the programmer can use that as a service without worrying about the lower details like storage capacity, data protection, encryption, replication, and so on. Renowned examples of PaaS are Google App Engine and Heroku.
- **Software as a Service (SaaS)**: This one is the topmost layer in the stack of cloud computation; it's actually the layer that provides the solution as a service. These services are charged on a per user or per month basis and this model ensures that the end users have flexibility to enroll for and use the service without any license fee or locking period. Some of the most widely known, and typical, examples are `Salesforce.com`, and Google Apps.

Now that we have been introduced to and acquainted with cloud, the next obvious point to understand is what this buzz is all about and why is it that the advent of the cloud is closing curtains on the era of traditional data centers. Let's understand some of the key benefits of cloud computing that have actually made this platform a hot selling cake for NRT and IOT applications

- **It's on demand**: The users can provision the computing components/resources as per the need and load. There is no need to make huge investments for the next X years on infrastructure in the name of future scaling and headroom. One can provision a cluster that's adequate to meet current requirements and that can then be scaled when needed by requesting more on–demand instances. So, the guarantee I get here as a user, is that I will get an instance when I demand for the same.
- It lets us build truly elastic applications, which means that depending upon the load and the need, my deployments can scale up and scale down. This is a huge advantage and the way the cloud does it is very cost effective too. If I have an application which sees an occasional surge in traffic on the first of every month, then, on the cloud I don't have to provision the hardware required to meet the demand of surge on the first of the month for the entire 30 days. Instead, I can provision what I need on an average day and build a mechanism to scale up my cluster to meet the surge on the first and then automatically scale back to average size on the second of the month.

- It's pay as you go: well, this is the most interesting feature of the cloud that beats the traditional hardware provisioning system, where to set up a data centers one has to plan up front for a huge investment. Cloud data centre, don't invite any such cost and one can pay only for the instances that are running, and that too, is generally handled on an hourly basis.

Summary

In this chapter we have discussed various aspects of the big data technology landscape and big data as an infrastructure and computation candidate. We walked the reader through various considerations and caveats to be taken into account while designing and deciding upon the big data infrastructural space. We had our uses introduced to reality of real–time analytics, the NRT architecture, and also touched upon the vast variety of use cases which can possibly be addressed by harnessing the power of IOT and NRT. Towards the end of the chapter, we briefly touched upon the concept of edge computing and cloud infrastructure for IOT.

In the next chapter, we will have the readers moving a little deeper into the real–time analytical application, architecture, and concepts. We will touch upon the basic building blocks of an NRT application, the technology stack required and the challenges encountered while developing it.

2
Real Time Applications – The Basic Ingredients

This chapter gets you acquainted with the basic building blocks of **near real-time** (**NRT**) systems. We introduce you to a high-level logical, physical, and technical view of such applications, and will touch upon various technology choices for each building block of the system:

- NRT system and its building blocks
- Data Collection
- Stream processing
- Analytical layer – serve it to the end user
- NRT – high-level system views
- NRT – technology views

The NRT system and its building blocks

The first and foremost question that strikes us here is "when do we call an application an NRT application?" The simple and straightforward answer to this is a software application that is able to consume, process, and generate results very close to real-time; that is, the lapse between the time the event occurred to the time results arrived is very small, an order of a few nanoseconds to at most a couple of seconds.

It's very important to understand the key aspects where the traditional monolithic application systems are falling short to serve the need of the hour:

- **Backend DB**: Single point monolithic data access.
- **Ingestion flow**: The pipelines are complex and tend to induce latency in end to end flow.
- **Failure & Recovery**: The Systems are failure prone, but the recovery approach is difficult and complex.
- **Synchronization and state capture**: It's very difficult to capture and maintain the state of facts and transactions in the system. Getting diversely distributed systems and real-time system failures further complicates the design and maintenance of such systems.

The answer to the previous issues is an architecture that supports streaming and thus provides its end users access to actionable insights in real-time over forever flowing in streams of real-time fact data. Couple of challenges to think through by design of a stream processing system and captured in in the following points:

- Local state and consistency of the system for large scale high velocity systems
- Data doesn't arrive at intervals, it keeps flowing in, and it's streaming in all the time
- No single state of truth in the form of backend database, instead the applications subscribe or tap into the stream of fact data

Before we delve further, it's worthwhile understanding the notation of time:

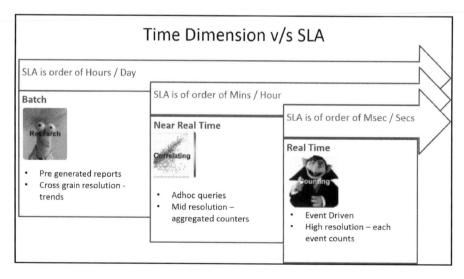

The image has made it, very clear to correlate the SLAs with each type of implementation (batch, near real-time, and real-time) and the kinds of use cases each implementation caters for. For instance, batch implementations have SLAs ranging from a couple of hours to days and such solutions are predominantly deployed for canned/pre-generated reports and trends. The real-time solutions have an SLA magnitude of a few seconds to hours and cater for situations requiring ad-hoc queries, mid-resolution aggregators, and so on. Where the real-time application is the most mission critical in terms of SLA and resolutions is where each event accounts for and the results have to return within an order of milliseconds to seconds.

Now that we understand the time dimensions and SLAs with respect to NRT, real-time, and batch systems, let's walk to the next step that talks about understanding the building blocks of NRT systems.

In essence, it consists of four main components/layers, as depicted in the following figure:

- The message transport pipeline
- The stream processing component
- The low-latency data store
- Visualization and analytical tools

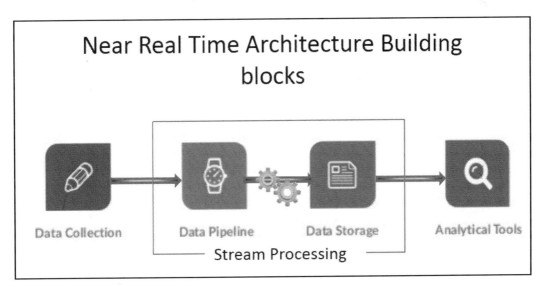

The first step is the collection of data from the source and providing it to the **Data Pipeline**, which actually is a logical pipeline that collects the continuous events or streaming data from various producers and provides it to the consumer stream processing applications. These applications transform, collate, correlate, aggregate, and perform a variety of other operations on this live streaming data and then finally store the results in the low-latency data store. Then, there are a variety of analytical, business intelligence, and visualization tools and dashboards that read this data from the data store and present it to the business user.

Data collection

This is the beginning of the journey of all data processing. Be it batch or real-time, the foremost challenge is getting the data from its source to the systems for processing. We can look at the processing unit as a black box and a data source, and at consumers as publishers and subscribers. This is captured in the following diagram:

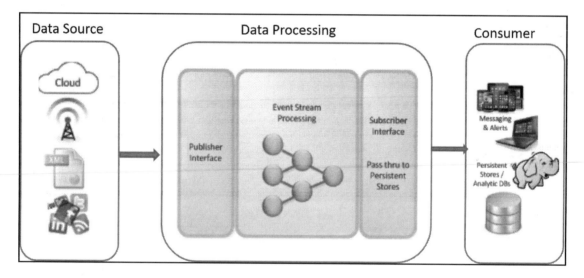

The key aspects that come under the criteria of data collection tools, in the general context of big data and real-time specifically, are as follows:

- Performance and low latency
- Scalability
- Ability to handle structured and unstructured data

Apart from this, any data collection tool should be able to cater for data from a variety of sources such as:

- **Data from traditional transnational systems**: When considering software applications, we must understand that the industry has been collating and collecting data in traditional warehouses for a long time. This data can be in the form of sequential files on tapes, Oracle, Teradata, Netezza, and so on. So, starting with a real-time application and its associated data collection, the three options the system architects have are:
  - To duplicate the ETL process of these traditional systems and tap the data from the source
  - Tap the data from these ETL systems
  - The third and a better approach is to go the virtual data lake architecture for data replication
- **Structured data from IOT/Sensors/Devices, or CDRs**: This is the data that comes at a very high velocity and in a fixed format—the data can be from a variety of sensors and telecom devices. The main complexity or challenge of data collection/ingestion of this data is the variety and the speed of data arrival. The collection tools should be capable of handling both the variety and the velocity aspects, but one good aspect of this kind of data for the upstream processing is that the formats are pretty standardized and fixed.
- **Unstructured data from media files, text data, social media, and so on**: This is the most complex of all incoming data where the complexity is due to the dimensions of volume, velocity, variety, and structure. The data formats may vary widely and could be in non-text format such as audio/ videos, and so on. The data collection tools should be capable of collecting this data and assimilating it for processing.

Stream processing

The stream processing component itself consists of three main sub-components, which are:

- **The Broker**: that collects and holds the events or data streams from the data collection agents
- **The Processing Engine**: that actually transforms, correlates, aggregates the data, and performs other necessary operations
- **The Distributed Cache**: that actually serves as a mechanism for maintaining common datasets across all distributed components of the **Processing Engine**

The same aspects of the stream processing component are zoomed out and depicted in the diagram that follows:

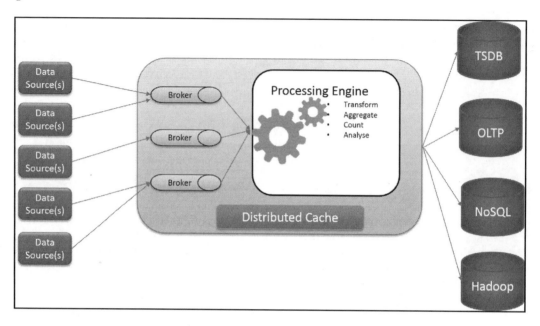

There are a few key attributes that should be catered for by the stream processing component:

- Distributed components thus offering resilience to failures
- Scalability to cater for the growing needs of an application or sudden surge of traffic
- Low latency to handle the overall SLAs expected from such applications
- Easy operationalization of a use case to be able to support evolving use cases
- Built for failures, the system should be able to recover from inevitable failures without any event loss, and should be able to reprocess from the point it failed
- Easy integration points with respect to off-heap/distributed cache or data stores
- A wide variety of operations, extensions, and functions to work with the business requirements of the use case

These aspects are basically considered while identifying and selecting the stream processing application/framework for a real-time use case implementation.

Analytical layer – serve it to the end user

The analytical layer is the most creative and interesting of all the components of an NRT application. So far, all we have talked about is backend processing, but this is the layer where we actually present the output/insights to the end user graphically, visually in the form of an actionable item.

The most crucial aspect of the data visualization technique that needs to be chosen as part of the solution is actually presenting the information to the intended audience in a format that they can comprehend and act upon. The crux here is that just smart processing of the data and arriving to an actionable insight is not sufficient; it has to reach the actors, be they humans or processes.

Before delving further into the nitty-gritties of business intelligence and visualization components, first let's understand the challenges big data and high velocity NRT/RT applications have brought to the mix of the problem statement.

A few of the challenges these visualization systems should be capable of handling are:

- **Need for speed**: The world is evolving and rationalizing the power of now—more and more companies are leaning towards real-time insights to gain an edge over their competition. So, the visualization tools should complement the speed of the application they are part of, so that they are quick to depict and present the key actors with accurate facts in meaningful formats so that informed decisions can be taken.

- **Understanding the data and presenting it in the right context**: At times, the same result needs to be modulated and presented differently, depending upon the audience being catered for. So, the tool should provide for this flexibility and for the capability to design a visual solution around the actionable insight in the most meaningful format. For instance, if you are charting vehicle location in a city, then you may want to use a heat map, where variance in color shows the concentration/number of vehicles, rather than plotting every vehicle on the graph. While you are presenting an itinerary of a particular flight/ship, you may not want to merge any data point and would plot each of them on the graph.

- **Dealing with outliers**: Graphical data representations easily denote the trends and outliers, which further enable the end users to spot the issues or pick up the points that need attention. Generally, outliers are 1-5% of the data, but when dealing with big data and handling a massive volume and velocity of data, even 5% of the total data is huge and may cause plotting issues.

The following figure depicts the overall application flow and some popular visualizations, including the Twitter heat map:

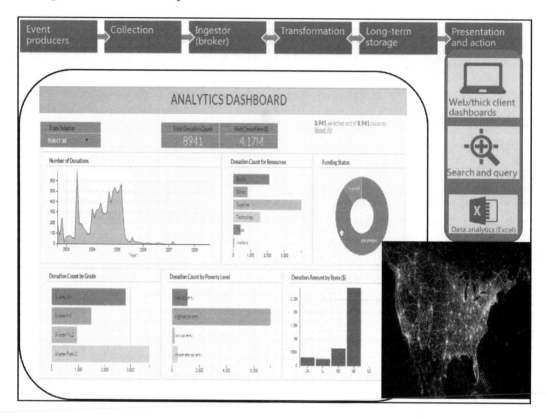

The figure depicts the flow of information from event producers to collection agents, followed by the brokers and processing engine (transformation, aggregation, and so on) and then long term storage. From the storage unit, the visualization tools reap the insights and present them in form of graphs, alerts, charts, Excel sheets, dashboards, or maps, to the business owners, who can assimilate the information and take some action based upon it.

NRT – high-level system view

The previous section of this chapter is dedicated to providing you with an understanding of the basic building blocks of an NRT application and its logical overview. The next step is to understand the functional and systems view of the NRT architectural framework. The following figure clearly outlines the various architectural blocks and cross cutting concerns:

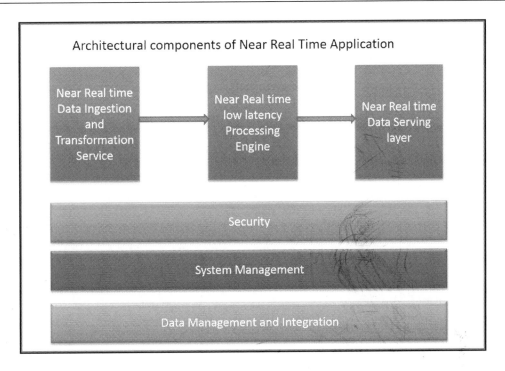

So, if I get to describe the system as a horizontal scale from left to right, the process starts with data ingestion and transformation in near real-time using low-latency components. The transformed data is passed on to the next logical unit that actually performs highly optimized and parallel operations on the data; this unit is actually the near real-time processing engine. Once the data has been aggregated and correlated and actionable insights have been derived, it is passed on to the presenting layer, which along with real-time dash boarding and visualization, may have a persistence component that retains the data for long term deep analytics.

The cross cutting concerns that exist across all the components of the NRT framework as depicted in the previous figure are:

- Security
- System management
- Data integrity and management

Next, we are going to get you acquainted with four basic streaming patterns, so you are acquainted with the common flavors that streaming use cases pose and their optimal solutions (in later sections):

- **Stream ingestion**: Here, all we are expected to do is to persist the events to the stable storage, such as HDFS, HBase, Solr, and so on. So all we need are low-latency stream collection, transformation, and persistence components.
- **Near real-time (NRT) processing**: This application design allows for an external context and addresses complex use cases such as anomaly or fraud detection. It requires filtering, alerting, de-duplication, and transformation of events based on specific sophisticated business logic. All these operations are required to be performed at extremely low latency.
- **NRT event partitioned processing**: This is very close to NRT processing, but with a variation that helps it deriving benefits from partitioning the data, to quote a few instances, it is like storing more relevant external information in memory. This pattern also operates at extremely low latencies.
- **NRT and complex models/machine learning**: This one mostly requires us to execute very complex models/operations over a sliding window of time over the set of events in the stream. They are highly complex operations, requiring micro batching of data and operate over very low latencies.

NRT – technology view

In this section, we introduce you to various technological choices for NRT components and their pros and cons in certain situations. As the book progresses, we will revisit this section in more detail to help you understand why certain tools and stacks are better suited to solving certain use cases.

Before moving on, it's very important to understand the key aspects against which all the tools and technologies are generally evaluated. The aspects mentioned here are generic to software, we move on to the specifics of NRT tools later:

- **Performance**: This is basically gauging the performance of the software component on a given set of hardware at a given load.
- **Capacity**: This is a very crucial aspect because it decides the breaking point for any application.
- **Management**: How easy or cumbersome is the management of the component? Would I need specialized engineers to maintain it?

- **Scalability**: Is the component scalable so it can accommodate an increasing load of traffic and new use cases? Can I grow over the same architecture?
- **Total cost of ownership** (**TCO**): This refers to the total cost that would be spent to own the solution end to end.

Now that we have rules of thumb set, let's look at the technology view of the NRT application framework to understand what all technological choices it presents to us—please refer to the following diagram:

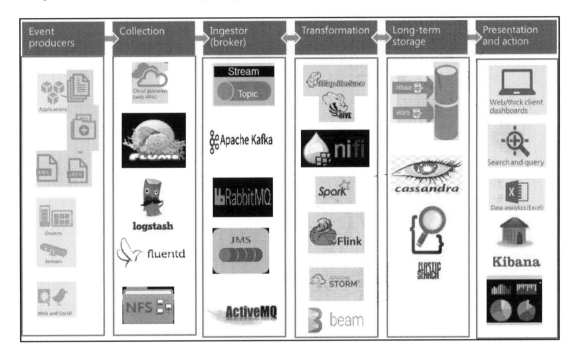

This figure captures various key technology players which are contenders as parts of the solution design for an NRT framework. Let's have a closer look at each segment and its contenders.

Event producer

This is the source where the events are happening. These individual events or tuples stringed in continuous never-ending flow actually form the streams of data which are the input source for any NRT application system. These events could be any of the following or more, which are tapped in real-time:

- Application or telecom logs and CDR
- Facebook, Twitter, and other social media
- Data from sensors and satellites
- Videos from CCTV and security cameras
- The format of such data could be image, free text, structured, semi-structured, non-text (audio, video), JSON, XML, and so on

Collection

Now that we have identified the source of data and its characteristics and frequency of arrival, next we need to consider the various collection tools available for tapping the live data into the application:

- **Apache Flume**: Flume is a distributed, reliable, and available service for efficiently collecting, aggregating, and moving large amounts of log data. It has a simple and flexible architecture based on streaming data flows. It is robust and fault tolerant with tenable reliability mechanisms and many fail over and recovery mechanisms. It uses a simple extensible data model that allows for online analytic application. (Source: `https://flume.apache.org/`). The salient features of Flume are:
    - It can easily read streaming data, and has a built in failure recovery. It has memory and disk channels to handle surges or spikes in incoming data without impacting the downstream processing system.
    - **Guaranteed delivery**: It has a built-in channel mechanism that works on acknowledgments, thus ensuring that the messages are delivered.
    - **Scalability**: Like all other Hadoop components, Flume is easily horizontally scalable.

- **FluentD**: FluentD is an open source data collector which lets you unify data collection and consumption for a better use and understanding of data. (Source: `http://www.fluentd.org/architecture`). The salient features of FluentD are:
  - **Reliability**: This component comes with both memory and file-based channel configurations which can be configured based on reliability needs for the use case in consideration
  - **Low infrastructure foot print**: The component is written in Ruby and C and has a very low memory and CPU foot print
  - **Pluggable architecture**: This component leads to an ever-growing contribution to the community for its growth
  - **Uses JSON**: It unifies the data into JSON as much as possible thus making unification, transformation, and filtering easier
- **Logstash**: Logstash is an open source, server-side data processing pipeline that ingests data from a multitude of sources simultaneously, transforms it, and then sends it to your favorite stash (ours is Elasticsearch, naturally). (Source: `https://www.elastic.co/products/logstash`). The salient features of Logstash are:
  - **Variety**: It supports a wide variety of input sources, varying from metrics to application logs, real-time sensor data, social media, and so on, in streams.
  - **Filtering the incoming data**: Logstash provides the ability to parse, filter, and transform data using very low latency operations, on the fly. There could be situations where we want the data arriving from a variety of sources to be filtered and parsed as per a predefined, a common format before landing into the broker or stash. This makes the overall development approach decoupled and easy to work with due to convergence to the common format. It has the ability to format and parse very highly complex data, and the overall processing time is independent of source, format, complexity, or schema.
  - It can club the transformed output to a variety of storage, processing, or downstream application systems such as Spark, Storm, HDFS, ES, and so on.
  - **It's robust, scalable and extensible**: where the developers have the choice to use a wide variety of available plugins or write their own custom plugins. The plugins can be developed using the Logstash tool called **plugin generator**.

- **Monitoring API**: It enables the developers to tap into the Logstash clusters and monitor the overall health of the data pipeline.
- **Security**: It provides the ability to encrypt data in motion to ensure that the data is secure.

	FluentD	Flume	Logstash
Installation	Gem/rpm/deb	Jar/rpm/deb	apt/yum
Footprint	3,000 lines Ruby	50,000 lines Java	5,000 lines JRuby
Plugin	Ruby	Java	JRuby
Plugin distribution	RubyGems.org	N/A	Logstash-plugins
Master Server	No	Yes	No
License	Apache	Apache	Apache
Scalable	Yes	Yes	Yes
Distributed	Yes	Yes	Yes

- **Cloud API for data collection**: This is yet another method of data collection where most cloud platforms offer a variety of data collection API's such as:
  - AWS Amazon Kinesis Firehose
  - Google Stackdriver Monitoring API
  - Data Collector API
  - IBM Bluemix Data Connect API

Broker

One of the fundamental architectural principles is the decoupling of various components. Broker is precisely the component in NRT architecture that not only decouples the data collection component and processing unit but also provides elasticity to hold data in a queue when there are sudden surges in traffic.

Amongst the vast variety of tools and technologies available under this segment, the key ones we would like to touch on are:

- **Apache Kafka**: Kafka is used for building real-time data pipelines and streaming apps. It is horizontally scalable, fault-tolerant, wickedly fast, and runs in production in thousands of companies. (Source: `https://kafka.apache.org/`). The salient features of this broker component are:
  - It's highly scalable
  - It's fail safe; it provides for fault tolerance and high availability
  - It is open source and extensible
  - It's disk-based and can store vast amounts of data (this is a USP of Kafka that enables it to virtually cater for any amount of data)
  - It allows replication and partitioning of data

- **ActiveMQ**: Apache ActiveMQ is fast, supports many cross language clients and protocols, and comes with easy-to-use enterprise integration patterns and many advanced features while fully supporting JMS 1.1 and J2EE 1.4. Apache ActiveMQ is released under the Apache 2.0 License. Key aspects of this protocol are:
  - It supports a variety of clients and protocols
  - It supports JMS 1.1 and J2EE 1.4
  - High performance
  - Support persistence
  - It exposes technology agnostic layer of web services

- **RabbitMQ**: This is an in-memory, durable, and persistent, low-latency, distributed queue system that has the following salient features:
  - It's robust
  - It's easy to use
  - It supports all major operating systems
  - It is available in both open source and commercial versions

The following table captures the critical aspects of the two close contenders for the broker:

	RabbitMQ	Apache Kafka
Definition	This is a general purpose, low-latency brokering system that supports a variety of industry protocols such as AMQP	This is an enterprise-grade service bus that is created and optimized for high-performance and low-latency data streaming

License	Mozilla Public License	Apache License
Written in	Erlang	Scala (JVM)
High Availability	Yes	Yes
Federated Queues	Yes	No
Complex Routing	Yes	No
Scalable	Generally vertical	Horizontal

Transformation and processing

This is the heart of the NRT framework, where all the processing actually takes place, starting from data transformation to complex aggregation and other business operations.

The key technology options that are available here are Apache Storm, Apache Flink, and Apache Spark. We will be delving into each in detail in the coming chapters, but the following is a quick comparison of each of them.

The following figure depicts key aspects of all of these scalable, distributed, and highly available frameworks for easy comparison and assimilation:

	Apache Storm	Apache Spark	Apache Flink
Stream processing	Supported		Supported
Api		High Level	High Level
Fault tolerance	Y (tuple ack)	RDD – based (lineage)	Coarse ceckpoints
Stateful			internal
Exactly once		Supported	Supported
Windowing			flexible
Low Latency	Very Low		low
High Throughput	Good	High	high

Storage

This is the stable storage to which intermittent or end results and alerts are written into. It's a very crucial component in the NRT context because we need to store the end results in a persistent store. Secondly, it serves as an integration point for further downstream applications which draw data from these low latency stores and evolve further insights or deep learning around them.

The following table clearly captures the various data stores and their alignment to the time SLA of NRT applications:

Data Systems		Analytical	Operational
"Commodity" Hardware Scale Out	Big Data	**Big Data Analytics** Hadoop, MapReduce, Hive, Spark	**NoSQL** Cassandra, Hbase, MongoDB
Large Servers using Shared Storage Scale Up	Conventional Scale	**Data Warehousing** SQL Server, Oracle, SAS, Tableau	**Relational Database** SQL Server, Oracle, DB2
		Batch Processing Minutes-to-Hours Range Queries Visualization / Dashboards	Real-time Processing Milliseconds Discrete Seeks/Updates Line of Business Apps

Source, http://image.slidesharecdn.com/cassandrameetuppresentation-160519132626/95/5-ways-to-use-spark-to-enrich-your-cassandra-environment-4-638.jpg?cb=1463664473

I would like to add a note here that we are skipping the plethora of options available for storage and visualization for now, but will touch upon these specifically in later sections of the book.

Summary

In this chapter we got you acquainted and introduced to various components of the NRT architectural framework and technology choices for it. You gained understanding of the challenges of real-time and the key aspects to be considered and the USPs of each technology available in stack. The intent here was to get you familiarized with the available choices in terms of tools and tech stack conceptually, so that you can pick and choose what works best for your use-case solutions, depending upon your functional and non-functional requirements.

3
Understanding and Tailing Data Streams

This chapter does a deep dive on the most critical aspect of the real-time application, which is about getting the streaming data from the source to the compute component. We will discuss the expectations and choices which are available. We will also walk the reader through which ones are more appropriate for certain use cases and scenarios. We will give high-level setup and some basic use cases for each of them. In this chapter, we will also introduce technologies related to data ingestion for the use cases.

The following is the list of components:

- Understanding data streams
- Setting up infrastructure for data ingestion
- Taping data from the source to the processor: expectations and caveats
- Comparing and choosing what works best for your use case
- Do it yourself

Understanding data streams

A data stream is the continuous flow of any type of data using any medium. Out of 4 Vs of big data, two are velocity and variety. A data stream refers to both velocity and variety of data. Data stream is real-time data coming from sources such as social media sites or different monitoring sensors installed in manufacturing units or vehicles. Another example of streaming data processing is IOT, that is the Internet Of Things, where data is coming from different components though the internet.

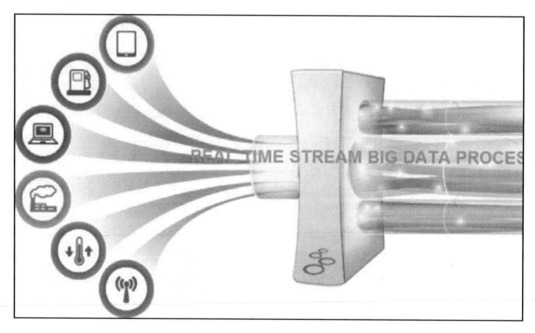

Real-time data stream processing

There are two different kinds of streaming data: bounded and unbounded streams, as shown in the following images. Bounded streams have a defined start and a defined end of the data stream. Data processing stops once the end of the stream is reached. Generally, this is called batch processing. An unbounded stream does not have an end and data processing starts from the beginning. This is called real-time processing, which keeps the states of events in memory for processing. It is very difficult to manage and implement use cases for unbounded data streams, but tools are available which give you the chance to play with them, including **Apache Storm**, **Apache Flink**, **Amazon Kinesis**, **Samaza**, and so on.

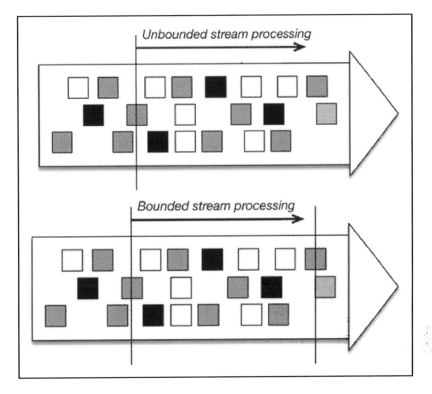

We will discuss data processing in the following chapters. Here, you will read about data ingestion tools which feed in to data processing engines. Data ingestion can be from live running systems generating log files or come directly from terminals or ports.

Setting up infrastructure for data ingestion

There are multiple tools and frameworks available on the market for data ingestion. We will discuss the following in the scope of this book:

- Apache Kafka
- Apache NiFi
- Logstash
- Fluentd
- Apache Flume

Apache Kafka

Kafka is message broker which can be connected to any real-time framework available on the market. In this book, we will use Kafka often for all types of examples. We will use Kafka as a data source which keeps data from files in queues for further processing. Download Kafka from
`https://www.apache.org/dyn/closer.cgi?path=/kafka/0.10.1.1/kafka_2.11-0.10.1.1.tgz` to your local machine. Once the `kafka_2.11-0.10.1.1.tgz` file is downloaded, extract the files using the following command:

```
cp kafka_2.11-0.10.1.1.tgz /home/ubuntu/demo/kafka
cd /home/ubuntu/demo/kafka
tar -xvf kafka_2.11-0.10.1.1.tgz
```

The following files and folders are extracted as seen in the following screenshot:

```
                              /kafka_2.11-0.10.1.1$ ls
bin  config  libs  LICENSE  NOTICE  site-docs
```

 Change the listener's property in the `server.properties` file. It should be `PLAINTEXT://localhost:9092`.

To start Kafka use the following commands:

```
/bin/zookeeper-server-start.sh config/zookeeper.properties
/bin/kafka-server-start.sh config/server.properties
```

Kafka will start on your local machine. Topics will be created later on as per the need. Let's move on to the NiFi setup and example.

Apache NiFi

Apache NiFi is the tool to read from the source and distribute data across different types of sinks. There are multiple types of source and sink connectors available. Download NiFi Version 1.1.1 from
`https://archive.apache.org/dist/nifi/1.1.1/nifi-1.1.1-bin.tar.gz` to your local machine. Once the `nifi-1.1.1-bin.tar.gz` file is downloaded, extract the files:

```
cp nifi-1.1.1-bin.tar.gz /home/ubuntu/demo
cd /home/ubuntu/demo
tar -xvf nifi-1.1.1-bin.tar.gz
```

The following files and folder are extracted, as shown in the following screenshot:

Start NiFi as follows:

```
/bin/nifi.sh start
```

NiFi is started in the background. To check whether NiFi is running successfully or not, use:

```
/bin/nifi.sh status
```

When NiFi is started, you can access the NiFi UI by accessing the following URL: `http://localhost:8080/nifi`. The following screenshot shows the UI interface for NiFi:

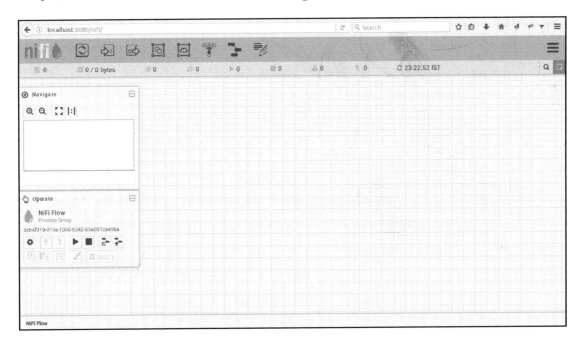

Now, let's a create flow file in NiFi which will read the file and push each line as an event in the Kafka topic named as `nifi-example`.

First, create a topic in Kafka using the following command:

```
/bin/kafka-topics.sh --create --topic nifi-example --zookeeper
localhost:2181 --partitions 1 --replication-factor 1
```

 You should have the right entry of the IP address of your system in `/etc/hosts`; otherwise, you will face problems while creating topics in Kafka.

Now, go to the NiFi UI. Select `Processor` and drag it into the window. It will show all available processors in NiFi. Search for GetFile and select it. It will display in your workspace area as in the following screenshot:

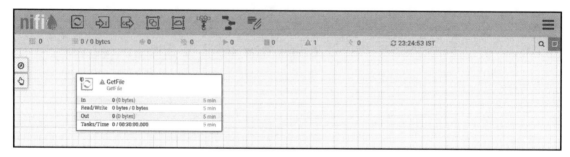

To configure processor, right click on the **GetFile** processor and select **Configure** as shown in the following screenshot:

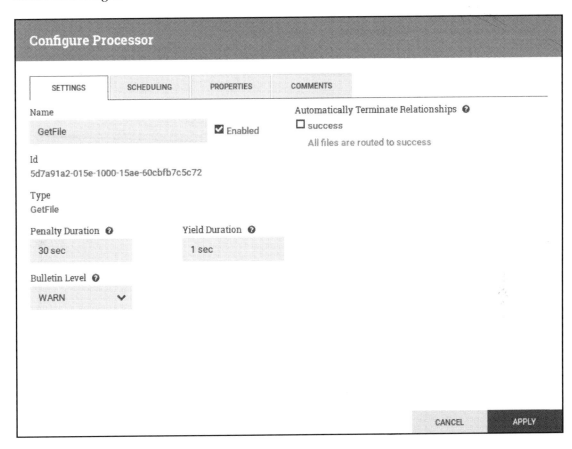

It will give you the flexibility to change all possible configurations related to the processor type. As per the scope of this chapter, let's go to properties directly.

Apply the properties as shown in the following screenshot:

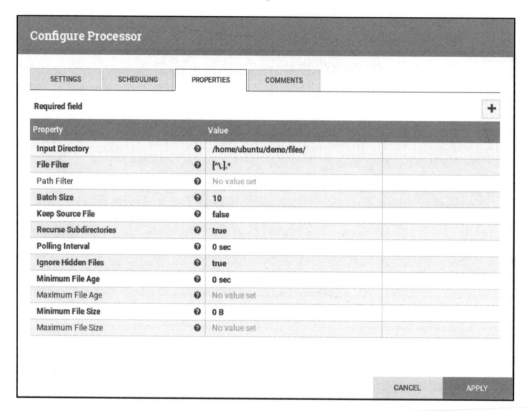

Input Directory is the directory where the logs/files are kept. **File Filter** is a regular expression to filter out the files in the directory. Let's suppose that the directory has application level logs as well as system level logs and we want to process only application level logs. In this case, the file filter can be used. **Path Filter** is a filter for sub directories. If log directory has multiple sub directories, then this filter can be used. **Batch Size** is the maximum number of files that will be fetched in one iteration of the run. If you don't want to delete source files, then set **Keep Source File** as true. **Recurse Subdirectories** is the property used whenever we need to scan sub directories in the log directory. If so, then set it to true; otherwise, set it to false. **Polling Interval** is the time after which the process will look for new files in the log directory. If you want to process hidden files in the log directory, then set **Ignore Hidden Files** as false.

To read the file we used the **GetFile** processor, now we want to push each line on the Kafka topic, then use the **PutKafka** processor. Again, click on processor and drag it into the workspace area.

After the mouse drop, it will ask for the type of processor. Search processor as **PutKafka** and select it. It will be shown *in* the following screenshot:

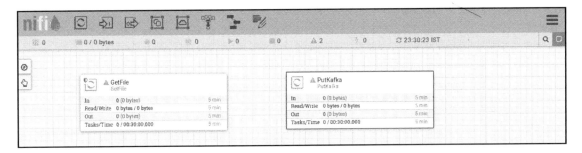

Now, right click on **PutKafka** and select configure for configuration. Set the configurations as shown in the following screenshot:

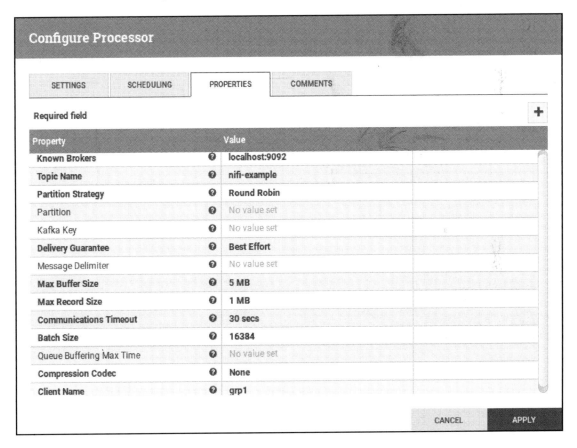

Some of the important configurations are **Known Brokers**, **Topic Name**, **Partition**, and **Client Name**.

You can specify the broker host name along with port number in **Known Brokers**. Multiple brokers are separated by a comma. Specify the topic name which is created on Kafka broker. Partition is used when a topic is partitioned. **Client Name** should be any relevant name for the client to make a connection with Kafka.

Now, make a connection between **GetFile** processor and **PutKafka** processor. Drag the arrow from **GetFile** processor and drop to **PutKafka** processor. It will create a connection between them.

Create a test file in `/home/ubuntu/demo/` files and some words or statements, as follows:

```
hello
this
is
nifi
kafka
integration
example
```

Before running NiFi Pipeline, start a process from the console to read from the Kafka topic `nifi-example`:

```
/bin/kafka-console-consumer.sh --topic nifi-example --bootstrap-server
localhost:9092 --from-beginning
```

Let's start the NiFi Pipeline which reads from the test file and puts it into Kafka. Go to the NiFi workspace, press select all (*Shift + A*) and press the **Play** button from the operate window.

The output is as shown in the following screenshot:

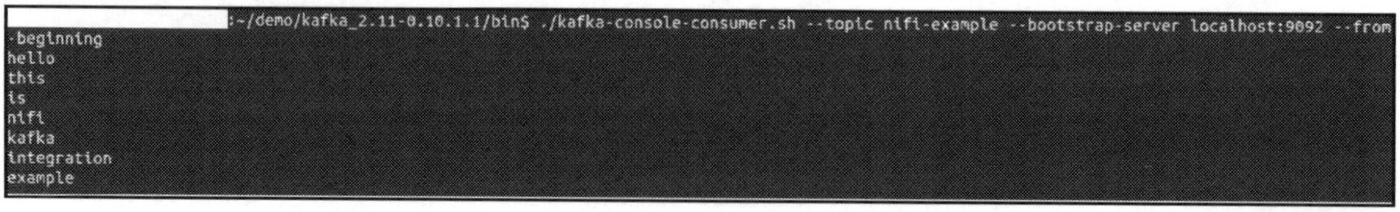

NiFi output is as seen in the following screenshot:

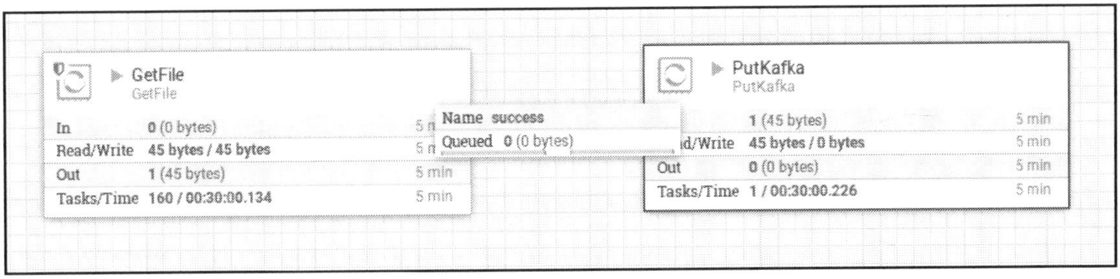

Logstash

Download **Logstash** version 5.2.1 from
`https://artifacts.elastic.co/downloads/logstash/logstash-5.2.1.tar.gz` on your
local machine. Once the `logstash-5.2.1.tar.gz` file is downloaded, extract the files
using the following command:

```
cp logstash-5.2.1.tar.gz ~/demo/.
tar -xvf ~/demo/logstash-5.2.1.tar.gz
```

The following folders and files will be extracted as seen in the following screenshot:

We will repeat the same example explained for NiFi, that is, reading from a file and pushing
an event on a Kafka topic. Let's create topic on Kafka for Logstash:

```
./kafka-topics.sh --create --topic logstash-example --zookeeper
localhost:2181 --partitions 1 --replication-factor 1
```

To run the example in Logstash, we have to create a configuration file, which will define the
input, filter, and output. Here, we will not apply any filters, so the configuration file will
contain two components: input as reading from file and output as writing into Kafka topic.
The following is the configuration file required to execute the example:

```
input {
    file {
            path => "/home/ubuntu/demo/files/test"
            start_position => "beginning"
        }
    }
```

```
output {
        stdout { codec => plain }
        kafka {
                codec => plain {format => "%{message}"}
                topic_id => "logstash-example"
                client_id => "logstash-client"
                bootstrap_servers => "localhost:9092"
        }
}
```

Create a file with the name `logstash-kafka-example.conf` and paste the previous configuration into that file. Create an input file of `test` in `/home/ubuntu/demo/files` and add the following content:

```
hello
this
is
logstash
kafka
integration
```

Before running Logstash Pipeline, start a process from the console to read from the Kafka topic `logstash-example,` using the following command:

```
/bin/kafka-console-consumer.sh --topic logstash-example --bootstrap-server localhost:9092 --from-beginning
```

Now, run the example using the following command:

```
/bin/logstash -f config/logstash-kafka-example.conf
```

The output on Kafka will be as shown in the following screenshot:

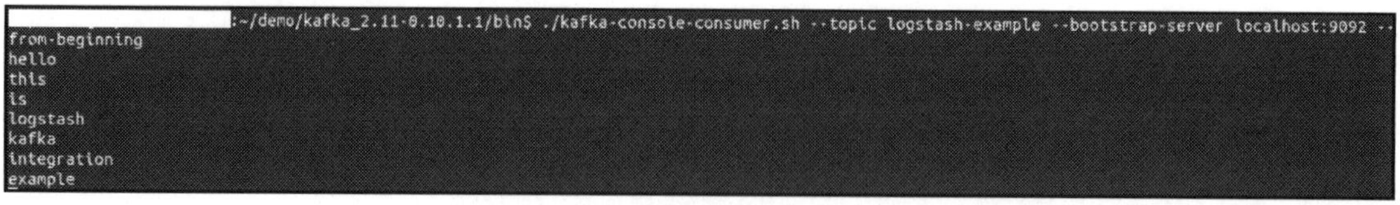

Fluentd

Fluentd is another tool to process log files. There are three components of Fluentd, the same as in Logstash, which are input, filter, and output. There are multiple input and output plugins are available as per the needs of your use case. Here, we will demonstrate a similar example to those seen previously, that is, reading from the log file and pushing it into Kafka.

Download **Fluentd** from `https://www.fluentd.org/download`. As we are using Ubuntu, select Debian installation. Download `td-agent_2.3.4-0_amd64.deb` and install it using Software Center in Ubuntu.

Once it is installed on the system, validate it using the following command:

```
sudo td-agent --dry-run
```

The following output will be generated and certify that everything is good:

```
2017-02-25 16:19:49 +0530 [info]: reading config file path="/etc/td-
agent/td-agent.conf"
2017-02-25 16:19:49 +0530 [info]: starting fluentd-0.12.31 as dry run
mode
2017-02-25 16:19:49 +0530 [info]: gem 'fluent-mixin-config-
placeholders' version '0.4.0'
2017-02-25 16:19:49 +0530 [info]: gem 'fluent-mixin-plaintextformatter'
version '0.2.6'
2017-02-25 16:19:49 +0530 [info]: gem 'fluent-plugin-kafka' version
'0.5.3'
2017-02-25 16:19:49 +0530 [info]: gem 'fluent-plugin-kafka' version
'0.4.1'
2017-02-25 16:19:49 +0530 [info]: gem 'fluent-plugin-mongo' version
'0.7.16'
2017-02-25 16:19:49 +0530 [info]: gem 'fluent-plugin-rewrite-tag-
filter' version '1.5.5'
2017-02-25 16:19:49 +0530 [info]: gem 'fluent-plugin-s3' version
'0.8.0'
2017-02-25 16:19:49 +0530 [info]: gem 'fluent-plugin-scribe' version
'0.10.14'
2017-02-25 16:19:49 +0530 [info]: gem 'fluent-plugin-td' version
'0.10.29'
2017-02-25 16:19:49 +0530 [info]: gem 'fluent-plugin-td-monitoring'
version '0.2.2'
2017-02-25 16:19:49 +0530 [info]: gem 'fluent-plugin-webhdfs' version
'0.4.2'
2017-02-25 16:19:49 +0530 [info]: gem 'fluentd' version '0.12.31'
2017-02-25 16:19:49 +0530 [info]: adding match pattern="td.*.*"
type="tdlog"
```

```
       2017-02-25 16:19:49 +0530 [info]: adding match pattern="debug.**"
type="stdout"
       2017-02-25 16:19:49 +0530 [info]: adding source type="forward"
       2017-02-25 16:19:49 +0530 [info]: adding source type="http"
       2017-02-25 16:19:49 +0530 [info]: adding source type="debug_agent"
       2017-02-25 16:19:49 +0530 [info]: using configuration file: <ROOT>
         <match td.*.*>
           @type tdlog
           apikey xxxxxx
           auto_create_table
           buffer_type file
           buffer_path /var/log/td-agent/buffer/td
           buffer_chunk_limit 33554432
           <secondary>
             @type file
             path /var/log/td-agent/failed_records
             buffer_path /var/log/td-agent/failed_records.*
           </secondary>
         </match>
         <match debug.**>
           @type stdout
         </match>
         <source>
           @type forward
         </source>
         <source>
           @type http
           port 8888
         </source>
         <source>
           @type debug_agent
           bind 127.0.0.1
           port 24230
         </source>
       </ROOT>
```

In Fluentd, to create a Pipeline, you need to write a configuration file, which is readable by Fluentd, and process the Pipeline. The default location of the Fluentd configuration file is /etc/td-agent/td-agent.conf. The following is a configuration file which reads from the log file and pushes each event into Kafka topic:

```
<source>
  @type tail
  path /home/ubuntu/demo/files/test
  pos_file /home/ubuntu/demo/fluentd/test.log.pos
  tag fluentd.example
  format none
</source>
```

```
<match *.**>
  @type kafka_buffered
  brokers localhost:9092
  default_topic fluentd-example
  max_send_retries 1
</match>
```

In the configuration file, there are two directives defined previously, out of six available directives. The `Source` directive is where all data comes from. `@type` tells us which type of input plugin is being used. Here, we are using tail, which will tail the log file. This is good for the use case where the input log file is running a log file in which events/logs are getting appended at the end of the file. It is same as the `tail -f` operation in Linux. There are multiple parameters of the tail input plugin. Path is the absolute path of the log file. `Pos_file` is the file which will keep track of last read position of the input file. Tag is the tag of the event. If you want to define the input format like CSV, or apply regex, then use format. As this parameter is mandatory, we used none which will use the input text as is.

The `Match` directive tells Fluentd what to do with the input, `*`. The `**` pattern is telling us that whatever is coming in through the log files, just push it into the Kafka topic. If you want to use a different topic for error and information logs, then define the pattern as error or info and tag the input as the same. Brokers is a host and port where Kafka broker is running on a system. Default-topic is the topic name where you want to push the events. If you want to retry after message failure, then set `max_send_reties` to one or more.

Replace the previous configuration in `/etc/td-agent/td-agent.conf`.

Now, create topic on Kafka, as follows:

```
/bin/kafka-topics.sh --create --topic fluentd-example --zookeeper
localhost:2181 --partitions 1 -replication-factor 1
```

Start the Fluentd agent, as follows:

```
sudo td-agent
```

Start Kafka consumer, as follows:

```
/bin/kafka-console-consumer.sh --topic fluentd-example --bootstrap-
server localhost:9092
```

Once the process is started without any exceptions, then start adding statements in `/home/ubuntu/demo/files/test` as shown in the following screenshot:

```
:~/demo/files$ echo hi >> test
:~/demo/files$ echo this >> test
:~/demo/files$ echo is >> test
:~/demo/files$ echo fluentd >> test
:~/demo/files$ echo kafka >> test
:~/demo/files$ echo integration >> test
:~/demo/files$ echo eaxmple >> test
```

The output on Kafka will be as shown in the following screenshot:

```
:~/demo/kafka_2.11-0.10.1.1/bin$ ./kafka-console-consumer.sh --topic fluentd-example --bootstrap-server localhost:9092 --f
rom-beginning
{"message":"hi"}
{"message":"this"}
{"message":"is"}
{"message":"fluentd"}
{"message":"kafka"}
{"message":"integration"}
{"message":"example"}
```

Flume

Flume is the most famous project of Apache for log processing. To download it, refer to the following link: `https://flume.apache.org/download.html`. Download the `apache-flume-1.7.0-bin.tar.gz` Flume setup file and unzip it, as follows:

```
cp apache-flume-1.7.0-bin.tar.gz ~/demo/
tar -xvf ~/demo/apache-flume-1.7.0-bin.tar.gz
```

The extracted folders and files will be as per the following screenshot:

```
:~/demo/apache-flume-1.7.0-bin$ ls
bin  CHANGELOG  conf  DEVNOTES  doap_Flume.rdf  docs  lib  LICENSE  logs  NOTICE  README.md  RELEASE-NOTES  tools
```

We will demonstrate the same example that we executed for the previous tools, involving reading from a file and pushing to a Kafka topic. First, let's configure the Flume file:

```
a1.sources = r1
a1.sinks = k1
a1.channels = c1
a1.sources.r1.type = TAILDIR
a1.sources.r1.positionFile = /home/ubuntu/demo/flume/tail_dir.json
a1.sources.r1.filegroups = f1
a1.sources.r1.filegroups.f1 = /home/ubuntu/demo/files/test
a1.sinks.k1.type = org.apache.flume.sink.kafka.KafkaSink
```

```
a1.sinks.k1.kafka.topic = flume-example
a1.sinks.k1.kafka.bootstrap.servers = localhost:9092
a1.channels.c1.type = memory
a1.channels.c1.capacity = 1000
a1.channels.c1.transactionCapacity = 6
a1.sources.r1.channels = c1
a1.sinks.k1.channel = c1
```

Flume has three components that define flow. The first are sources, from which the logs or events come. There are multiple sources available in Flume to define the flow. A few are `kafka`, `TAILDIR`, and HTTP, and you can also define your own custom source. The second component is sink, which is the destination of events where it will be consumed. The third is channels, which defines the medium between source and sink. The most commonly used channels are `Memory`, `File`, and `Kafka`, but there are also many more. Here, we will use `TAILDIR` as source, Kafka as sink, and Memory as channel. As of previously configuration `a1` is the agent name, `r1` is the source, `k1` is the sink, and `c1` is the channel.

Let's start with source configuration. First of all, you have to define the type of source using `<agent-name>.<sources/sinks/channels>.<alias name>.type`. The next parameter is `positionFile` which is required to keep track of the tailing file. `filegroups` indicates a set of files to be tailed. `filegroups.<filegroup-name>` is the absolute path of the file directory. Sink configuration is simple and straightforward. Kafka requires bootstrap servers and topic names. Channels configuration is long, but here we used only the most important ones. Capacity is the maximum number of events stored in the channel and transaction Capacity is the maximum number of events the channel will take from a source or give to a sink per transaction.

Now, start the Flume agent using the following command:

```
bin/flume-ng agent --conf conf --conf-file conf/flume-conf.properties -
-name a1 -Dflume.root.logger=INFO,console
```

It will be started and the output will be as follows:

```
17/09/08 00:18:35 INFO instrumentation.MonitoredCounterGroup: Monitored counter group for type: SOURCE, name: r1: Successfully registered new MBe
an.
17/09/08 00:18:35 INFO instrumentation.MonitoredCounterGroup: Component type: SOURCE, name: r1 started
17/09/08 00:18:35 INFO utils.AppInfoParser: Kafka version : 0.9.0.1
17/09/08 00:18:35 INFO utils.AppInfoParser: Kafka commitId : 23c69d62a0cabf86
17/09/08 00:18:35 INFO instrumentation.MonitoredCounterGroup: Monitored counter group for type: SINK, name: k1: Successfully registered new MBean
17/09/08 00:18:35 INFO instrumentation.MonitoredCounterGroup: Component type: SINK, name: k1 started
```

Create a Kafka topic and name it `flume-example`:

```
bin/kafka-topics.sh --create --topic flume-example --zookeeper
localhost:2181 --partitions 1 --replication-factor 1
```

Next, start the Kafka console consumer:

```
bin/kafka-console-consumer.sh --topic flume-example --bootstrap-server
localhost:9092
```

Now, push some messages in the file /home/ubuntu/demo/files/test as in the following screenshot:

The output from Kafka will be as seen in the following screenshot:

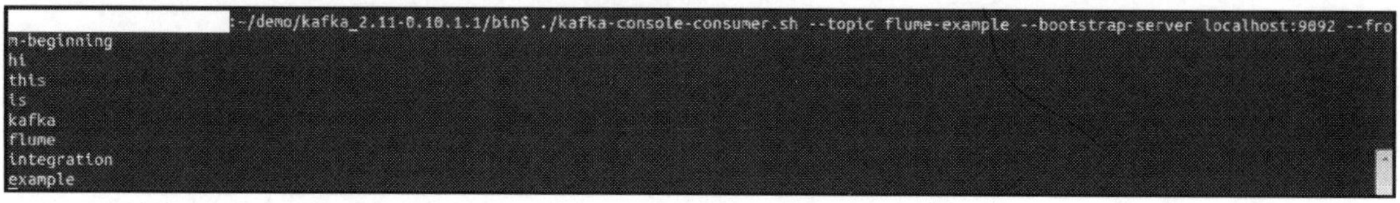

Taping data from source to the processor - expectations and caveats

In this section, we will discuss the expectations of log streaming tools in terms of performance, reliability, and scalability. The reliability of the system can be identified by message delivery semantics. There are three types of delivery semantics:

- **At most once**: Messages are immediately transferred. If the transfer succeeds, the message is never sent out again. However, many failure scenarios can cause lost messages.
- **At least once**: Each message is delivered at least once. In failure cases, messages may be delivered twice.
- **Exactly once**: Each message is delivered once and only once.

Performance consists of I/O, CPU, and RAM usage and impact. By definition, scalability is the capability of a system, network, or process to handle a growing amount of work, or its potential to be enlarged in order to accommodate that growth. So, we will identify whether tools are scalable to handle increased loads or not. Scalability can be achieved horizontally and vertically. Horizontally means adding more computing machines and distributing the work, while vertically means increasing the capacity of a single machine in terms of CPU, RAM, or IOPS.

Let's start with NiFi. It is a guaranteed delivery processing engine (exactly once) by default, which maintains write-ahead logs and a content repository to achieve this. Performance depends on the reliability that we choose. In the case of NiFi guaranteed message delivery, all messages are written to the disk and then read from there. It will be slow, but you have to pay in terms of performance if you don't want to lose even a single message. We can create a cluster of NiFi controlled by the NiFi cluster manager. Internally, it is managed by zookeeper to sync all of the nodes. The model is master and slave, but if the master dies then all nodes continue to operate. A restriction will be that no new nodes can join the cluster and you can't change the NiFi flow. So, NiFi is scalable enough to handle the cluster.

Fluentd provides *At most once* and *At least once* delivery semantics. Reliability and performance is achieved by using the Buffer plugin. Memory Buffer structure contains a queue of chunks. When the top chunk exceeds the specified size or time limit, a new empty chunk is pushed to the top of the queue. The bottom chunk is written out immediately when a new chunk is pushed. File Buffer provides a persistent buffer implementation. It uses files to store buffer chunks on a disk. As per its documentation, Fluentd is a well-scalable product where $M*N$, is resolved by $M+N$ where M is the number of input plugins and N is the number of output plugins. By configuring multiple log forwarders and log aggregators, we can achieve scalability.

Logstash reliability and performance is achieved by using third party message brokers. Logstash fits best with Redis. Other input and output plugins are available to integrate with message brokers, like Kafka, **RabbitMQ,** and so on. Using `Filebeat` as leaf nodes, we can get scalability with Logstash to read from multiple sources, from the same source with a different log directory, or from the same source and the same directory with a different file filter.

Flumes get its reliability using channels and syncs between sink and channel. The sink removes an event from the channel only after the event is stored into the channel of the next agent or stored in the terminal repository. This is single hop message delivery semantics. Flume uses a transactional approach to guarantee the reliable delivery of the events. To read data over a network, Flume integrates with `Avro` and `Thrift`.

Comparing and choosing what works best for your use case

The following table shows comparisons between Logstash, Fluentd, Apache Flume, Apache NiFi, and Apache Kafka:

	Logstash	Fluentd	Apache Flume	Apache NiFi	Apache Kafka
Concerns	No UI and hard to write filters	Windows installation is still in the experiment stage.	Hard to manage multiple connections.	Not mature enough when compared to other tools available on the market.	No UI and hard to maintain offsets.
Main Features	Flexibility and Interoperability	Simplicity and robustness	Provides best integration with HDFS, reliable and scalable.	Flow management, ease of use, security, flexible scaling model.	Fast, provides pub/sub based data streams, easy to integrate and use, partitioned.
Plugins	90+ plugins	125+ plugins	50+ plugins and custom components	An ample amount of processors are available. Also you can write your own easily.	No plugin, you can write your own code.
Scalability	Yes	Yes	Yes	Yes	Yes
Reliability	At least once using Filebeat	At most once or at least once	At least once using transactions	Exactly once by default	Supports at least once, at most once and exactly once based on configuration.

Do it yourself

In this section, we will provide the problem for the reader so that they can create their own application after reading the previous content.

Here, we will extend the example given previous regarding the setup and configuration of NiFi. The problem statement is read from a real-time log file and put into Cassandra. The pseudo code is as follows:

- Tail log file
- Put events into Kafka topic

- Read events from Kafka topic
- Filter events
- Push event into Cassandra

You have to install Cassandra and configure it so that NiFi will be able to connect it.

Logstash is made to process the logs and throw them to other tools for storage or visualization. The best fit here is **Elastic Search, Logstash and Kibana (ELK)**. As per the scope of this chapter, we will build integration between Elastic Search and Logstash and, in the next chapters, we will integrate Elastic Search with Kibana for complete workflow. So all you need to do to build ELK is:

- Create a program to read from `PubNub` for real-time sensor data. The same program will publish events to the Kafka topic
- Install Elasticsearch on the local machine and start
- Now, write a Logstash configuration which reads from a Kafka topic, parse and format them and push them into the Elasticsearch engine

Setting up Elasticsearch

Execute the following steps to set up Elasticsearch:

1. Download the Elasticsearch setup file using the following command:

```
wget
https://artifacts.elastic.co/downloads/elasticsearch/elasticsearch-
5.2.2.tar.gz
```

2. Extract `elasticsearch-5.2.2.tar.gz` using the following command:

```
tar -xzf elasticsearch-5.2.2.tar.gz
```

3. Go to the `elasticsearch-5.2.2 directory`:

```
cd elasticsearch-5.2.2/
```

4. Start Elasticsearch using the given command:

```
./bin/elasticsearch
```

Summary

In this chapter, we explained what a data stream is and gave related examples, as well as looking at the real-time use cases related to data streams. We got readers acquainted and introduced setup and quick execution for different real-time data ingestion tools like Flume, NiFi, Logstash, and Fluentd. We also explained where these data ingestion tools stand in terms of reliability and scalability. Then, we tried to compare the data ingestion tools so that the reader could pick the tools as per the need for their use case, after comparing pros and cons. They can run the examples by running the code bundled in JAR easily on standalone as well as in cluster mode. In the end, we gave the reader a real-time problem to solve using data ingestion tools along with pseudo code, so that we could focus on coding the example rather than finding right solution.

As we are now aware of different types of data streaming tools, in the next chapter we will focus on setting up Storm. Storm is an open source distributed, resilient, real-time processing engine. Setting up includes download, installation, configuration, and running an example to test whether setup is working or not.

4
Setting up the Infrastructure for Storm

This chapter will guide users through setting up and configuring Storm in single and distributed mode. It will also help them to write and execute their first real-time processing job on Storm.

The following topics will be covered:

- Overview of Storm
- Storm architecture and its components
- Setting up and configuring Storm
- Real-time processing job on Storm

Overview of Storm

Storm is an open source, distributed, resilient, real-time processing engine. It was started by *Nathan Marz* in late 2010. He was working at **BackType.** On his blog, he mentioned the challenges he faced while building Storm. It is a must read:

`http://nathanmarz.com/blog/history-of-apache-storm-and-lessons-learned.html`.

Here is the crux of the whole blog: initially, real-time processing was implemented like pushing messages into a queue and then reading the messages from it using Python or any other language and processing them one by one. The challenges with this approach are:

- In case of failure of the processing of any message, it has to be put back into the queue for reprocessing
- Keeping queues and the worker (processing unit) up and running all the time

What follows are two sparking ideas by Nathan that make Storm capable of being a highly reliable and real-time engine:

- **Abstraction**: Storm is a distributed abstraction in the form of streams. Streams can be produced and processed in parallel. Spouts can produce new streams and a bolt is a small unit of processing in a stream. Topology is top-level abstraction. The advantage of abstraction here is that nobody need worry about what is going on internally, such as serialization/deserialization, sending/receiving messages between different processes, and so on. The user can focus on writing the business logic.
- A guaranteed message processing algorithm is the second idea. Nathan developed an algorithm based on random numbers and XORs that would only require about 20 bytes to track each spout tuple, regardless of how much processing was triggered downstream.

In May 2011 BackType was acquired by Twitter. After becoming popular in public forums, Storm started to be called "real-time Hadoop". In September, 2011, Nathan officially released Storm. In September, 2013, he officially proposed Storm in Apache Incubator. In September, 2014, Storm became a top-level project in Apache.

Storm architecture and its components

Let's discuss Storm architecture and how it works. The following figure depicts the Storm cluster:

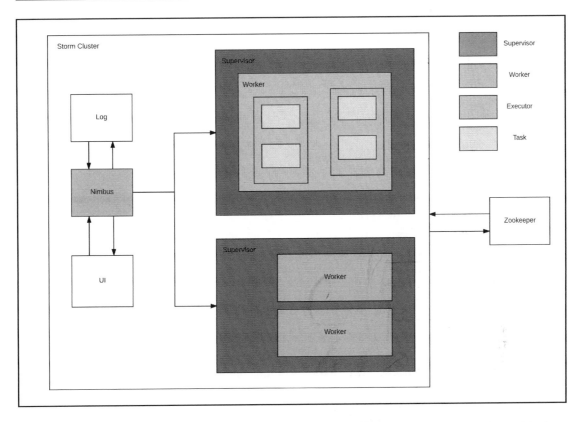

- The **Nimbus node** acts as the master node in a Storm cluster. It is responsible for analyzing topology and distributing tasks to different supervisors as per their availability. Also, it monitors failure; if one of the supervisors dies, it redistributes the tasks among available supervisors. The **Nimbus** node uses Zookeeper to keep track of tasks to maintain it's state. If the **Nimbus** node fails, it can be restarted so that it reads the state of Zookeeper and starts from same point where it failed earlier.
- **Supervisors** act as slave nodes in the Storm cluster. One or more workers, that is, JVM processes, can run in each supervisor node. A supervisor coordinates with workers to complete the tasks assigned by Nimbus node. In the case of worker process failure, the supervisor finds available workers to complete the tasks.

- A worker process is a JVM running in a supervisor node. It has executors. There can be one or more executors in a worker process. A worker coordinates with an executor to finish up the task.
- An executor is a single thread process spawned by a worker. Each executor is responsible for running one or more tasks.
- A task is a single unit of work. It performs actual processing on data. It can be either a spout or a bolt.
- Apart from previous processes, there are two important parts of a Storm cluster; they are logging and Storm UI. The `logviewer` service is used to debug logs for workers and supervisors on Storm UI.

Characteristics

The following are important characteristics of Storm:

- **Fast**: As per Hortonworks, the benchmark is to process one million 100-bytes of messages per second per node. It is lighting fast.
- **Reliable**: Storm guarantees message processing either at least once or at most once.
- **Scalable**: Storm can scale to a massive number of messages per second. You need to add more supervisor nodes along with increasing the parallelism of spouts and bolts in a topology.
- **Fault-tolerant**: In case any **Supervisor** dies, then Nimbus node redistributes the task to another **Supervisor**. If any worker dies, then **Supervisor** redistributes the task to another worker. The same applies to the **Executor** and the **Task**.
- **Programing language agnostic**: Topology can be written in any language.

Components

The following are components of Storm:

- **Tuple**: This is the basic data structure of Storm. It can hold multiple values and the data types of each value can be different. Storm serializes the primitive types of values by default but if you have any custom class then you must provide serializer and register it in Storm. A tuple provides very useful methods such as `getInteger`, `getString` and `getLong` so that the user does not need to cast the value in a tuple.

- **Topology**: As mentioned earlier, topology is the highest level of abstraction. It contains the flow of processing including spouts and bolts. It is a kind of graph computation. Each flow is represented in the form of a graph. So, nodes are spouts or bouts and edges are a stream grouping which connects them. The following figure showsa simple example of topology:

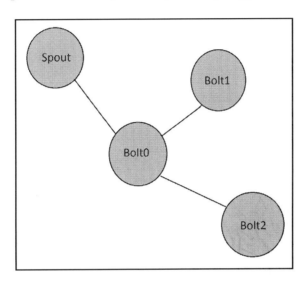

- **Stream**: The stream is the core abstraction of Storm. It is a sequence of unbounded tuples. A stream can be processed by different types of bolts, which result in a new stream. Every stream is provided an ID. If the user does not provide with an ID, then `default` is the default ID of the stream. You can define the ID of a stream by defining it in the `OutputFieldDeclare` class.

- **Spout**: A Spout is the source of a stream. It reads messages from sources such as Kafka, RabbitMQ, and so on as tuples and emits them in a stream. A Spout can produce more than one stream by defining the `declareStream` method of `OutputFieldDeclare`. There are two types of spouts:
  - **Reliable**: The Spout keeps track of each tuple and replays the tuple in case of any failure
  - **Unreliable**: The Spout does not care about the tuple once it is emitted as a stream to another bolt or spout

The following are methods of Spouts:

- `Ack`: This method is called when tuple is successfully processed in topology. The user should mark the tuple as processed or completed.
- `Fail`: This method is called when tuple is not processed successfully. The user must implement this method in such a way that the tuple should be sent for processing again in `nextTuple`.
- `nextTuple`: This method is called to get the tuple from the input source. The logic to read from the input source should be written in this method and emitted to the tuple for further processing.
- `Open`: This method is called only once when spout is initialized. Here, making a connection with input source or the output sink or configuring the memory cache,e configured, will ensure that it will not be repeated in the `nextTuple` method.

`IRichSpout` is the interface available in Storm to implement custom spout. All of the previous methods need to be implemented.

- **Bolt**: A bolt is a processing unit of Storm. All types of processing such as filtering and aggregations join the database operations. A bolt is a transformation that takes input as a stream of tuples and generates no or more streams as output. It is possible that types of values or more values in tuple might also change. A bolt can emit more than one stream by the defining `declareStream` method of `OutputFieldDeclare`. You can't subscribe to all streams at once. You must subscribe to them one by one. The following are methods of bolt:
  - **Execute**: This method is executed for each tuple in a stream to which the bolt subscribed as an input. In this method, any processing can be defined either by transforming value or persisting values in a database. A bolts must call the `ack` method on the `OutputCollector` for every tuple they process, so that Storm knows when tuples are completed.
  - **Prepare**: This method executes only once, when a bolt is initialized, so whatever connection or initializing of class variable can go into this method.

`IRichBolt` and `IBasicBolt` are available in Storm to implement the processing unit of Storm. The differences between the two are that `IBasicBolt` auto `acks` each tuple and provides basic filter and simple functions.

Stream grouping

The following are different types of grouping available with Storm:

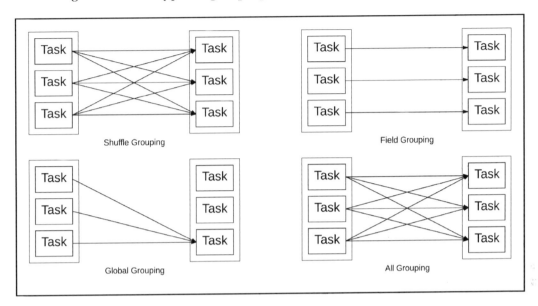

- **Shuffle grouping**: Shuffle grouping distributes tuples equally across the tasks. An equal number of tuples are received by all tasks.
- **Field grouping**: In this grouping, tuples are sent to the same bolt based on one or more fields, for example, in Twitter if we want to send all tweets from the same tweet to the same bolt then we can use this grouping.
- **All grouping**: All tuples are sent to all bolts. Filtering is one operation where we need all grouping.
- **Global grouping**: All tuples send a single bolt. Reduce is one operation where we need global grouping.
- **Direct grouping**: The producer of the tuple decides which of the consumer's task will receive the tuple. This is possible for only streams that are declared as direct streams.
- **Local or shuffle grouping**: If the source and target bolt are running in the same worker process then it is local grouping, as no network hops are required to send the data across the network. If this is not the case, then it is the same as shuffle grouping.
- **Custom grouping**: You can define your own custom grouping.

Setting up and configuring Storm

Before setting up Storm, we need to set up Zookeeper, which is required by Storm:

Setting up Zookeeper

What follows are instructions on how to install, configure and run Zookeeper in standalone and cluster mode.

Installing

Download Zookeeper from
`http://www-eu.apache.org/dist/zookeeper/zookeeper-3.4.6/zookeeper-3.4.6.tar.gz`.
After the download, extract `zookeeper-3.4.6.tar.gz` as follows:

```
tar -xvf zookeeper-3.4.6.tar.gz
```

The following files and folders will be extracted:

Configuring

There are two types of deployment with Zookeeper; they are standalone and cluster. There is no big difference in configuration, just new extra parameters for cluster mode.

Standalone

As shown in the previous figure, go to the `conf` folder and change the `zoo.cfg` file as follows:

```
tickTime=2000 # Length of single tick in milliseconds. It is used to
# regulate heartbeat and timeouts.
initLimit=5 # Amount of time to allow followers to connect and sync
# with leader.
syncLimit=2 # Amount of time to allow followers to sync with
# Zookeeper
dataDir=/tmp/zookeeper/tmp # Directory where Zookeeper keeps
# transaction logs
```

```
clientPort=2182 # Listening port for client to connect.
maxClientCnxns=30 # Maximum limit of client to connect to Zookeeper
# node.
```

Cluster

In addition to thepreviousconfiguration, add the following configuration to the cluster as well:

```
server.1=zkp-1:2888:3888
server.2=zkp-2:2888:3888
server.3=zkp-3:2888:3888
```

`server.x=[hostname]nnnn:mmmm`: Here x is id assigned to each Zookeeper node. In `datadir`, configured previously, create a file calledmyid and put the corresponding ID of Zookeeper in it. It should be unique across the cluster. The same ID is used as x here. nnnn is port used by followers to connect with leader node and mmmm is port used for leader election.

Running

Use the following command to run Zookeeper from the Zookeeper home directory:

```
/bin/zkServer.sh start
```

The console will come out after the followingmessage and the process will run in the background:

```
Starting zookeeper ... STARTED
```

The following command can be used to check the status of the Zookeeper process:

```
/bin/zkServer.sh status
```

The following output would be in standalone mode:

```
Mode: standalone
```

The following output would be in cluster mode:

```
Mode: follower # in case of follower node
Mode: leader      # in case of leader node
```

Setting up Apache Storm

What follows are instructions on how to install, configure, and run Storm with Nimbus and supervisors.

Installing

Download Storm from
`http://www.apache.org/dyn/closer.lua/storm/apache-storm-1.0.3/apache-storm-1.0.3.tar.gz`. After the download, extract `apache-storm-1.0.3.tar.gz`, as follows:

```
tar -xvf apache-storm-1.0.3.tar.gz
```

The following are the files and folders that will be extracted:

```
impadmin@Impetus-NL163U:~/tools/apache-storm-1.0.3$ ls
bin  CHANGELOG.md  conf  examples  external  extlib  _extlib-daemon  lib  LICENSE  log4j2  NOTICE  public  README.markdown  RELEASE  SECURITY.md
```

Configuring

As shown in previous screenshot, go to the `conf` folder and add/edit thefollowingproperties in `storm.yaml`:

- Set the Zookeeper hostname in the Storm configuration:

  ```
  storm.zookeeper.servers:
  - "zkp-1"
  - "zkp-2"
  - "zkp-3"
  ```

- Set the Zookeeper port:

  ```
  storm.zookeeper.port: 2182
  ```

- Set the Nimbus node host name so that the Storm supervisor can communicate with it:

  ```
  nimbus.host: "nimbus"
  ```

- Set the Storm local data directory to keep small information such as `conf`, JARs, and so on:

  ```
  storm.local.dir: "/usr/local/storm/tmp"
  ```

- Set the number of workers that will run on the current supervisor node. It is best practice to use same number of workers as the number of cores in the machine.

```
supervisor.slots.ports:
    - 6700
    - 6701
    - 6702
    - 6703
    - 6704
    - 6705
```

- Perform memory allocation to the worker, supervisor, and Nimbus:

```
worker.childopts: "-Xmx1024m"
nimbus.childopts: "-XX:+UseConcMarkSweepGC -
XX:+UseCMSInitiatingOccupancyOnly -
XX:CMSInitiatingOccupancyFraction=70"
supervisor.childopts: "-Xmx1024m"
```

- **Topologies related configuration**: The first configuration is to configure the maximum amount of time (in seconds) for a tuple's tree to be acknowledged (fully processed) before it is considered to have failed. The second configuration is that debug logs are false, so Storm will generate only info logs:

```
topology.message.timeout.secs: 60
topology.debug: false
```

Running

There are four services needed to start a complete Storm cluster:

- `nimbus`: First of all, we need to start Nimbus service in Storm. The following is the command to start it:

```
/bin/storm nimbus
```

- `supervisor`: Next, we need to start supervisor nodes to connect with the Nimbus node. The following is the command:

```
/bin/storm supervisor
```

- `ui`: To start Storm UI, execute the following command:

```
/bin/storm ui
```

You can access the UI on `http://nimbus-host:8080`. It is shown in the following figure:

- `logviewer`: The`logviewer` service helps to see the worker logs in the Storm UI. Execute the following command to start it:

```
/bin/storm logviewer
```

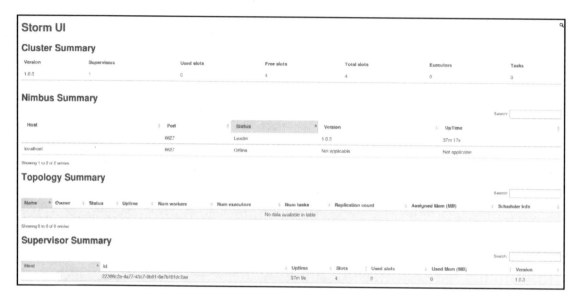

Real-time processing job on Storm

After discussing setup and configuration, let's look at an example of a real-time processing job. Here, we will discuss a very basic example of Storm, that is, word count. To implement word count in Storm, we need one spout that should emit sentences at regular intervals, one bolt to split the sentence into words based on space, one bolt that collects all the words and finds the count, and finally, we need one bolt to display the output on the console.

Let's discuss them one by one as follows:

- **Sentence spout**: To create a custom spout, first you must extend theBaseRichSpout class in which you can provide implementation of that required methods. To create a fixed spout, which means that it emits the same set of sentences per iteration, create a constant string array of sentences. declareOutputFields is the method that defines the ID of the stream. This stream is the input for the bolt. nextTuple is the method that iterates over the sentence array and emits each sentence to the next bolt.

```
public class FixedSentenceSpout extends BaseRichSpout {
        private static final long serialVersionUID = 1L;
        private SpoutOutputCollector collector;

private String[] sentences = { "This is example of chapter 4",
"This is word count example", "Very basic example of Apache
Storm","Apache Storm is open source real-time processing
engine"};
        private int index = 0;

        public void declareOutputFields(OutputFieldsDeclarer
declarer) {
                declarer.declare(new Fields("sentence"));
        }

public void open(@SuppressWarnings("rawtypes") Map config,
TopologyContext context, SpoutOutputCollector collector) {
                this.collector = collector;
        }

                public void nextTuple() {
                String sentence = sentences[index];
                System.out.println(sentence);
                this.collector.emit(new Values(sentence));
                index++;
                if (index >= sentences.length) {
                        index = 0;
                }
        }
}
```

- **Splitter bolt**: First, extend with `BaseRichBolt` class and implement the required methods. In the `execute` method, we read a tuple with the ID `sentence` which we defined in the spout. Then, split each sentence based on space and emit each word as tuple to the next bolt. `declareOutputFields` is a method used to define the ID of the stream for each bolt:

```
public class SplitSentenceBolt extends BaseRichBolt {
        private static final long serialVersionUID = 1L;
        private OutputCollector collector;

public void prepare(@SuppressWarnings("rawtypes") Map config,
TopologyContext context, OutputCollector collector) {
                this.collector = collector;
        }

        public void execute(Tuple tuple) {
                String sentence =
tuple.getStringByField("sentence");
                String[] words = sentence.split(" ");
                for (String word : words) {
                        this.collector.emit(new Values(word));
                }
        }

        public void declareOutputFields(OutputFieldsDeclarer
declarer) {
                declarer.declare(new Fields("word"));
        }
}
```

- **Word count bolt**: In this bolt, we keep a map with the key as word and value as count. We implement the value with one `execute` method for each tuple. In the `declareOutputFields` method, we make a tuple of two values and send it to next bolt. In Storm, you can send more than one value to the next bolt/spout, as shown in the following example:

```
public void execute(Tuple tuple) {
        String word = tuple.getStringByField("word");
        Long count = this.counts.get(word);
        if (count == null) {
                count = 0L;
        }
        count++;
        this.counts.put(word, count);
        this.collector.emit(new Values(word, count));
}
```

```
public void declareOutputFields(OutputFieldsDeclarer declarer)
{
        declarer.declare(new Fields("word", "count"));
}
```

- **Display bolt**: This bolt is the last bolt in topology so, there is nothing to define in the declareOutputFields method. Also, nothing is emitted in the execute method. Here, we are collecting all the tuples and putting them into a map. In the cleanup method, which is called when the topology kills, we display values present in the map:

```
public class DisplayBolt extends BaseRichBolt {
        private static final long serialVersionUID = 1L;
        private HashMap<String, Long> counts = null;

        public void prepare(@SuppressWarnings("rawtypes") Map
config, TopologyContext context, OutputCollector collector) {
                this.counts = new HashMap<String, Long>();
        }

        public void execute(Tuple tuple) {
                String word = tuple.getStringByField("word");
                Long count = tuple.getLongByField("count");
                this.counts.put(word, count);
        }

        public void declareOutputFields(OutputFieldsDeclarer
declarer) {
                // this bolt does not emit anything
        }

        public void cleanup() {
                System.out.println("--- FINAL COUNTS ---");
                List<String> keys = new ArrayList<String>();
                keys.addAll(this.counts.keySet());
                Collections.sort(keys);
                for (String key : keys) {
                        System.out.println(key + " : " +
this.counts.get(key));
                }
                System.out.println("-------------");
        }
}
```

- **Creating topology and submitting**: After defining all spouts and bolts, let's bind them into one program, that is, topology. Here, two things are very important, the sequence of bolts with ID and the grouping of streams.

  First, create TopologyBuilder in line 1, which is required to build the complete topology of spouts and bolts. Set a spout in line 2, which is the FixedSentenceSpout spout. Set the first bolt in line 3, which is the SplitSentenceBolt bolt. Now we have used shuffleGrouping, which means all tuples will be evenly distributed among all tasks. Set the second bolt in line 4, which is the WordCountBolt bolt. Here, we used fieldsGrouping as we want that same word go to the same process to perform the word count. Set the last bolt which is the DisplayBolt bolt. This bolt will display the final output once the topology is shut down:

```
TopologyBuilder builder = new TopologyBuilder(); # line 1
builder.setSpout("sentence-spout", new FixedSentenceSpout()); #
line 2
builder.setBolt("split-bolt", new
SplitSentenceBolt()).shuffleGrouping("sentence-spout"); # line 3
builder.setBolt("count-bolt", new
WordCountBolt()).fieldsGrouping("split-bolt", new Fields("word"));
# line 4
builder.setBolt("display-bolt", new
DisplayBolt()).globalGrouping("count-bolt"); # line 5
Config config = new Config();

if (mode.equals("cluster")) {
StormSubmitter.submitTopology("word-count-topology", config,
builder.createTopology()); # line 6
} else {
    LocalCluster cluster = new LocalCluster();
    cluster.submitTopology("word-count-topology", config,
    builder.createTopology()); # line 7
    Thread.sleep(20000);
    cluster.killTopology("word-count-topology");
    cluster.shutdown();
}
```

Running job

To run the previous example, there are two ways, one is local mode and the second is cluster mode.

Local

Local mode means running your topology on the local cluster. You can run it in Eclipse without the need to set up and configure Storm. To run it in the local cluster, right-click on **BasicStormWordCountExample** and select **Run As | Java Application**. Logs will start printing on the console. Before shutting down in 20 seconds, the final output will be displayed on the console, as as shown in following figure:

```
--- FINAL COUNTS ---
4 : 4073
Apache : 8145
Storm : 8145
This : 8146
Very : 4073
basic : 4073
chapter : 4073
count : 4073
engine : 4072
example : 12219
is : 12218
of : 8146
open : 4072
processing : 4072
real : 4072
source : 4072
time : 4072
word : 4073
```

Cluster

To run the example in cluster mode, execute the following steps:

1. Go to the project directory where `pom.xml` is placed and make build using the following command:

   ```
   mvn clean install
   ```

2. Submit the topology JAR on the Storm cluster:

```
./storm jar ~/workspace/Practical-Real-time-
Analytics/chapter4/target/chapter4-0.0.1-SNAPSHOT.jar
com.book.realtime.job.BasicStormWordCountExample cluster
```

3. You will check the status of topology on UI, as shown in the following screenshot:

4. When you click on the topology, you will find details of the spouts and bolts as shown in the following screenshot:

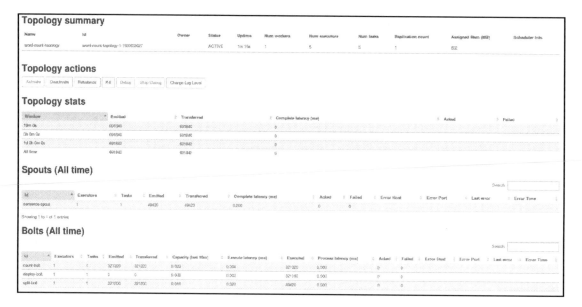

5. Kill the topology from the UI, as shown in the previous screenshot.

6. Check the worker logs to get the final output. Go to
   STORM_HOME/logs/workers-artifacts/word-count-topology-1-
   <Topology ID>/<worker port>/worker.log.

Summary

In this chapter, we acquainted the reader with the basics of Storm. We started with the history of Storm, where we discussed how Nathan Marz got the idea for Storm and what types of challenges he faced while releasing Storm as open source software and then in Apache. We discussed the architecture of Storm and its components. Nimbus, supervisor workers, executors, and tasks are all part of Storm's architecture. Its components are tuples, stream, topology, spouts, and bolts. We discussed how to set up Storm and configure it to run in the cluster. Zookeeper is required to be set up first, as Storm requires it.

At the end of the chapter, we discussed a word count example implemented in Storm using a spout and multiple bolts. We showed how to run an example locally, as well as on the cluster.

5

Configuring Apache Spark and Flink

This chapter helps the readers do the basic setup of various computation components that will be required throughout the book. We will do the setup and some basic set of examples validating these setups. Apache Spark, Apache Flink, and Apache Beam are computation engines we will discuss in this chapter. There are more computational engines available in market.

As per the definitions on official websites of computation engines, Apache Spark is a fast and general engine for large-scale data processing engine, Apache Flink is an open source stream processing framework for distributed, high-performing, always-available, and accurate data streaming applications and Apache Beam is an open source, unified model for defining both batch and streaming data-parallel processing pipelines. Using Apache Beam, you can run the program on your choice of computation engine like Apache Spark, Apache Flink, and many more.

The following are the list of components:

- Setting up and a quick execution of Spark
- Setting up and a quick execution of Flink
- Setting up and a quick execution of Apache Beam
- Balancing act of Apache Beam

Setting up and a quick execution of Spark

There are two different ways to set up Spark, build it from the source or download and extract it. Both ways are explained in the following sections.

Building from source

Download the source code from the link,`http://spark.apache.org/downloads.html`, which is also shown in the following screenshot:

You will require Maven 3.3.6 and Java 7+ to compile Spark 2.1.0. Also, you need to update the `MAVEN_OPT` as the default setting will not be able to compile the code:

```
exportMAVEN_OPTS="-Xmx2g -XX:ReservedCodeCacheSize=512m"
```

Use the following command to trigger the build. It will compile Spark 2.1.0 with Hadoop Version 2.4.0:

```
./build/mvn -Pyarn -Phadoop-2.4 -Dhadoop.version=2.4.0 -DskipTests
clean package
```

Downloading Spark

Download the latest version (2.1.0) using the same link (`http://spark.apache.org/downloads.html`) as given for *Building from source* section. Select the Spark release version if the user wants to install anything other than the latest version and pre-built to select version of Hadoop. The user can also download the source from same page and build it. Spark 2.1.0 version requires:

- Java 7+
- Python 3.4+
- Scala 2.11

The following are the commands to extract the downloaded `spark-2.1.0-bin-hadoop2.7.tar` file:

```
mkdir demo
mv /home/ubuntu/downloads/spark-2.1.0-bin-hadoop2.7.tar ~/demo
cd demo
tar -xvf spark-2.1.0-bin-hadoop2.7.tar
```

The following list of files and folders will be extracted, as seen in the following screenshot:

Other ways to download or install Spark are to use a virtual image of Spark provided by **Cloudera Distribution Hadoop (CDH)**, **Hortonworks Data Platform (HDP)**, or **MapR**. If the user wants customer support on Spark then use Databricks, which is on the cloud.

Running an example

The Spark package comes with examples. So, to test whether all required dependencies are working fine, execute the following commands:

```
cd spark-2.1.0-bin-hadoop2.7
./bin/run-example SparkPi 10
```

The output of this will be:

```
Pi is roughly 3.1415431415431416
```

Before starting spark-shell, we need to setup Hadoop on the local machine. Download Hadoop 2.7.4 version from the following link:

`http://www-eu.apache.org/dist/hadoop/common/hadoop-2.7.4/hadoop-2.7.4.tar.gz`.
Untar the files and folders extracted using the following command:

```
tar -xvf hadoop-2.7.4.tar.gz
```

The output is as shown in the following screenshot:

Copy the configuration in the `.bashrc` file at the home location of user:

```
export HADOOP_PREFIX=/home/impadmin/tools/hadoop-2.7.4
export HADOOP_HOME=/home/impadmin/tools/hadoop-2.7.4
export HADOOP_MAPRED_HOME=${HADOOP_HOME}
export HADOOP_COMMON_HOME=${HADOOP_HOME}
export HADOOP_HDFS_HOME=${HADOOP_HOME}
export YARN_HOME=${HADOOP_HOME}
export HADOOP_CONF_DIR=${HADOOP_HOME}/etc/hadoop
# Native Path
export HADOOP_COMMON_LIB_NATIVE_DIR=${HADOOP_PREFIX}/lib/native
export HADOOP_OPTS="-Djava.library.path=$HADOOP_PREFIX/lib"
export PATH=$PATH:$HADOOP_HOME/bin:$HADOOP_HOME/sbin
```

Start all Hadoop services using the following command:

```
/bin/start-all.sh
```

The output is as shown in the following screenshot:

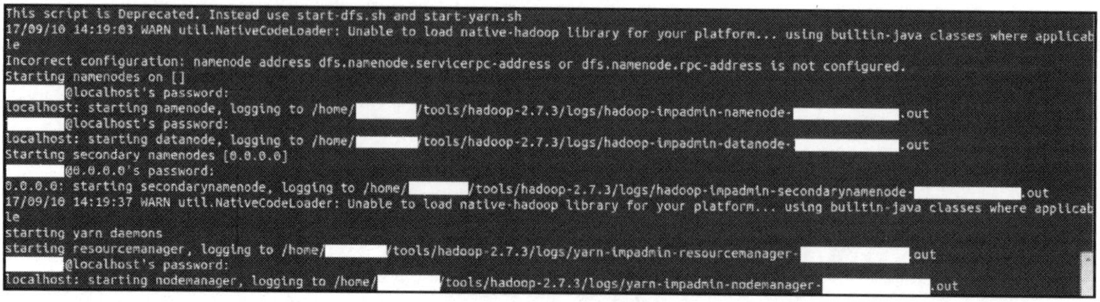

Now, create a file in the /tmp folder with name as input.txt and add the given lines as shown in following screenshot:

```
Apache Spark is a fast and general engine for large-scale data processing.
Run programs up to 100x faster than Hadoop MapReduce in memory, or 10x faster on disk.
Write applications quickly in Java, Scala, Python, R.
Combine SQL, streaming, and complex analytics.
Spark runs on Hadoop, Mesos, standalone, or in the cloud. It can access diverse data sources including HDFS, Cassandra, HBase, and S3.
```

Let's create a word count example using Scala in Spark. Spark is giving shell where we can write the code and execute it as a command line:

```
cdspark-2.1.0-bin-hadoop2.7
./bin/spark-shell
```

The output of this command is as shown in the preceding screenshot:

```
Welcome to

      ____              __
     / __/__  ___ _____/ /__
    _\ \/ _ \/ _ `/ __/  '_/
   /___/ .__/\_,_/_/ /_/\_\   version 2.1.0
      /_/

Using Scala version 2.11.8 (Java HotSpot(TM) 64-Bit Server VM, Java 1.8.0_45)
Type in expressions to have them evaluated.
Type :help for more information.

scala> █
```

The following are the steps to create the word count example:

1. Define the file name. Take the file name in a variable named fileName:

   ```
   valfileName = ""/tmp/input.txt"
   ```

2. Take file name in a variable fileName. Get file pointer. Construct the file object using Spark context sc, which holds the file content:

   ```
   valfile = sc.textFile(fileName)
   ```

3. Construct the file object using spark context sc which holds the file content. Perform word count. Read each line and split each line delimiter as space " ":

   ```
   valwordCount = file.flatMap(line =>line.split(" "))
   ```

[95]

4. Map transformation creates a key-value pair of word and its count as 1. Before going to the next step, the key-value pair will contain each word with count as 1:

```
map(word => (word, 1))
```

5. Similar keys are added up and give the final count of word of word which is 1. The key-value pair will contain each word with count as 1:

```
reduceByKey(_ + _)
```

6. Collect and print the output. The collect action will collect the values of key-value contains word and its counts from all workers:

```
wordCount.collect()
```

7. Print each key-value on the console. The collect action will collect the values of key-value contains word and its counts from all workers.

```
foreach(println)
```

8. Print each key-value on the console. Save output in a file:

```
wordCount.saveAsTextFile ("/tmp/output")
```

9. The output is shown in the following screenshots:

```
                        :/tmp/output$ ls
part-00000   part-00001   _SUCCESS
                        :/tmp/output$ cat part-00000
(is,1)
(can,1)
(runs,1)
(general,1)
(fast,1)
(Cassandra,,1)
(Java,,1)
(Apache,1)
(MapReduce,1)
(data,2)
(complex,1)
(large-scale,1)
(sources,1)
(S3.,1)
(analytics.,1)
(diverse,1)
(streaming,,1)
(access,1)
(quickly,1)
(Scala,,1)
(Python,,1)
(R.,1)
(engine,1)
(SQL,,1)
```

```
                          :/tmp/output$ cat part-00001
(cloud.,1)
(Run,1)
(up,1)
(Spark,2)
(faster,2)
(than,1)
(Mesos,,1)
(processing.,1)
(HDFS,,1)
(a,1)
(on,2)
(or,2)
(Hadoop,,1)
(to,1)
(10x,1)
(including,1)
(in,3)
(Write,1)
(100x,1)
(disk.,1)
(applications,1)
(Combine,1)
(programs,1)
(for,1)
(It,1)
(HBase,,1)
(and,3)
(standalone,,1)
(memory,,1)
(the,1)
(Hadoop,1)
```

Here is the complete program:

```
val fileName = "/tmp/input.txt"
val file = sc.textFile(fileName)
val wordCount = file.flatMap(line=>line.split(" ")).map(word =>(word,
1)).reduceByKey(_+_)
wordCount.collect().foreach(println)
wordCount.saveAsTextFile("/tmp/output")
```

Setting up and a quick execution of Flink

There are different ways to set up Flink, that is building from source or downloading and extracting it. Both ways are explained in the following sections.

Build Flink source

Download the source from `http://Flink.apache.org/downloads.html` or clone Git repository `https://github.com/apache/Flink`.

To clone from Git, enter the following command:

```
git clone https://github.com/apache/Flink
```

Maven 3.0.3 and Java 8 are required to build Flink. Use the following command to build Flink using Maven:

```
mvn clean install -DskipTests
If you want to build Flink with different version of hadoop then use:
mvn clean install -DskipTests -Dhadoop.version=2.6.1
```

Download Flink

Download the latest version of Flink (1.1.4) from `http://Flink.apache.org/downloads.html`, as shown in the following screenshot:

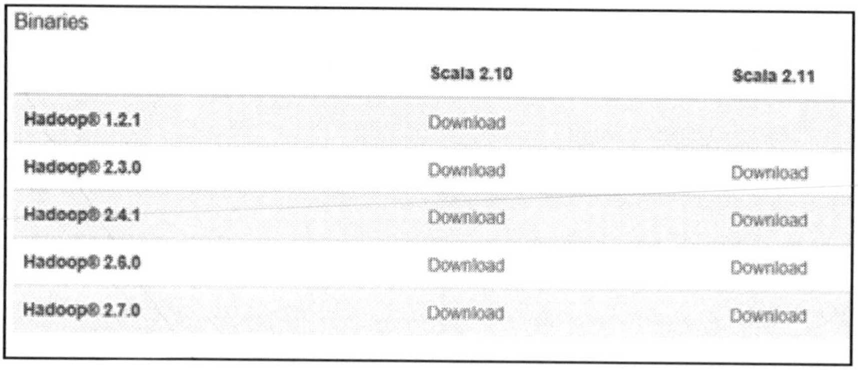

Binaries	Scala 2.10	Scala 2.11
Hadoop® 1.2.1	Download	
Hadoop® 2.3.0	Download	Download
Hadoop® 2.4.1	Download	Download
Hadoop® 2.6.0	Download	Download
Hadoop® 2.7.0	Download	Download

Extract the downloaded `Flink-1.1.4-bin-hadoop27-scala_2.11.tgz` file using the following commands:

```
mkdir demo
mv /home/ubuntu/downloads/Flink-1.1.4-bin-hadoop27-scala_2.11.tgz ~/demo
cd demo
tar -xvfFlink-1.1.4-bin-hadoop27-scala_2.11.tgz
```

A list of files and folders will be extracted as shown in the following screenshot:

```
README.txt
log
bin
tools
resources
NOTICE
LICENSE
lib
examples
conf
```

Use the following command to start Flink:

```
./bin/start-local.sh
```

Apache Flink provides a dashboard which shows all the jobs that are running or completed and submits a new job. The dashboard is accessible though `http://localhost:8081`. It also shows that everything is up and running.

Running example

Flink provides a streaming API called `Flink DataStream` API to process continuous unbounded streams of data in realtime.

To start using `Datastream` API, you should add the following dependency to the project. Here, we are using `sbt` for build management.

```
org.apache.Flink" %% "Flink-scala" % "1.0.0
```

In the next few steps, we will create a word count program which reads from a socket and displays the word count in realtime.

1. **Get the Streaming environment**: First of all we have to create the streaming environment on which the program runs. We will discuss deployment modes later in this chapter:

    ```
    val environment =
    StreamExecutionEnvironment.getExecutionEnvironment
    ```

    `StreamExecutionEnvironment` is similar to spark context.

2. Import streaming API for Java or Scala:

    ```
    importorg.apache.Flink.streaming.api.scala._
    ```

3. Create the DataStream from the socket:

    ```
    valsocketStream = environment.socketTextStream("localhost",9000)
    ```

    `socketStream` will be of the type `DataStream`. `DataStream` is basic abstraction of Flink's streaming API.

4. Implement `wordcount` logic:

    ```
    valwordsStream = socketStream.flatMap(value
    =>value.split("\\s+")).map(value => (value,1))
    valkeyValuePair = wordsStream.keyBy(0)
    valcountPair = keyValuePair.sum(1)
    ```

The `keyBy` function is the same as the`groupBy` function and the sum function is the same as the reduce `function`. 0 and 1 in `keyBy` and `sum` respectively indicates the index of columns in tuple.

5. Print the word counts:

   ```
   countPair.print()
   ```

6. Trigger program execution: We need to explicitly call the execute function to trigger execution:

   ```
   env.execute()
   ```

We need to explicitly call the execute function to trigger execution.

Here is the complete code:

```
importorg.apache.Flink.streaming.api.scala._
objectStreamingWordCount {
def main(args: Array[String]) {
valenv = StreamExecutionEnvironment.getExecutionEnvironment

    // create a stream using socket
valsocketStream = env.socketTextStream("localhost",9000)

    // implement word count
valwordsStream = socketStream.flatMap(value
=>value.split("\\s+")).map(value => (value,1))
valkeyValuePair = wordsStream.keyBy(0)
valcountPair = keyValuePair.sum(1)

    // print the results
countPair.print()

    // execute the program
env.execute()
  }
}
```

You can build the above program using `sbt` and create a `.jar` file. The word count program is pre-built and comes with a Flink installed package. You can find the JAR file at:

```
~/demo/Flink-1.1.4/examples/streaming/SocketWindowWordCount.jar
```

Start the socket at 9000 using following command:

```
nc -lk 9000
```

The following command will submit the job on Flink (replace your JAR file name):

```
/demo/ Flink-1.1.4/bin/Flink run
examples/streaming/SocketWindowWordCount.jar --port 9000
```

The Flink dashboard starts showing the running job and all its relevant details as shown in the following screenshot:

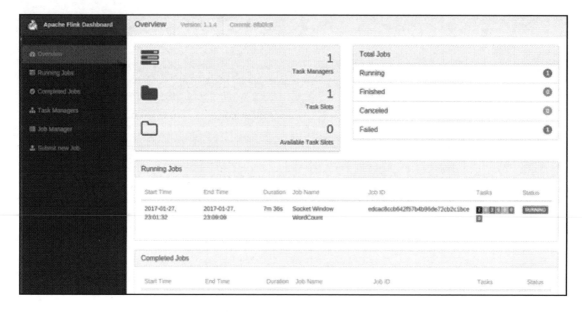

The following screenshot shows the job details with each subtask:

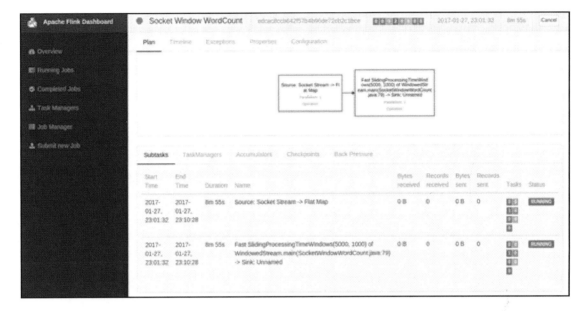

Now, enter the words or statement on the console as shown in the following screenshot:

The output is as shown in the following screenshot:

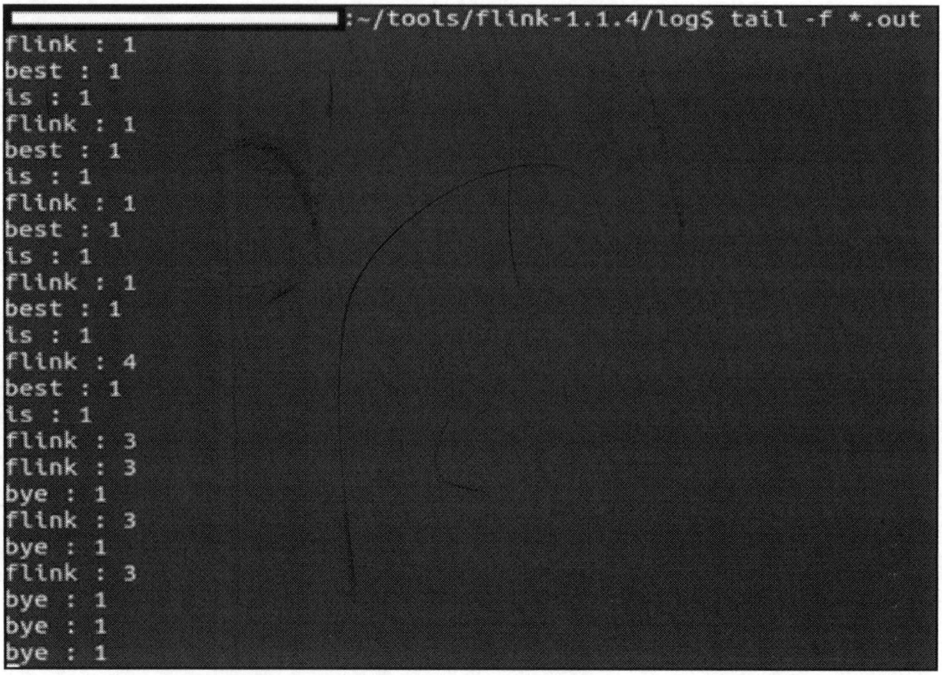

```
                                :~/tools/flink-1.1.4/log$ tail -f *.out
flink : 1
best : 1
is : 1
flink : 1
best : 1
is : 1
flink : 1
best : 1
is : 1
flink : 1
best : 1
is : 1
flink : 4
best : 1
is : 1
flink : 3
flink : 3
bye : 1
flink : 3
bye : 1
flink : 3
bye : 1
bye : 1
bye : 1
```

When multiple options are available for streaming on the market, then which technology to pick up depends on factors like performance, features provided, reliability, and how it fits in your use case. The given table shows a small comparison between Storm, Spark, and Flink:

	Storm	Spark	Flink
Version	1.0	2.1.0	1.1.4
Stateful processing	Storm 1.0 introduces Stateful processing - Redis backed. State is maintained at a bolt instance level. Not a distributed store.	Update State By Key	Yes - Partitioned state store (backed by Filesystem or **RocksDB**).

Window	Sliding and tumbling windows based on time duration and/or event count.	Sliding Window	Sliding window, Tumbling window, Custom window, Event Count based window.
Task isolation	Tasks are not isolated in its execution. Multiple tasks can execute in single JVM and one can be affected by other.	Standalone, YARN, Mesos	Jobs Run in YARN containers
Resource manager	Nimbus.	Standalone, YARN, Mesos	Standalone, YARN
SQL compatibility	No	Yes	Yes - Table API and SQL. SQL is not matured enough.
Language	Java, Javascript, Python, Ruby	Java, Scala, Python	Java, Scala

Setting up and a quick execution of Apache Beam

What is **Apache Beam**? According to the definition from `beam.apache.org`, Apache Beam is a unified programming model, allowing us to implement batch and streaming data processing jobs that can run on any execution engine.

Why Apache Beam? Because of the following points:

- **UNIFIED**: Use a single programming model for both batch and streaming use cases.
- **PORTABLE**: The runtime environment is decoupled from code. Execute pipelines on multiple execution environments, including Apache Apex, Apache Flink, Apache Spark, and Google Cloud Dataflow.
- **EXTENSIBLE:** Write and share new SDKs, IO connectors, and transformation libraries. You can create your own Runner in case to support new runtime.

Beam model

Any transformation or aggregation performed in Beam is called `Ptransform` and the connection between these transforms is called `PCollection`.

`PCollection` can be bounded (finite) or unbounded (infinite). One or many sets of `PTransform` and `PCollection` makes a pipeline in Beam.

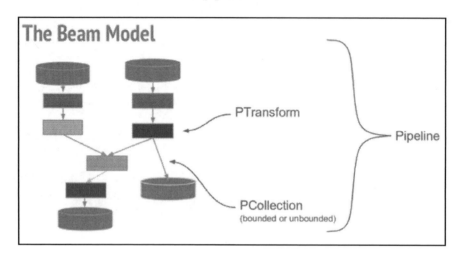

Running example

You need Java 7 or a later version and Maven to build the code. Let's get ready and run the tech world famous word count example with Apache Beam.

The preceding Maven command generates a Maven project that contains Apache Beam's `WordCount` example:

```
$ mvnarchetype:generate \
    -DarchetypeRepository=https://repository.apache.org/content
    /groups/snapshots \
    -DarchetypeGroupId=org.apache.beam \
    -DarchetypeArtifactId=beam-sdks-java-maven-archetypes-examples \
    -DarchetypeVersion=LATEST \
    -DgroupId=org.example \
    -DartifactId=word-count-beam \
    -Dversion="0.1" \
    -Dpackage=org.apache.beam.examples \
    -DinteractiveMode=false
```

This will create a folder named word-count-beam which contains the code:

```
$ cd word-count-beam/
$ ls
pom.xml   src
$ lssrc/main/java/org/apache/beam/examples/
DebuggingWordCount.java     WindowedWordCount.java   common
MinimalWordCount.java                WordCount.java
```

There are different versions of WordCount available provided by Apache Beam as an example. Let's focus on WordCount.java for now. Beam pipeline can run multiple runners. While executing any pipeline, you have to specify the runner using argument --runner=<runner>.

To run the WordCount example, execute the command as per the runner:

- **Direct Runner**: There is no need to specify the runner as it is the default. Direct Runner runs on local machine and no specific setup will be required

    ```
    mvn compile exec:java -
    Dexec.mainClass=org.apache.beam.examples.WordCount -Dexec.args="--
    inputFile=pom.xml --output=counts" -Pdirect-runner
    ```

- **Flink Runner**:

    ```
    mvn compile exec:java -
    Dexec.mainClass=org.apache.beam.examples.WordCount -Dexec.args="--
    runner=FlinkRunner --inputFile=pom.xml --output=counts" -PFlink-
    runner
    ```

- **Spark Runner**:

    ```
    mvn compile exec:java -
    Dexec.mainClass=org.apache.beam.examples.WordCount -Dexec.args="--
    runner=SparkRunner --inputFile=pom.xml --output=counts" -Pspark-
    runner
    ```

- **DataFlow Runner**:

    ```
    mvn compile exec:java -
    Dexec.mainClass=org.apache.beam.examples.WordCount -Dexec.args="--
    runner=DataflowRunner --gcpTempLocation=gs://<your-gcs-bucket>/tmp
    --inputFile=gs://apache-beam-samples/shakespeare/* --
    output=gs://<your-gcs-bucket>/counts" -Pdataflow-runner
    ```

After running the previous command, the file names starting with count are created in the same folder. When we execute the command to check the entries in files, it will be as shown in the given screenshot:

```
                                                    /word-count-beam$ ls
counts-00000-of-00003   counts-00001-of-00003   counts-00002-of-00003  pom.xml  src  target
                                                    /word-count-beam$ ls counts-0000*
counts-00000-of-00003   counts-00001-of-00003   counts-00002-of-00003
                                                    /word-count-beam$ more counts-0000*
::::::::::::::::
counts-00000-of-00003
::::::::::::::::
removed: 1
time: 2
plugin: 15
loaded: 1
examples: 1
Snapshot: 1
ASF: 2
agreements: 1
codec: 2
NOTICE: 1
a: 17
```

 If your program fails due to missing dependencies in Maven, then cleanup the .m2/repository/org/apache/maven and try again.

MinimalWordCount example walk through

We will walk through the MinimalWordCount.java example given on the Apache Beam site and run it on the Flink server that we setup in the previous section. The WordCount that we ran in the above example is the same implementation as MinimalWordCount.java, but with best coding practices and reusable code. So, here we would discuss the MinimalWordCount example so that the user can understand the concept clearly. For more details, visit https://beam.apache.org/get-started/wordcount-example. The key concepts for building the minimal word count example in the Beam Pipeline are:

- **Creating Pipeline**:

    ```
    PipelineOptions options = PipelineOptionsFactory.create();
    ```

The `PipelineOption` object contains information about the runner and runner-specific configuration. By default, it runs on Default Runner. To make it specific to the Flink or Spark Runner then make the runner specific changes:

```
FlinkPipelineOptions options =
PipelineOptionsFactory.create().as(FlinkPipelineOptions.class);
options.setRunner(FlinkRunner.class);
```

Create the `Pipeline` object with the options we defined above.

```
Pipeline p = Pipeline.create(options);
```

- **Applying Pipeline transforms**: Each transformation takes input and produces output in the form of `PCollection`. Apply the read transformation which sets the input path and reads the file:

```
p.apply(TextIO.Read.from("gs://apache-beam-samples/shakespeare/*"))
```

`gs://` is Google Cloud Storage. You can specify the local file with a complete path, but keep in mind that if you are running code on a Spark cluster or Flink cluster then it might be possible that the file is not present in the directory mentioned in `Readfrom` function.

Apply the `ParDo` transformation which calls `DoFn`. `DoFn` splits each element in `PCollection` from `TextIO` and generates a new `PCollection` with each individual word as an element:

```
.apply("ExtractWords", ParDo.of(new DoFn<String, String>() {
          @ProcessElement
public void processElement(ProcessContext c) {
for (String word : c.element().split("[^a-zA-Z']+")) {
if (!word.isEmpty()) {
c.output(word);
                }
            }
        }
    })))
```

Apply count transformation which counts the occurrence of each element in `PCollection` and produces a `PCollection` of the key/value pair. Each key represents a unique word and the value is the total count.

```
.apply(Count.<String>perElement())
```

To convert the output into a readable/meaningful format then apply `MapElement` composite transformation which executes the user defined function for each element in `PCollection` and produces a `PCollection` of string or any type. Here, it converts the key/value pair in a printable format:

```
.apply("FormatResults", MapElements.via(new
SimpleFunction<KV<String, Long>, String>() {
        @Override
public String apply(KV<String, Long> input) {
returninput.getKey() + ": " + input.getValue();
        }
    }))
```

To save the output in the file apply write transformation which takes `PCollection` and produces `PDone`.

```
.apply(TextIO.Write.to("wordcounts"));
```

- **Running the Pipeline**: Run the Pipeline using the following statement in code:

```
p.run().waitUntilFinish();
```

Pictorial representation is as shown in the following figure:

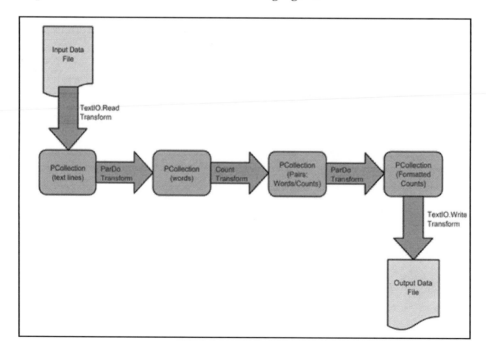

Here is the complete program:

```
packageorg.apache.beam.examples;

importorg.apache.beam.runners.Flink.FlinkPipelineOptions;
importorg.apache.beam.runners.Flink.FlinkRunner;
importorg.apache.beam.sdk.Pipeline;
importorg.apache.beam.sdk.io.TextIO;
importorg.apache.beam.sdk.options.PipelineOptionsFactory;
importorg.apache.beam.sdk.transforms.Count;
importorg.apache.beam.sdk.transforms.DoFn;
importorg.apache.beam.sdk.transforms.MapElements;
importorg.apache.beam.sdk.transforms.ParDo;
importorg.apache.beam.sdk.transforms.SimpleFunction;
importorg.apache.beam.sdk.values.KV;

public class MinimalWordCount {

public static void main(String[] args) {
FlinkPipelineOptions options =
PipelineOptionsFactory.create().as(FlinkPipelineOptions.class);
   options.setRunner(FlinkRunner.class);
    Pipeline p = Pipeline.create(options);
p.apply(TextIO.Read.from("gs://apache-beam-samples/shakespeare/*"))
    .apply("ExtractWords", ParDo.of(new DoFn<String, String>() {
                        @ProcessElement
public void processElement(ProcessContext c) {
for (String word : c.element().split("[^a-zA-Z']+")) {
if (!word.isEmpty()) {
c.output(word);
                                }
                            }
                        }
                    }))
    .apply(Count.<String>perElement())
    .apply("FormatResults", MapElements.via(new SimpleFunction<KV<String,
Long>, String>() {
                        @Override
public String apply(KV<String, Long> input) {
returninput.getKey() + ": " + input.getValue();
                        }
                    }))
    .apply(TextIO.Write.to("wordcounts"));
p.run().waitUntilFinish();
  }
}
```

Balancing in Apache Beam

Apache Beam provides a way to keep balance between completeness, latency, and cost. Completeness refers here to how all events should process, latency is the time taken to execute an event and cost is the computing power required to finish the job. The following are the right questions that should be asked to build a Pipeline in Apache Beam which maintains balance between the above three parameters:

- **What results are calculated?** By using the transformations available in Pipeline, the system is calculating results.
- **Where in the event time results are calculated?** This is achieved by using event-time windowing. Event time windowing is further categorized into fixed, sliding, and session window.
- **When in processing time are results materialized?** This is achieved by using watermark and triggers. Watermark is the way to measure the completeness of a sequence of events in an unbounded stream. The trigger defines when the output will be emitted from the window. These are the important factors to create balance.
- **How do the refinements of the results relate?** Accumulators are used to refine the results generated from the above process.

We saw the example of transformation above which computes the word count for a batch of files. Now, we will continue on window, watermark, triggers, and accumulators. We will discuss the same example given in the Apache Beam examples coming with package.

This example illustrates the different scenarios of trigger where results are generated partially, including late arriving data by recalculating the results. Data is real time traffic from San Diego. It contains readings from sensor stations set up along each freeway. Each sensor reading includes a calculation of the `total_flow` across all lanes in that freeway direction. The input would be a text file and the output would be written in **Big Query**.

The following table is a sequence of records:

Key (`freeway`)	Value (`total_flow`)	Event time	Processing time
5	50	10:00:03	10:00:47
5	30	10:01:00	10:01:03
5	30	10:02:00	11:07:00
5	20	10:04:10	10:05:15

5	60	10:05:00	11:03:00
5	20	10:05:01	11.07:30
5	60	10:15:00	10:27:15
5	40	10:26:40	10:26:43
5	60	10:27:20	10:27:25
5	60	10:29:00	11:11:00

Take a window of duration 5 minutes:

```
PCollection<TableRow>defaultTriggerResults = flowInfo
.apply("Default", Window.<KV<String,
Integer>>into(FixedWindows.of(Duration.standardMinutes(30)))
```

The trigger emits the output when the system's watermark passes the end of the window:

```
.triggering(Repeatedly.forever(AfterWatermark.pastEndOfWindow()))
```

Data which arrives after the watermark has passed the event timestamp of the arriving element is considered as late data and in this example we will drop the event if it is late arriving:

```
.withAllowedLateness(Duration.ZERO)
```

Discard the elements when the window is finished. It will not be carried forward to the next window:

```
.discardingFiredPanes())
```

The result will be as follows:

Key (freeway)	Value (total_flow)	number_of_records	isFirst	isFirst	Timing
5	260	6	True	True	ON_TIME

Each pane produced by the default trigger with no allowed lateness will be the first and last pane in the window and will be ON_TIME. At 11:03:00 (processing time), the system watermark may have advanced to 10:54:00. As a result, when the data record with event time 10:05:00 arrives at 11:03:00, it is considered late and dropped.

We can change the duration for allowed late arriving data in the above example as follows:

```
.withAllowedLateness(Duration.standardDays(1)))
```

If we do this, then the result will be as follows:

Key (freeway)	Value (total_flow)	number_of_records	isFirst	isFirst	timing
5	260	6	True	True	ON_TIME
5	60	1	False	False	LATE
5	30	1	False	False	LATE
5	20	1	False	False	LATE
5	60	1	False	False	LATE

This leads to each window staying open for ONE_DAY after the watermark has passed the end of the window. If we want to accumulate the value across the panes and also want to emit the results irrespective of the watermark, we can implement the code in the following example:

The trigger emits the element after the processing time whenever the element is received in the pane:

```
triggering(Repeatedly.forever(AfterProcessingTime.pastFirstElementInPane()
```

This accumulates the elements, so that each approximation includes all of the previous data in addition to the newly arrived data:

```
accumulatingFiredPanes()
```

The following table shows the result:

Key (freeway)	Value (total_flow)	number_of_records	isFirst	isFirst	timing
5	80	2	True	False	EARLY
5	100	3	False	False	EARLY
5	260	6	False	False	EARLY
5	320	7	False	False	LATE
5	370	9	False	False	LATE
5	430	10	False	False	LATE

Since we don't have any triggers that depend on the watermark, we don't get an ON_TIME firing. Instead, all panes are either EARLY or LATE.

The complete program is available in the Apache beam GitHub location: https://github.com/apache/beam/blob/master/examples/java/src/main/java/org/apache/beam/examples/cookbook/TriggerExample.java.

Summary

In this chapter, we get the readers acquainted with and introduced to the setup and quick execution of Spark, Flink, and Beam. They can run the examples by running the code bundled in the jar easily on standalone as well as on cluster mode.

Storm is also computation engine. We will discuss Storm in next few chapters. In the next chapter, we will discuss about integration of Storm with different data sources.

6
Integrating Storm with a Data Source

This is the chapter where we integrate the source of data with Storm distributed compute engine. It involves stringing together the source of streaming data to a broker service like RabbitMQ and then wiring the streaming pipeline to Storm. We have a very interesting sensor data recipe here, which streams live data from a free real-time sensor data channel and pushes that into RabbitMQ and further to a Storm topology for business analysis .

- RabbitMQ – messaging that works
- RabbitMQ Exchanges
- RabbitMQ Setup
- RabbitMQ – publish and subscribe
- RabbitMQ – integration with Storm
- PubNub data stream publisher
- Sensor data processing topology

RabbitMQ – messaging that works

RabbitMQ is one of the most sought after broker/queue services that works in production implementation with Storm. It's a very robust and versatile messaging system, that is supported both in open source as well as in a commercial version across all major operating systems. It has both durable and in-memory configuration on queues where the developers get enough flexibility to decide and choose on trade-offs between reliability and performance.

A few terms that would be used very often in context to RabbitMQ in particular, or any other queuing system are described as follows:

- **Producer/publisher**: It's the client component that writes or sends the messages to the queue
- **Queue**: It's actually the in-memory buffer that stores the message, from the time it's sent to the queue to the time it's read off the queue by a consumer application
- **Consumer/subscriber**: It's the client component that receives or reads the messages off the queue

In the case of RabbitMQ, the producer/publisher never publishes any messages to the queue, but it actually writes the messages to an **exchange** which in turn further pushes the messages into the queue, based on the exchange type and routing key.

RabbitMQ exchanges

RabbitMQ is versatile and provides for a variety of exchanges which are at the disposal of its developers to cater to a myriad of problems that come across for implementation.

Direct exchanges

In this type of exchange, we have a routing key bound to the queue, which serves as a pass key to direct the messages to the queue. So every message that is published to the exchange has a routing key associated with it, which decides the destination queue the exchange writes it to. For example, in the preceding figure, the message is written to the green queue because the message routing queue **"green"** binds to the green queue:

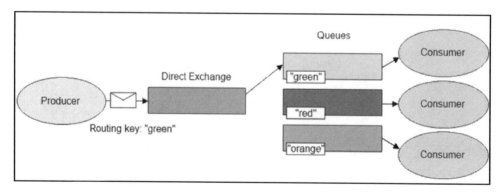

Fanout exchanges

They can also be called broadcast exchange, because when a message is published to a **Fanout Exchange** it's written/sent to all the queues bound to the exchange. The preceding figure demonstrates its working. Here the message published by the producer is sent to all the three queues; green, red, and orange. So in a nutshell each queue bound to the exchange receives a copy of the message. It is analogue to the pub-sub broker pattern:

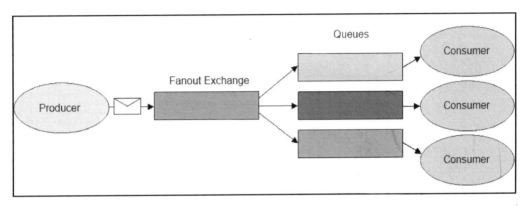

Topic exchanges

When a message is published to a topic exchange, it is sent to all the queues whose routing key matches all, or a portion of the routing key of the message published—for example, if we publish a message to a topic exchange with a key as green.red, then the message would be published to the queue green queue and red queue. To understand it better, here is the figurative explanation for the same:

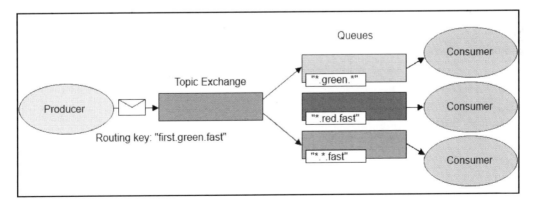

The message routing key is **"first.green.fast"** and with topic exchange it's published onto the **"green"** queue because the word green occurs in there, the **"red.fast"** queue because the word fast occurs in there, and the **"*.fast"** queue because the word **"fast"** occurs in there.

Headers exchanges

This exchange actually publishes the messages to specific queues by matching the message headers with the binding queue headers. These exchanges hold a very strong similarity to the topic based exchange, but they differ in the concept that they have more than one matching criteria with complex ordered conditions:

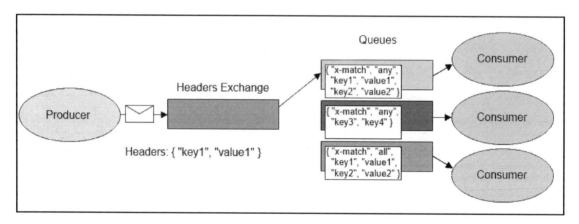

The message published in the previous exchange has a key ("**key1**") associated with it which maps to the value ("**value1**"); the exchange matches it against all the bindings in queue headers and the criteria actually matches with the first header value in the first queue which maps to "**key1**", "**value1**" and thus the message gets published only to the first queue—also note the match criteria as "**any**". In the last queue, the values are the same as the first queue but the match criteria is "**all**" which means both mappings should match, thus the message isn't published on the bottom queue.

RabbitMQ setup

Now let's actually start the setup and see some action with RabbitMQ. The latest version of RabbitMQ can be downloaded as a DEB file from rabbitMQ.com/github.com and can be installed using the Ubuntu software center:

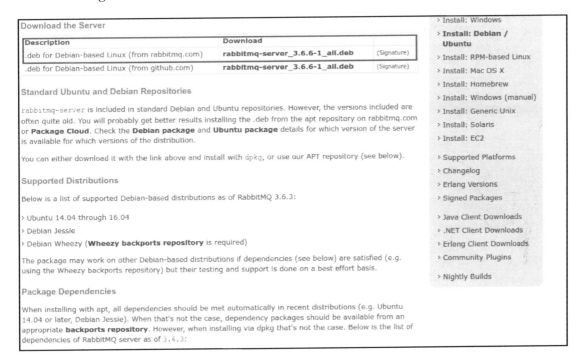

Another mechanism is using the command line interface using the following steps:

1. The given command is used to add the repository to your system:

```
echo 'deb http://www.rabbitmq.com/debian/ testing main' |
        sudo tee /etc/apt/sources.list.d/rabbitmq.list
```

2. Next, we need to add the public key to your trusted key configurations:

```
wget -O- https://www.rabbitmq.com/rabbitmq-release-signing-key.asc
|
        sudo apt-key add -
```

3. Once the previous steps are successfully executed we need to update the package list:

```
sudo apt-get update
```

4. We are all set to install the RabbitMQ server:

```
sudo apt-get install rabbitmq-server
```

5. Once set up is done we need to start the server:

```
sudo service rabbitmq-server start
```

6. The following command can be used to check the status of the server:

```
sudo service rabbitmq-server status
```

7. The following command is used to stop the RabbitMQ Server:

```
sudo service rabbitmq-server stop
```

8. Optionally users can/or rather should enable the RabbitMQ management console to provide access to the UI Application for the same using the given command:

```
sudo rabbitmq-plugins enable rabbitmq_management
```

9. Access the RabbitMQ UI:

```
http://localhost:15672/#/
```

On successful completion of the previous steps, you should have the following screenshot:

RabbitMQ — publish and subscribe

Once the RabbitMQ service is installed and it's up and running as can be verified from the RMQ, the management console's next obvious step is to write a quick publisher and consumer application. Following is the code snippet of the producer that publishes a message under an exchange called `MYExchange` on a queue called `MyQueue`.

```
package com.book.rmq;
...
public class RMQProducer {
        private static String myRecord;
```

```
private static final String EXCHANGE_NAME = "MYExchange";
private final static String QUEUE_NAME = "MYQueue";
private final static String ROUTING_KEY = "MYQueue";
public static void main(String[] argv) throws Exception {
        ConnectionFactory factory = new ConnectionFactory();
        Address[] addressArr = { new Address("localhost", 5672) };
        Connection connection = factory.newConnection(addressArr);
        Channel channel = connection.createChannel();
        channel.exchangeDeclare(EXCHANGE_NAME, "direct");
        channel.queueDeclare(QUEUE_NAME, true, false, false, null);
        channel.queueBind(QUEUE_NAME, EXCHANGE_NAME, ROUTING_KEY);
        int i = 0;
          while (i < 1) {
              try {
                    myRecord = "My Sample record";
                    channel.basicPublish(EXCHANGE_NAME, ROUTING_KEY,
MessageProperties.PERSISTENT_TEXT_PLAIN,
                              myRecord.getBytes());
                    System.out.println(" [x] Sent '" + myRecord + "'
                              sent at " + new Date());
                    i++;
                    Thread.sleep(2);
              } catch (Exception e) {
                    e.printStackTrace();

              }
        }
        channel.close();
        connection.close();
    }
}
```

Here we begin with:

- Declaring the exchange as MYExchange, queue as MYQueue bound to the exchange using the routing queue MYQueue

- Next we proceed to declare a ConnectFactory called factory, that binds to the RabbitMQ broker running on localhost (you can also specify local or remote IP for the same)

- We are using the following statement, to declare a direct exchange:
  channel.exchangeDeclare(EXCHANGE_NAME, "direct");

- Next we declare a channel, associate the exchanges and queue to the channel, and bind the queue to the exchange using the routing key

- Lastly, we create a test message and publish to the queue using the basicPublish method

The preceding screenshot shows the command line and UI output for the same for the execution of the program:

On the RabbitMQ console you can see the event published under MyQueue under the **Queues** tab:

Next, let's put together a quick consumer Java application to read this message from the queue:

```
package com.book.rmq;
..

public class RMQConsumer {
    private static final String EXCHANGE_NAME = "MYExchange";
    private final static String QUEUE_NAME = "MYQueue";
    private final static String ROUTING_KEY = "MYQueue";
```

```java
public static void main(String[] argv) {
    ConnectionFactory factory = new ConnectionFactory();
    Address[] addressArr = { new Address("localhost", 5672) };
    try {
        Connection connection = factory.newConnection(addressArr);
        Channel channel = connection.createChannel();
        connection = factory.newConnection();
        channel.exchangeDeclare(EXCHANGE_NAME, "direct");
        channel.queueDeclare(QUEUE_NAME, true, false, false, null);
        channel.queueBind(QUE    UE_NAME, EXCHANGE_NAME,
ROUTING_KEY);
        System.out.println("{N|T} Waiting for messages.");
        channel.queueDeclare(QUEUE_NAME, true, false, false, null);
        channel.queueBind(QUEUE_NAME, EXCHANGE_NAME, ROUTING_KEY);
        Consumer consumer = new DefaultConsumer(channel) {
            @Override
            public void handleDelivery(String consumerTag, Envelope
            envelope, AMQP.BasicProperties properties,
            byte[] body) throws IOException {
                String message = new String(body, "UTF-8");
                System.out.println("Java Queue - Message Received
'" +
                message + "'");
            }
        };
        // loop that waits for message
        channel.basicConsume(QUEUE_NAME, true, consumer);
    } catch (IOException e) {
        System.out.println("RabbitMQ server is Down !");
        System.out.println(e.getMessage());
    } catch (TimeoutException e) {
        e.printStackTrace();
    }
}
}
```

Here is the console output for the same that reads the sample:

```
Problems  @ Javadoc  Declaration  Console 23  Progress
<terminated> RMQConsumer [Java Application] /opt/java8/bin/java (14-Feb-2017 11:06:49am)
{N|T} Waiting for messages.
Java Queue - Message Received 'My Sample record'
```

The next progressive item would be to read the messages from RabbitMQ using a Storm topology.

RabbitMQ – integration with Storm

Now that we have accomplished basic setup and publish, and subscribe next let's move on to integration of RabbitMQ with Storm. We'll execute this as an end-to-end example.

AMQPSpout

Storm integrates with RabbitMQ using an AMQPSpout, which reads the messages from RabbitMQ and pushes them to Storm topology for further processing. The following code snippet captures the key aspects of encoding the AMQPSpout:

```
..
public class AMQPSpout implements IRichSpout {
        private static final long serialVersionUID = 1L;
        /**
         * Logger instance
         */
        private static final Logger log =
        LoggerFactory.getLogger(AMQPSpout.class);
        private static final long CONFIG_PREFETCH_COUNT = 0;
        private static final long DEFAULT_PREFETCH_COUNT = 0;
        private static final long WAIT_AFTER_SHUTDOWN_SIGNAL = 0;
        private static final long WAIT_FOR_NEXT_MESSAGE = 1L;

        private static final String EXCHANGE_NAME = "MYExchange";
        private static final String QUEUE_NAME = "MYQueue";
        private String amqpHost;
        private int amqpPort;
        private String amqpUsername;
        private String amqpPasswd;
        private String amqpVhost;
        private boolean requeueOnFail;
        private boolean autoAck;

        private int prefetchCount;

        private SpoutOutputCollector collector;

        private Connection amqpConnection;
        private Channel amqpChannel;
        private QueueingConsumer amqpConsumer;
        private String amqpConsumerTag;
        private boolean spoutActive;

        // The constructor where we set initialize all properties
```

```
    public AMQPSpout(String host, int port, String username, String
        password, String vhost, boolean requeueOnFail, boolean autoAck) {
            this.amqpHost = host;
            this.amqpPort = port;
            this.amqpUsername = username;
            this.amqpPasswd = password;
            this.amqpVhost = vhost;
            this.requeueOnFail = requeueOnFail;
            this.autoAck = autoAck;
    }

/*
 * Open method of the spout , here we initialize the prefetch count,
 this
 * parameter specified how many messages would be prefetched from the
 queue
 * by the spout - to increase the efficiency of the solution
 */
public void open(@SuppressWarnings("rawtypes") Map conf,
            TopologyContext context, SpoutOutputCollector collector) {
        Long prefetchCount = (Long) conf.get(CONFIG_PREFETCH_COUNT);
        if (prefetchCount == null) {
            log.info("Using default prefetch-count");
            prefetchCount = DEFAULT_PREFETCH_COUNT;
        } else if (prefetchCount < 1) {
            throw new IllegalArgumentException(CONFIG_PREFETCH_COUNT
                    + " must be at least 1");
        }
        this.prefetchCount = prefetchCount.intValue();

        try {
            this.collector = collector;

            setupAMQP();
        } catch (IOException e) {
            log.error("AMQP setup failed", e);
            log.warn("AMQP setup failed, will attempt to
            reconnect...");
            Utils.sleep(WAIT_AFTER_SHUTDOWN_SIGNAL);
            try {
                reconnect();
            } catch (TimeoutException e1) {
                // TODO Auto-generated catch block
                e1.printStackTrace();
            }
        } catch (TimeoutException e) {
            // TODO Auto-generated catch block
            e.printStackTrace();
```

```
            }
      }
   /**
    * Reconnect to an AMQP broker.in case the connection breaks at some
      point
    *
    * @throws TimeoutException
    */
   private void reconnect() throws TimeoutException {
         log.info("Reconnecting to AMQP broker...");
         try {
               setupAMQP();
         } catch (IOException e) {
               log.warn("Failed to reconnect to AMQP broker", e);
         }
   }
     /**
      * Setup a connection with an AMQP broker.
      *
      * @throws IOException
      *     This is the method where we actually connect to the queue
      *            using AMQP client api's
      * @throws TimeoutException
      */
   private void setupAMQP() throws IOException, TimeoutException {
         final int prefetchCount = this.prefetchCount;
           final ConnectionFactory connectionFactory = new
ConnectionFactory() {
               public void configureSocket(Socket socket) throws
IOException {
                     socket.setTcpNoDelay(false);
                     socket.setReceiveBufferSize(20 * 1024);
                     socket.setSendBufferSize(20 * 1024);
               }
         };
           connectionFactory.setHost(amqpHost);
         connectionFactory.setPort(amqpPort);
         connectionFactory.setUsername(amqpUsername);
         connectionFactory.setPassword(amqpPasswd);
         connectionFactory.setVirtualHost(amqpVhost);
          this.amqpConnection = connectionFactory.newConnection();
         this.amqpChannel = amqpConnection.createChannel();
           log.info("Setting basic.qos prefetch-count to " +
           prefetchCount);
         amqpChannel.basicQos(prefetchCount);
           amqpChannel.exchangeDeclare(EXCHANGE_NAME, "direct");
         amqpChannel.queueDeclare(QUEUE_NAME, true, false, false, null);
           amqpChannel.queueBind(QUEUE_NAME, EXCHANGE_NAME, "");
```

```
              this.amqpConsumer = new QueueingConsumer(amqpChannel);
          assert this.amqpConsumer != null;
          this.amqpConsumerTag = amqpChannel.basicConsume(QUEUE_NAME,
                    this.autoAck, amqpConsumer);
          System.out.println("***************");
     }
   /*
   * Cancels the queue subscription, and disconnects from the AMQP
   broker. */
  public void close() {
       try {
            if (amqpChannel != null) {
                 if (amqpConsumerTag != null) {
                      amqpChannel.basicCancel(amqpConsumerTag);
                 }
                 amqpChannel.close();
            }
       } catch (IOException e) {
            log.warn("Error closing AMQP channel", e);
       } catch (TimeoutException e) {
            // TODO Auto-generated catch block
            e.printStackTrace();
       }
         try {
            if (amqpConnection != null) {
                 amqpConnection.close();
            }
       } catch (IOException e) {
            log.warn("Error closing AMQP connection", e);
       }
    }
   /*
   * Emit message received from queue into collector
   */
  public void nextTuple() {
       // if (spoutActive &amp;&amp; amqpConsumer != null) {
       try {
            final QueueingConsumer.Delivery delivery = amqpConsumer
                      .nextDelivery(WAIT_FOR_NEXT_MESSAGE);
            if (delivery == null)
                 return;
            final long deliveryTag =
            delivery.getEnvelope().getDeliveryTag();
            String message = new String(delivery.getBody());
              if (message != null &amp;&amp; message.length() > 0) {
                   collector.emit(new Values(message), deliveryTag);
              } else {
                   log.debug("Malformed deserialized message, null or
```

```
                     zero-length. "
                              + deliveryTag);
                    if (!this.autoAck) {
                        ack(deliveryTag);
                    }
               }
        } catch (ShutdownSignalException e) {
             log.warn("AMQP connection dropped, will attempt to
             reconnect...");
             Utils.sleep(WAIT_AFTER_SHUTDOWN_SIGNAL);
             try {
                    reconnect();
             } catch (TimeoutException e1) {
                    // TODO Auto-generated catch block
                    e1.printStackTrace();
             }
        } catch (ConsumerCancelledException e) {
             log.warn("AMQP consumer cancelled, will attempt to
             reconnect...");
             Utils.sleep(WAIT_AFTER_SHUTDOWN_SIGNAL);
             try {
                    reconnect();
             } catch (TimeoutException e1) {
                    // TODO Auto-generated catch block
                    e1.printStackTrace();
             }
        } catch (InterruptedException e) {
             log.error("Interrupted while reading a message, with
             Exception : " + e);
        }
        // }
  }
  /*
  * ack method to acknowledge the message that is successfully processed
  */
  public void ack(Object msgId) {
        if (msgId instanceof Long) {
             final long deliveryTag = (Long) msgId;
             if (amqpChannel != null) {
                    try {
                           amqpChannel.basicAck(deliveryTag, false);
                    } catch (IOException e) {
                           log.warn("Failed to ack delivery-tag " +
                           deliveryTag, e);
                    } catch (ShutdownSignalException e) {
                           log.warn(
                                      "AMQP connection failed. Failed to
                                      ack delivery-tag "
```

```
                                                     + deliveryTag, e);
                    }
              }
        } else {
              log.warn(String.format("don't know how to ack(%s: %s)",
              msgId.getClass().getName(), msgId));
        }
    }
  public void fail(Object msgId) {
        if (msgId instanceof Long) {
              final long deliveryTag = (Long) msgId;
              if (amqpChannel != null) {
                    try {
                          if (amqpChannel.isOpen()) {
                                if (!this.autoAck) {
amqpChannel.basicReject(deliveryTag,
                                         requeueOnFail);
                                }
                          } else {
                                reconnect();
                          }
                    } catch (IOException e) {
                          log.warn("Failed to reject delivery-tag " +
                          deliveryTag, e);
                    } catch (TimeoutException e) {
                          // TODO Auto-generated catch block
                             e.printStackTrace();
                    }
              }
        } else {
              log.warn(String.format("don't know how to reject(%s:
              %s)", msgId.getClass().getName(), msgId));
        }
    }

    public void declareOutputFields(OutputFieldsDeclarer declarer) {
          declarer.declare(new Fields("messages"));

    }

    public void activate() {
          // TODO Auto-generated method stub

    }

    public void deactivate() {
          // TODO Auto-generated method stub
```

```
        }

        public Map<String, Object> getComponentConfiguration() {
                // TODO Auto-generated method stub
                return null;
        }
}
```

We'll quickly browse through the key methods of the previous code snippet and their internal workings:

- `public AMQPSpout(..)`: This is the constructor, where key variables are initialized with details such as host IP, port, username, and password for RabbitMQ. We also set up the `Requeue` flag in case the message fails to be processed by the topology for some reason.
- `public void open(..)`: This is the basic method of the `IRichSpout`; the prefetch count here tells us how many records should be read and kept ready in the spout buffer for the topology to consume.
- `private void setupAMQP()` `..`: This is the key method that does its namesake and sets up the spout and RabbitMQ connection by declaration of a connection factory, exchange, and queue and binds them together to the channel.
- `public void nextTuple()`: This is the method that receives the message from the RabbitMQ channel and emits the same into the collector for the topology to consume.
- The following code snippet retrieves the message and its body and emits the same into the topology:

```
..
final long deliveryTag = delivery.getEnvelope().getDeliveryTag();
String message = new String(delivery.getBody());
..
collector.emit(new Values(message), deliveryTag);
```

- Next let's capture the topology builder for holding an `AMQPSpout` component together with other bolts:

```
TopologyBuilder builder = new TopologyBuilder();
        builder.setSpout("spout", new AMQPSpout("localhost", 5672,
"guest", "guest", "/", true, false), 1);
```

- Next, we are going to plug in our queue declared under RabbitMQ with a continuous stream of sensor data. I suggest to connect you any free streaming data source such as Facebook or Twitter. For this book, I have resorted to `PubNub`: (`https://www.pubnub.com/developers/realtime-data-streams/`)

The following are some `pom.xml` entries that are required for the dependencies for this entire program to execute correctly out of your Eclipse setup.

Following are the Maven dependencies for Storm, RabbitMQ, Jackson, and `PubNub`:

```
. . .
  <properties>
    <project.build.sourceEncoding>UTF-8</project.build.sourceEncoding>
    <storm.version>0.9.3</storm.version>
</properties>
  <dependencies>
  <dependency>
      <groupId>com.rabbitmq</groupId>
      <artifactId>amqp-client</artifactId>
      <version>3.6.2</version>
</dependency>
<dependency>
      <groupId>org.apache.storm</groupId>
      <artifactId>storm-core</artifactId>
      <version>0.9.3</version>
      <scope>provided</scope>
</dependency>
<dependency>
    <groupId>com.pubnub</groupId>
    <artifactId>pubnub-gson</artifactId>
    <version>4.4.4</version>
</dependency>
<dependency>
      <groupId>com.fasterxml.jackson.core</groupId>
      <artifactId>jackson-databind</artifactId>
      <version>2.6.3</version>
</dependency>
  . .
```

PubNub data stream publisher

Let's put together a quick publisher that reads the live stream of sensor data messages from the PubNub and pushes them to RabbitMQ:

```java
..
 public class TestStream {

        private static final String EXCHANGE_NAME = "MYExchange";
        private final static String QUEUE_NAME = "MYQueue";
        private final static String ROUTING_KEY = "MYQueue";
private static void RMQPublisher(String myRecord) throws IOException,
TimeoutException
{

        ConnectionFactory factory = new ConnectionFactory();
        Address[] addressArr = { new Address("localhost", 5672) };
        Connection connection = factory.newConnection(addressArr);
        Channel channel = connection.createChannel();
        channel.exchangeDeclare(EXCHANGE_NAME, "direct");
        channel.queueDeclare(QUEUE_NAME, true, false, false, null);
        channel.queueBind(QUEUE_NAME, EXCHANGE_NAME, ROUTING_KEY);
        int i = 0;
        while (i < 1) {
                try {
                        channel.basicPublish(EXCHANGE_NAME, ROUTING_KEY,
                                MessageProperties.PERSISTENT_TEXT_PLAIN,
                                myRecord.getBytes());
                        System.out.println(" [x] Sent '" + myRecord + "' sent at
                          " + new Date());
                        i++;
                        Thread.sleep(2);
                } catch (Exception e) {
                        e.printStackTrace();

                }
        }
        channel.close();
        connection.close();
}
public static void main ( String args[])
{
PNConfiguration pnConfiguration = new PNConfiguration();
pnConfiguration.setSubscribeKey("sub-c-5f1b7c8e-fbee-11e3-
aa40-02ee2ddab7fe");
PubNub pubnub = new PubNub(pnConfiguration);
```

```
pubnub.addListener(new SubscribeCallback() {
    @Override
    public void status(PubNub pubnub, PNStatus status) {
        if (status.getCategory() ==
PNStatusCategory.PNUnexpectedDisconnectCategory) {
            // This event happens when radio / connectivity is lost
        }

        else if (status.getCategory() ==
PNStatusCategory.PNConnectedCategory) {
//System.out.println("2");
            // Connect event. You can do stuff like publish, and know
you'll get it.
            // Or just use the connected event to confirm you are
subscribed for
            // UI / internal notifications, etc
            if (status.getCategory() ==
PNStatusCategory.PNConnectedCategory){
System.out.println("status.getCategory()="+status.getCategory());
            }
        }
        else if (status.getCategory() ==
PNStatusCategory.PNReconnectedCategory) {
            // Happens as part of our regular operation. This event happens
when
            // radio / connectivity is lost, then regained.
        }
        else if (status.getCategory() ==
PNStatusCategory.PNDecryptionErrorCategory) {
            // Handle messsage decryption error. Probably client configured
to
            // encrypt messages and on live data feed it received plain
text.
        }
    }

    @Override
    public void message(PubNub pubnub, PNMessageResult message) {
        // Handle new message stored in message.message
        String strMessage = message.getMessage().toString();
            System.out.println("******"+strMessage);
        try {
            RMQPublisher(strMessage);
        } catch (IOException e) {
            // TODO Auto-generated catch block
            e.printStackTrace();
        } catch (TimeoutException e) {
            // TODO Auto-generated catch block
```

```
                    e.printStackTrace();
        }

    }
    @Override
    public void presence(PubNub pubnub, PNPresenceEventResult presence) {

        }
    });

    pubnub.subscribe().channels(Arrays.asList("pubnub-sensor-
    network")).execute();
    }
}
```

This small snippet actually connects to the PubNub stream—https://www.pubnub.com/ developers/realtime-data-streams/sensor-network/ using the subscription keys mentioned as:

STREAM DETAILS
Channel: pubnub-sensor-network
Subscribe key: sub-c-5f1b7c8e-fbee-11e3-aa40-02ee2ddab7fe

To use this stream in your project, copy/paste the previous snippets or subscribe to this channel and subkey.

The PubNub listener previously binds to the subscription channel identified by the subscription key and emits the messages into the RabbitMQ — `MyExchange`, `MYQueue`. The following is screenshot of the program in execution and a screenshot of RabbitMQ with messages in the Queue and a sample message for reference:

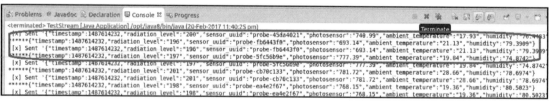

The following screenshot shows the messages showing up in the RabbitMQ, where you can see the messages from the PubNub sensor stream lined up in the `MyQueue`:

> Messages are coming as a real-time continuous stream—for this book and example I had actually shut down the PubNub stream publisher after a couple of seconds, thus you see only 33 messages.

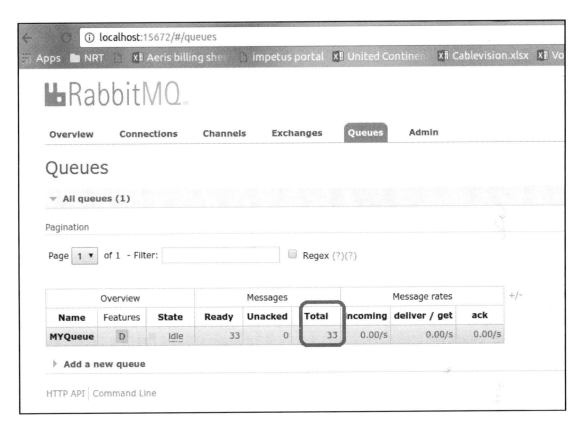

You can delve further into the Queue to retrieve and have a look at the message; click on the MyQueue, and scroll down to the **Get message** section on the next page and type the number of messages you wish to retrieve and view in the console:

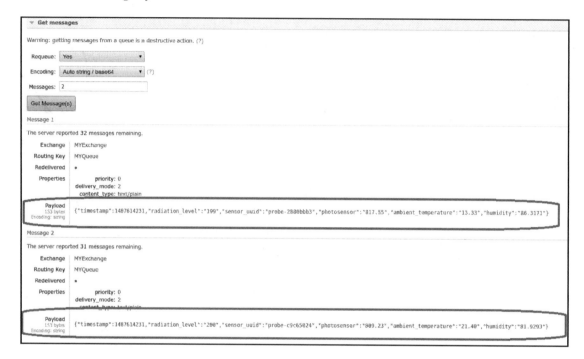

String together Storm-RMQ-PubNub sensor data topology

Let's wire in the JSON bolt to parse this JSON payload in our topology and see the execution:

```
...

public class JsonBolt implements IRichBolt {
..
        private static final long serialVersionUID = 1L;
        OutputCollector collector;

        public void prepare(Map arg0, TopologyContext arg1, OutputCollector
arg2) {
                this.collector = arg2;
```

```
        }

    public void execute(Tuple arg0) {
            String jsonInString = arg0.getStringByField("messages");
            System.out.println("message read from  queue" + jsonInString);
            JsonConverter jsonconvertor = new JsonConverter();
            MySensorData mysensorObj = jsonconvertor.run(jsonInString);
            this.collector.emit(new Values(mysensorObj));
            this.collector.ack(arg0);
        }
    ..


}
..


class JsonConverter {
..


    public MySensorData run(String jsonInString) {
            ObjectMapper mapper = new ObjectMapper();
            MySensorData mysensorObj = null;
            try {

                    mysensorObj = mapper.readValue(jsonInString,
                    MySensorData.class);

                    // Pretty print
                    String prettyStaff1 =
                    mapper.writerWithDefaultPrettyPrinter()
                            .writeValueAsString(mysensorObj);
                    System.out.println(prettyStaff1);

            } catch (JsonGenerationException e) {
            ..
            return mysensorObj;
        }

}
```

My JSONBolt basically accepts the message from the AMQPSpout of the topology and converts the JSON string into a JSON object that can be further processed based on business logic, for instance in our case we further stringed the SensorProcessorBolt:

```
TopologyBuilder builder = new TopologyBuilder();
builder.setSpout("spout", new AMQPSpout("localhost", 5672, "guest",
"guest", "/", true, false), 1);
builder.setBolt("split", new JsonBolt(), 8).shuffleGrouping("spout");
builder.setBolt("count", new SensorProcessorBolt(),
2).fieldsGrouping("split", new Fields("word"));
```

The SensorProcessorBolt checks for the radiationLevel in the sensor emitted data and filters and emits only the events that have a radiation level of more than 197:

```
..

public class SensorProcessorBolt extends BaseBasicBolt {

        public void execute(Tuple tuple, BasicOutputCollector collector) {
                MySensorData mysensordata = (MySensorData) tuple.getValue(0);
                if (mysensordata.getRadiation_level() > 197) {
System.out.println("###################################");
                        System.out.println(mysensordata.getSensor_uuid());
                        System.out.println(mysensordata.toString());
System.out.println("###################################");

        }

                collector.emit(new Values(mysensordata.toString()));
        }

    ..

}
```

The following screenshot is the complete topology in execution:

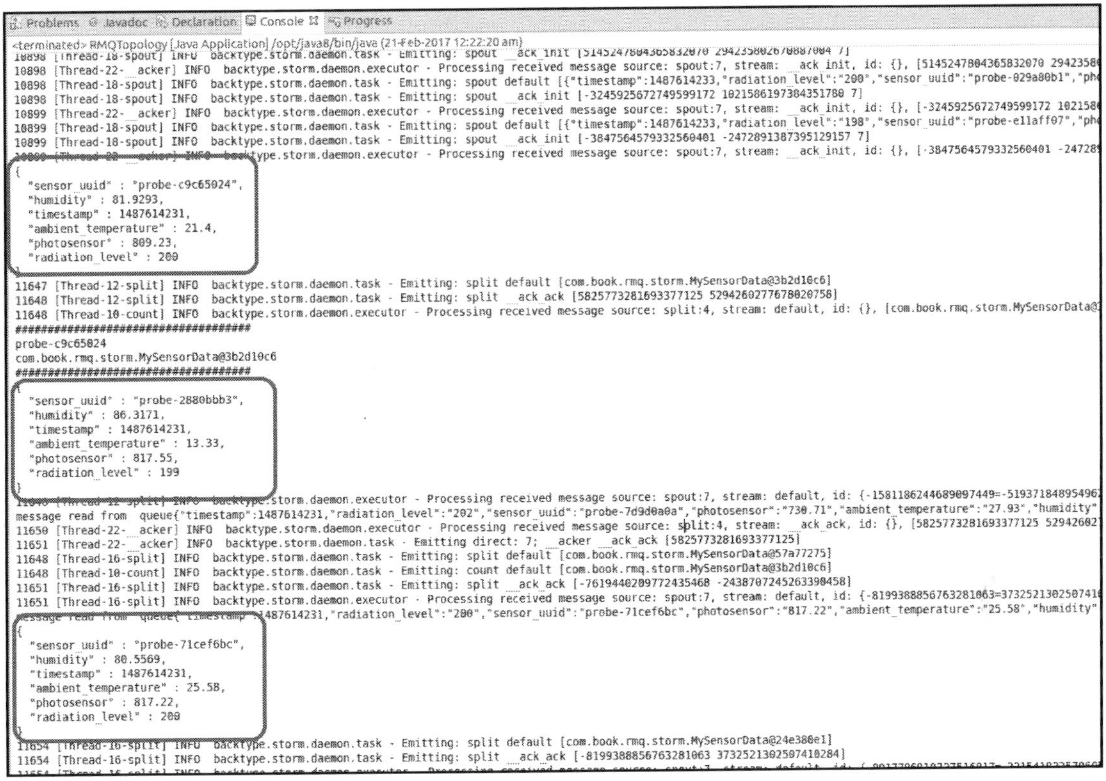

It's easy to deduce from the previous screenshot that we are emitting only the high (above 197) radiation level events as an output from this topology. One can further enhance this use case and apply a variety of business analytics on the stream of IOT sensor data or variety of other data sources available freely or at PubNub:

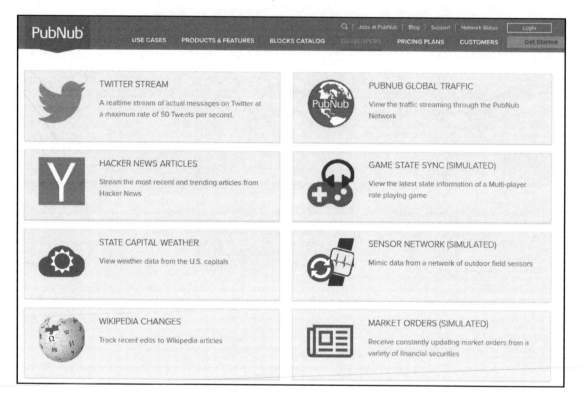

Summary

In this chapter, we introduce the readers to the RabbitMQ messaging system—they start with a setup followed by a basic publisher and subscriber and then graduate to the next level of integrating the broker service to a Storm topology. Then we further delve into end-to-end application building exercises by the introduction of PubNub sensor data as a real-time continuous stream of IOT events for consumption and processing by Storm topology. After walking the readers through examples and codes for each component in the topology, we leave them with a stimulated mind to delve further and try more sources at PubNub with advanced business logic under the processing topology.

7
From Storm to Sink

This is the chapter where we integrate the stable storage and sinks to the Storm topology. We begin with setting up Cassandra and then wiring integrations through Storm. The following topics will be covered in this chapter:

- Setting up and configuring Cassandra
- Storm and Cassandra topology
- Storm and IMDb integration for dimensional data
- Integrating the presentation layer with Storm
- Do It Yourself

Setting up and configuring Cassandra

Before moving towards setting up and configuring Cassandra, let's explain what Cassandra is and why it is so popular. Cassandra is a NoSQL columnar database. If you need high scalability with high availability then Cassandra is the best choice. It has high read and write performance but with eventual consistency.

Eventual consistency is when you insert a row in a database and at same time another user reads the same table, making it possible that the newly added row would be visible to the user or not. **Keyspace** in Cassandra is the same as a database in RDMS. The rest of the terminology is the same as RDMS. Cassandra is an open source tool but if you need to manage clusters with designed a UI, then go for DataStax. **DataStax** provides paid premium services and includes full-time support. Now, let's see how to set up Cassandra.

Setting up Cassandra

Download the latest version 3.10 from `http://cassandra.apache.org/download/`and the older version can be downloaded from `http://archive.apache.org/dist/cassandra/`. `apache-cassandra-3.10-bin.tar.gz` will be downloaded. The following commands are executed to extract it:

```
mw apache-cassandra-3.10-bin.tar.gz ~/demo
tar -xvf ~/demo/apache-cassandra-3.10-bin.tar.gz
```

Files and directories are extracted, as seen in the following screenshot:

```
                            /demo/apache-cassandra-3.10$ ls
bin  CHANGES.txt  conf  doc  interface  javadoc  lib  LICENSE.txt  NEWS.txt  NOTICE.txt  pylib  tools
```

Now run Cassandra as a standalone on the localhost:

```
/bin/Cassandra
```

Cassandra is started as the backend process. Press *Enter* to exit from the logs. To verify whether Cassandra is working or not, execute the following command:

```
/bin/nodetool status
```

The output is as shown in the following screenshot:

```
Datacenter: datacenter1
=======================
Status=Up/Down
|/ State=Normal/Leaving/Joining/Moving
--  Address    Load        Tokens       Owns (effective)  Host ID                                Rack
UN  127.0.0.1  140.38 KiB  256          100.0%            c4248a64-328f-4e9c-80ee-86952783f6be   rack1
```

There is the concept of Virtual Nodes (vnodes) in Cassandra. vnodes are created automatically by Cassandra on each node. By default, 256 vnodes are created when you start Cassandra. To check the vnodes on the current node, use the following command:

```
/bin/nodetool ring
```

It shows a long list of token IDs along with the load, as seen in the following screenshot:

```
Datacenter: datacenter1
===========
Address      Rack     Status State   Load          Owns         Token
                                                                 9082964654361184224
127.0.0.1    rack1    Up     Normal  140.38 KiB    100.00%      -9110336601702226265
127.0.0.1    rack1    Up     Normal  140.38 KiB    100.00%      -9101444158216710526
127.0.0.1    rack1    Up     Normal  140.38 KiB    100.00%      -8896467633216707558
127.0.0.1    rack1    Up     Normal  140.38 KiB    100.00%      -8887579311965894736
127.0.0.1    rack1    Up     Normal  140.38 KiB    100.00%      -8851910265753833933
127.0.0.1    rack1    Up     Normal  140.38 KiB    100.00%      -8808830478669524597
127.0.0.1    rack1    Up     Normal  140.38 KiB    100.00%      -8719892936278247869
127.0.0.1    rack1    Up     Normal  140.38 KiB    100.00%      -8635350951218162545
127.0.0.1    rack1    Up     Normal  140.38 KiB    100.00%      -8532306360683834438
127.0.0.1    rack1    Up     Normal  140.38 KiB    100.00%      -8528437378771948471
```

Configuring Cassandra

The `Conf` file in the installation directory contains all the configuration files that you configure. Let's divide the configurations in to sections to understand them better:

The following properties must be shown in the next lines:

- `cluster_name`: The name of your cluster.
- `seeds`: A comma separated list of the IP addresses of your cluster seeds. These nodes are used to help gossip protocol, which checks the health of the nodes.

> Two or three nodes are sufficient to perform this role. Also, use the same seeds node in your whole cluster.

- `listen_address`: The IP address of your node.This is what allows other nodes to communicate with this node, so it is important that you change it.
- Never set `listen_address` to `0.0.0.0`.
- Alternatively, you can set `listen_interface` to tell Cassandra which interface to use, and consecutively which address to use.
- Set either `listen_address` or `listen_interface`, but not both.
- `native_transport_port`: As for `storage_port`, this is used by clients to communicate with Cassandra.
- Make sure this port is not blocked by firewalls.

- Location of data log files:
  - `data_file_directories`: Location of one or more directories where data files are kept
  - `commitlog_directory`: Location of the directory where `commitlog` files are kept
  - `saved_caches_directory`: Location of the directory where saved caches are kept
  - `hints_directory`: Location of directory where hints are kept

 For performance reasons, if you have multiple disks, consider putting `commitlog` and data files on different disks.

- **Environment variables**: To set up environment variables, use `cassandra.in.sh` located at `installation_dir/bin/cassandra.in.sh`. It is mainly used to set up the JVM level of settings.
- **Logging**: The `Logback` framework is used as the logger in Cassandra. You can change the log level settings by making changes in `logback.xml` located at `installation_dir/conf/logback.xml`.

Storm and Cassandra topology

As discussed in `Chapter 4`, *Setting up the Infrastructure for Storm*, Storm has spouts and bolts. The Casandra bolt is required to persist records. There are two common ways to integrate Storm with Cassandra. The first is by using the `storm-cassandra` built-in library where you just need to call `CassndraBolt` and the required parameters. The second way is by using the DataStax Cassandra library, which needs to be imported using the build manager and using the wrapper classes to make a connection with Cassandra. The following are the steps to integrate Storm with Cassandra using the `DataStax` library:

1. Add the following dependencies:

```
<dependency>
    <groupId>com.datastax.cassandra</groupId>
    <artifactId>cassandra-driver-core</artifactId>
    <version>3.1.0</version>
</dependency>
<dependency>
    <groupId>com.datastax.cassandra</groupId>
```

```
        <artifactId>cassandra-driver-mapping</artifactId>
        <version>3.1.0</version>
</dependency>
<dependency>
        <groupId>com.datastax.cassandra</groupId>
        <artifactId>cassandra-driver-extras</artifactId>
        <version>3.1.0</version>
</dependency>
```

Add the dependencies in your `pom.xml`.

2. Create a class:

```
public class CassandraBolt extends BaseBasicBolt
```

Create a class and extend it with `BaseBasicBolt`. It will ask you to implement two methods to execute and `declareOutputFields`.

3. Implement the `prepare` and `cleanup` methods:

```
public void prepare(Map stormConf, TopologyContext context) {
    cluster =
Cluster.builder().addContactPoint("127.0.0.1").build();// Line #1
    session = cluster.connect("demo"); // Line #2
}
@Override
public void cleanup() {
    cluster.close();// Line #3
}
```

Override the two methods, `prepare` and `cleanup`. Line #1 is creating a cluster of Cassandra where you have to provide the IPs of all Cassandra's nodes. If you have a port number configured other than 9042 then provide IPs with the port number separated by :. Line #2 is creating a session from the cluster in which it will create a connection with one of the nodes provided in the Cassandra node cluster list. Also you need to provide a `keyspace` name while creating the session. Line #3 is closing the cluster after the job is completed. In Storm, the `prepare` method calls up only once when the topology is deployed on the cluster and the `cleanup` method calls up only once when killing the topology.

4. Definition of the `execute` method. The `execute` method executes for each tuple for processing to Storm:

```
session.execute("INSERT INTO users (lastname, age, city, email,
firstname) VALUES ('Jones', 35, 'Austin', 'bob@example.com',
'Bob')");
```

The preceding code statement inserts a row into the Cassandra table `users` in a demo keyspace. Fields are available in the tuple parameter. Therefore, you can read the fields and change the previous statement like following:

```
String userDetail = (String) input.getValueByField("event");
String[] userDetailFields = userDetail.split(":");
session.execute("INSERT INTO users (lastname, age, city, email,
firstname) VALUES ('userDetailFields[0]', userDetailFields[1], '
userDetailFields[2]', ' userDetailFields[3]', '
userDetailFields[4]')");
```

You can execute any valid SQL in the `session.execute` method. The session also provides `PreparedStatement` which can be used for bulk insert/update/delete.

Storm and IMDB integration for dimensional data

IMDB stands for **In-Memory Database**. An IMDB is required to keep intermediate results while processing the streaming of events or to keep static information related to events, which is not provided in events, for example. Employee details can be stored in IMDB on the basis of employee IDs and events that are coming in and out of an office. In this case, an event does not contain complete information about employees to save the network costs and for better performance, Therefore, when Storm processes the event, it will take static information regarding the employee from the IMDB and persist it along with the event details in Cassandra or any other database for further analytics. There are numerous open source IMDB tools available on the market, but some famous ones are **Hazelcast**, **Memcached**, and **Redis**.

Let's see how to integrate Storm and Hazelcast. No special setup is required for Hazelcast. Perform the following steps:

1. Add the dependencies:

```
<dependency>
    <groupId>com.hazelcast</groupId>
```

```
        <artifactId>hazelcast</artifactId>
        <version>3.8</version>
    </dependency>
    <dependency>
        <groupId>com.hazelcast</groupId>
        <artifactId>hazelcast-client</artifactId>
        <version>3.8</version>
    </dependency>
```

Add the dependencies in pom.xml to include hazelcast in your project.

2. Create the Hazelcast cluster and load the data:

```
Config cfg = new Config(); // Line #1
HazelcastInstance instance = Hazelcast.newHazelcastInstance(cfg);
// Line #2
Map<Integer, String> mapCustomers = instance.getMap("employees");
// Line #3
mapCustomers.put(1, "Joe"); // Line #4
mapCustomers.put(2, "Ali"); // Line #5
mapCustomers.put(3, "Avi"); // Line #6
```

Line #1 is creating a configuration object, cfg. Here it is just an empty object but you can provide the IP and port of the Hazelcast cluster already running on remote machines. Line #2 is creating an instance of Hazelcast using the configuration. Its default configuration is used and then it searches Hazelcast running on the localhost with port 5701. If any instance is already running on 5701 then it makes a cluster with port number 5702; otherwise, it creates a single instance running on the localhost with port 5701.

Line #3 is creating a map on Hazelcast named employees. The key is Integer and the value is string. Line #4, Line #5, and Line #6 illustrate how to insert/add values in Map. It is the same as Map in Java.

3. Use Hazelcast Map in the Storm topology:

```
public class EmployeeBolt extends BaseBasicBolt {
    public void prepare(Map stormConf, TopologyContext context)
    {
        ClientConfig clientConfig = new ClientConfig(); // Line #1
clientConfig.getNetworkConfig().addAddress("127.0.0.1:5701");
        // Line #2
        HazelcastInstance client =
        HazelcastClient.newHazelcastClient(clientConfig);} // Line #3
    public void execute(Tuple input, BasicOutputCollector arg1)
    {
```

```
            String inoutDetails = (String)
input.getValueByField("event");
            IMap map = client.getMap("employees"); // Line #4
            System.out.println("Employee Name:" +
            map.get(inoutDetails.split(":")[0])); // Line #5
    }
    @Override
    public void cleanup() {
        cluster.close();// Line #7
    }
}
```

First create a class and extend it with `BaseBasicBolt`, as we did in the previous section. `Line #1` is creating an object of `ClientConfig`, which is used to create `HazelcastInstance`. In `line #2`, add the hostname along with the IP of the Hazelcast server in the `clientConfig` object. Create an instance of `HazelcastClientInstance` to communicate with the Hazelcast server. Get the `Map` reference of `employees` using the client object in `line #4`. Now you can use the Map in the same way as the Java `Map` to do add/update/delete operations. You can integrate Storm with Redis using the `storm-redis` library available in the market. For further details, refer to http://storm.apache.org/releases/1.0.3/storm-redis.html

Now we know how to persist data using Storm in Cassandra and how to use Hazelcast to get the static information about the events. Let's move on to integrate storm with the presentation layer.

Integrating the presentation layer with Storm

Visualization over data is adding power to know your data in the best way and also you can take key decisions based on those. There are numerous tools available on the market for visualization. Every visualization tool needs a database to store and process the data. Some combinations are Grafana over Elasticseach, Kibana over Elasticsearch, and Grafana over Influxdb. In this chapter, we will discuss the fusion of Grafana, Elasticsearch, and Storm.

In this example, we will use the data stream from `PubNub`, which provides real-time sensor data. `PubNub` provides all types of APIs to read data from the channel. Here, a program is required to get the values from the `PubNub` subscribed channel and push it into a Kafka topic. You will the find program in the code bundle.

Setting up Grafana with the Elasticsearch plugin

Grafana is analytics platform which understands your data and visualizes it on a dashboard.

Downloading Grafana

Download Grafana from `https://grafana.com/grafana/download` and it will give you all the possible options to download the setup with support platforms/OS. Here we are installing standalone binaries:

```
wget
https://s3-us-west-2.amazonaws.com/grafana-releases/release/grafana-4.2.0.1
inux-x64.tar.gz
    cp grafana-4.2.0.linux-x64.tar.gz ~/demo/.
    tar -zxvf grafana-4.2.0.linux-x64.tar.gz
```

The folders are extracted as shown in the following screenshot:

```
                                   :~/demo/grafana-4.2.0$ ls
bin   conf   data   LICENSE.md   NOTICE.md   public   README.md   scripts   vendor
```

Configuring Grafana

The following two configurations are required to change under the path section in the `defaults.ini` configuration file:

- `data`: The Path to where Grafana stores the `sqlite3` database (if used), file based sessions (if used), and other data.
- `logs`: The Path to where Grafana will store logs.

Installing the Elasticsearch plugin in Grafana

Use the following command to install the latest Elasticsearch version plugin in Grafana:

```
/bin/grafana-cli plugins install stagemonitor-elasticsearch-app
```

Running Grafana

Use the following command to run Grafana:

```
/bin/grafana-server
```

At first it will take some time to start as it needs to set up its own database. Once it has started successfully, the UI can be accessed using `http://localhost:3000`. Enter `admin` as the username and `admin` as the password. The dashboard will be displayed as shown in the following screenshot:

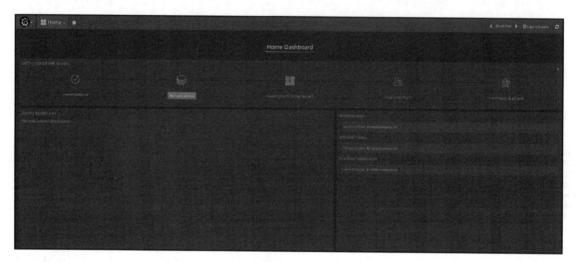

Adding the Elasticsearch datasource in Grafana

Now, click on the **Add data source** icon on the dashboard. Add/update the value as shown in the following screenshot:

- Enter the **Name** of the datasource as ES.
- Select **Elasticsearch** from the **Type** dropdown.
- Enter `http://localhost:9200` in **URL**.
- Select **Access** as **direct**.

   For this you have to add the following lines in `elasticsearch.yml`:

   ```
   http.cors.enabled: true
   http.cors.allow-origin: "*"
   ```

- Enter the **Index name** as pub-nub.
- Enter the **Time field name** as timestamp
- Select the **Version** as **5.x**
- Click the **Add** button.

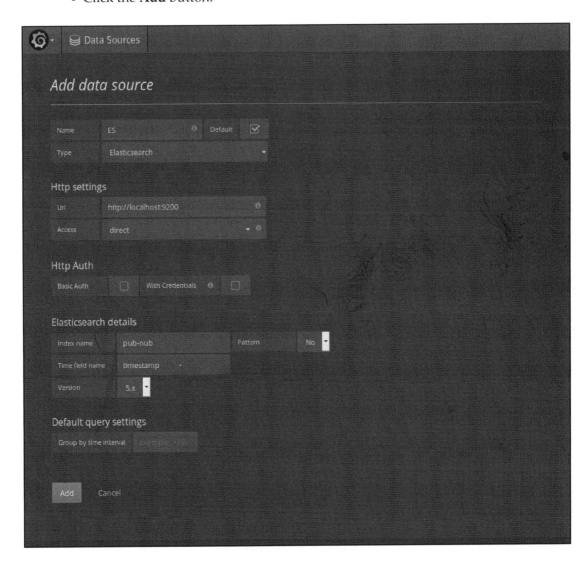

After that, you can test the connection by clicking **save and test**.

Writing code

The Elasticsearch setup and configuration has been described in Chapter 3,*Understanding and Tailing Data Streams,* under *DIY* section. Apart from the configuration mentioned there, change the given property in elasticsearch.yml:

```
cluster.name: my-application
```

We learned how to write topology code in previous sections. Now, we will discuss the Elasticsearch bolt that reads the data from other bolts/spouts and writes into Elasticsearch. Perform the following steps: .

1. Add the following dependencies in pom.xml:

```
<!-- Need for JSON parsing -->
<dependency>
    <groupId>com.fasterxml.jackson.core</groupId>
    <artifactId>jackson-databind</artifactId>
    <version>2.8.7</version>
</dependency>

<!-- Need for Elasticsearch java client API -->
<dependency>
    <groupId>org.elasticsearch.client</groupId>
    <artifactId>transport</artifactId>
    <version>5.2.2</version>
</dependency>

<!-- Need for Store core -->
<dependency>
    <groupId>org.apache.storm</groupId>
    <artifactId>storm-core</artifactId>
    <version>1.0.3</version>
    <exclusions>
        <exclusion>
            <groupId>org.slf4j</groupId>
            <artifactId>log4j-over-slf4j</artifactId>
        </exclusion>
    </exclusions>
</dependency>
<dependency>
    <groupId>org.apache.logging.log4j</groupId>
    <artifactId>log4j-api</artifactId>
    <version>2.7</version>
</dependency>
<dependency>
    <groupId>org.apache.logging.log4j</groupId>
```

```
        <artifactId>log4j-core</artifactId>
        <version>2.7</version>
</dependency>

<!-- Need for Store Kafka integration -->
<dependency>
        <groupId>org.apache.storm</groupId>
        <artifactId>storm-kafka</artifactId>
        <version>1.0.3</version>
</dependency>
<dependency>
        <groupId>org.apache.kafka</groupId>
        <artifactId>kafka_2.11</artifactId>
        <version>0.8.2.2</version>
        <exclusions>
            <exclusion>
                <artifactId>jmxri</artifactId>
                <groupId>com.sun.jmx</groupId>
            </exclusion>
            <exclusion>
                <artifactId>jms</artifactId>
                <groupId>javax.jms</groupId>
            </exclusion>
            <exclusion>
                <artifactId>jmxtools</artifactId>
                <groupId>com.sun.jdmk</groupId>
            </exclusion>
            <exclusion>
                <groupId>org.slf4j</groupId>
                <artifactId>slf4j-log4j12</artifactId>
            </exclusion>
            </exclusions>
</dependency>
```

2. Define a class and class level variables:

```
public class ElasticSearchBolt extends BaseBasicBolt
```

3. Declare class level variables:

```
Client client;
PreBuiltTransportClient preBuiltTransportClient;
ObjectMapper mapper;
```

4. Define the `prepare` method from `BaseBasicBolt`:

```
@Override
public void prepare(@SuppressWarnings("rawtypes") Map stormConf,
TopologyContext context) {
    mapper = new ObjectMapper(); // line #1
    Settings settings = Settings.builder().put("cluster.name",
    "my-application").build(); // line #2
    preBuiltTransportClient = new
PreBuiltTransportClient(settings);
    // line #3
    client = preBuiltTransportClient.addTransportAddress(new
    InetSocketTransportAddress(new
    InetSocketAddress("localhost", 9300))); // line #4
}
```

`Line #1` creates the object of `ObjectMapper` for JSON parsing. Any other library can be used for parsing. `Line #2`is creating the object of the settings, which is required by the client for Elasticsearch. The settings require the cluster name as mandatory. `Line #3`is creating the Elasticsearch client object which is taking the settings as a parameter. In `line #4,` we need to provide the Elastcisearch node details which include the hostname and port number. If there is a cluster of Elasticsearch, then use `InetAddresses`.

5. Define the `execute` method from `BaseBasicBolt`:

```
@Override
public void execute(Tuple input, BasicOutputCollector collector) {
    String valueByField = input.getString(0); // Line #1
    try {
        IndexResponse response = client.prepareIndex("pub-nub",
"sensor-
        data").setSource(convertStringtoMap(valueByField)).get();
        // Line #2
    } catch (IOException e) {
        e.printStackTrace();
    }
}
```

`Line #1`is getting values from the tuple at the zero position which contains the event. `Line #2` is creating an index, if one does not exist, as well as adding a document into the index. `client.prepareIndex` is creating an index which requires the index name as the first parameter and the type as the second parameter. `setSource` is a method which adds a document in the index. The `get` method will return the object of the class `IndexResponse`, which contains information about whether a request for creating the index and adding the document is successfully completed or not. `convertStringtoMap` is converting a string into a map that changes the datatype of the field. It is required to make it presentable on the `Grafana` dashboard. If an event is already in the desired format, then we do not need to convert the type.

Now, we have to integrate the Elasticsearch bolt with the Kafka spout to read the data. Perform the following steps:

6. Write the topology that binds the Kafka spout and the Elasticsearch bolt:

```
TopologyBuilder topologyBuilder = new TopologyBuilder();//Line #1
BrokerHosts hosts = new ZkHosts("localhost:2181");//Line #2
SpoutConfig spoutConfig = new SpoutConfig(hosts, "sensor-data" ,
"/" + topicName, UUID.randomUUID().toString()); //Line #3
spoutConfig.scheme = new SchemeAsMultiScheme(new StringScheme());
//Line #4
KafkaSpout kafkaSpout = new KafkaSpout(spoutConfig); //Line #5
topologyBuilder.setSpout("spout", kafkaSpout, 1);//Line #6
topologyBuilder.setBolt("es-bolt", new ElasticSearchBolt(),
1).shuffleGrouping("spout"); //Line #7
```

`Line #1` is creating the object of `TopologyBuilder` which contains information for spouts and all bolts. Here, in this example, we are using predefined the Storm-Kafka integrated spout provided by Storm. Create the Zookeeper host details as `BrokerHosts` in `line #2`. In `line #3`, we are creating the `spoutConfig` required for the Kafka spout which contains information about Zookeeper hosts, topic name, Zookeeper root directory, and client ID to communicate with the Kafka broker. `Line #4` sets the scheme as string; otherwise, by default, it is bytes. Create the `KafkaSpout` object with `spoutConfig` as the parameter. Now, first set the spout into `topologyBuilder` with parameters as Id, `kafkaSpout` and parallelism hint in `line #6`. In the same way, set the ElasticSearch bolt into `topologyBuilder` as described in `line #7`.

7. Submit the topology:

```
Config config = new Config(); // Line #1
config.setNumWorkers(3); // Line #2
LocalCluster cluster = new LocalCluster(); // Line #3
cluster.submitTopology("storm-es-example", config,
topologyBuilder.createTopology()); // Line #4
```

Line #1 is creating the object of `config` that is required by Storm. Line #2 sets the minimum number of workers required in the Storm supervisor. Now, create `LocalCluster` as the cluster to submit the topology. Call the `submitTopology` method with parameters as the name of the topology, configuration, and `topologyBuilder`. You will find the complete code in the code bundle.

Executing code

Import the code in Eclipse, available in the code bundle. Once you have imported the program in eclipse, execute the following steps:

1. Run `PubNubDataStream.java`.
2. Run `SenorTopology.java`.

Visualizing the output on Grafana

You can configure the dashboard, as shown in the following screenshot:

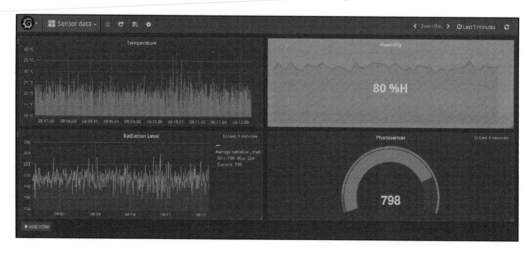

Code:

```
package com.book.chapter7.visualization.example;

import java.util.Arrays;
import java.util.Properties;

import org.apache.kafka.clients.producer.KafkaProducer;
import org.apache.kafka.clients.producer.ProducerRecord;

import com.pubnub.api.PNConfiguration;
import com.pubnub.api.PubNub;
import com.pubnub.api.callbacks.SubscribeCallback;
import com.pubnub.api.enums.PNStatusCategory;
import com.pubnub.api.models.consumer.PNStatus;
import com.pubnub.api.models.consumer.pubsub.PNMessageResult;
import com.pubnub.api.models.consumer.pubsub.PNPresenceEventResult;
```

Data stream from PubNub:

```
public class PubNubDataStream {

    public KafkaProducer<Integer, String> producer;

    public PubNubDataStream() {
        Properties properties = new Properties();
        properties.put("bootstrap.servers", "localhost:9092");
        properties.put("key.serializer",
        "org.apache.kafka.common.serialization.StringSerializer");
        properties.put("value.serializer",
        "org.apache.kafka.common.serialization.StringSerializer");
        properties.put("acks", "1");
        producer = new KafkaProducer<Integer, String>(properties);
    }

    private void pubishMessageToKafka(String message) {
        ProducerRecord<Integer, String> data = new ProducerRecord<Integer,
        String>(
            "sensor-data", message);
            producer.send(data);
    }

    private void getMessageFromPubNub() {
        PNConfiguration pnConfiguration = new PNConfiguration();
        pnConfiguration
        .setSubscribeKey("sub-c-5f1b7c8e-fbee-11e3-aa40-02ee2ddab7fe");
         PubNub pubnub = new PubNub(pnConfiguration);
```

```
pubnub.addListener(new SubscribeCallback() {
    @Override
    public void status(PubNub pubnub, PNStatus status) {
        System.out.println(pubnub.toString() + "::" + status.toString());

        if (status.getCategory() ==
        PNStatusCategory.PNUnexpectedDisconnectCategory) {
            // This event happens when radio / connectivity is lost
        }
        else if (status.getCategory() ==
        PNStatusCategory.PNConnectedCategory) {
            // Connect event. You can do stuff like publish, and know
            // you'll get it.
            // Or just use the connected event to confirm you are
            // subscribed for
            // UI / internal notifications, etc
            if (status.getCategory() ==
            PNStatusCategory.PNConnectedCategory) {
                System.out.println("status.getCategory()="+
                status.getCategory());
            }
        } else if (status.getCategory() ==
            PNStatusCategory.PNReconnectedCategory) {
            // Happens as part of our regular operation. This event
            // happens when
            // radio / connectivity is lost, then regained.
        } else if (status.getCategory() ==
            PNStatusCategory.PNDecryptionErrorCategory) {
            // Handle messsage decryption error. Probably client
            // configured to
            // encrypt messages and on live data feed it received plain
            // text.
        }
    }
    @Override
    public void message(PubNub pubnub, PNMessageResult message) {
        // Handle new message stored in message.message
        String strMessage = message.getMessage().toString();
        System.out.println("******" + strMessage);
        pubishMessageToKafka(strMessage);
        /*
         * log the following items with your favorite logger -
         * message.getMessage() - message.getSubscription() -
         * message.getTimetoken()
         */
    }

    @Override
```

```
    public void presence(PubNub pubnub, PNPresenceEventResult presence) {

    }
});

    pubnub.subscribe().channels(Arrays.asList("pubnub-sensor-
    network")).execute();
    }
    public static void main(String[] args) {
        new PubNubDataStream().getMessageFromPubNub();
    }
}
```

Elasticsearch persistence bolt:

```
package com.book.chapter7.visualization.example;

import java.io.IOException;
import java.net.InetSocketAddress;
import java.util.Date;
import java.util.HashMap;
import java.util.Map;

import org.apache.storm.task.TopologyContext;
import org.apache.storm.topology.BasicOutputCollector;
import org.apache.storm.topology.OutputFieldsDeclarer;
import org.apache.storm.topology.base.BaseBasicBolt;
import org.apache.storm.tuple.Tuple;
import org.elasticsearch.action.index.IndexResponse;
import org.elasticsearch.client.Client;
import org.elasticsearch.common.settings.Settings;
import org.elasticsearch.common.transport.InetSocketTransportAddress;
import org.elasticsearch.transport.client.PreBuiltTransportClient;

import com.fasterxml.jackson.core.JsonParseException;
import com.fasterxml.jackson.core.type.TypeReference;
import com.fasterxml.jackson.databind.JsonMappingException;
import com.fasterxml.jackson.databind.ObjectMapper;

public class ElasticSearchBolt extends BaseBasicBolt {
    private static final long serialVersionUID = -9123903091990273369L;
    Client client;
    PreBuiltTransportClient preBuiltTransportClient;
    ObjectMapper mapper;

    @Override
        public void prepare(@SuppressWarnings("rawtypes") Map stormConf,
        TopologyContext context) {
            // instance a json mapper
```

```
        mapper = new ObjectMapper(); // create once, reuse
        Settings settings = Settings.builder()
        .put("cluster.name", "my-application").build();
        preBuiltTransportClient = new
        PreBuiltTransportClient(settings);
        client = preBuiltTransportClient.addTransportAddress(new
InetSocketTransportAddress(new InetSocketAddress("localhost", 9300)));
    }

@Override
public void cleanup() {
    preBuiltTransportClient.close();
    client.close();
}

@Override
public void declareOutputFields(OutputFieldsDeclarer declarer) {
}

@Override
public void execute(Tuple input, BasicOutputCollector collector) {
    String valueByField = input.getString(0);
    System.out.println(valueByField);
    try {
        IndexResponse response = client.prepareIndex("pub-nub", "sensor-
        data").setSource(convertStringtoMap(valueByField)).get();
        System.out.println(response.status());
    } catch (IOException e) {
        e.printStackTrace();
    }
}

public Map<String,Object> convertStringtoMap(String fieldValue) throws
JsonParseException, JsonMappingException, IOException {
    System.out.println("Orignal value  "+ fieldValue);
    Map<String,Object> convertedValue = new HashMap<>();
    Map<String,Object> readValue = mapper.readValue(fieldValue, new
    TypeReference<Map<String,Object>>() {});

    convertedValue.put("ambient_temperature",
Double.parseDouble(String.valueOf(readValue.get("ambient_temperature"))));
convertedValue.put("photosensor",
Double.parseDouble(String.valueOf(readValue.get("photosensor"))));
convertedValue.put("humidity",
Double.parseDouble(String.valueOf(readValue.get("humidity"))));
convertedValue.put("radiation_level",
Integer.parseInt(String.valueOf(readValue.get("radiation_level"))));
convertedValue.put("sensor_uuid", readValue.get("sensor_uuid"));
```

```
convertedValue.put("timestamp", new Date());

System.out.println("Converted value  "+ convertedValue);
return convertedValue;
}
}
```

Topology Builder binds spout and bolts.

```
package com.book.chapter7.visualization.example;

import java.util.UUID;

import org.apache.storm.Config;
import org.apache.storm.LocalCluster;
import org.apache.storm.kafka.BrokerHosts;
import org.apache.storm.kafka.KafkaSpout;
import org.apache.storm.kafka.SpoutConfig;
import org.apache.storm.kafka.StringScheme;
import org.apache.storm.kafka.ZkHosts;
import org.apache.storm.spout.SchemeAsMultiScheme;
import org.apache.storm.topology.TopologyBuilder;

public class SensorTopology {
    public static void main(String args[]) throws InterruptedException {
    Config config = new Config();
    config.setNumWorkers(3);
    TopologyBuilder topologyBuilder = new TopologyBuilder();

    String zkConnString = "localhost:2181";
    String topicName = "sensor-data";

    BrokerHosts hosts = new ZkHosts(zkConnString);
    SpoutConfig spoutConfig = new SpoutConfig(hosts, topicName , "/" +
    topicName, UUID.randomUUID().toString());
    spoutConfig.scheme = new SchemeAsMultiScheme(new StringScheme());
    KafkaSpout kafkaSpout = new KafkaSpout(spoutConfig);
    topologyBuilder.setSpout("spout", kafkaSpout, 1);
    topologyBuilder.setBolt("es-bolt", new ElasticSearchBolt(),
    1).shuffleGrouping("spout");

        LocalCluster cluster = new LocalCluster();
        cluster.submitTopology("storm-es-example", config,
        topologyBuilder.createTopology());
    }
}
```

Do It Yourself

Here we will string Storm, Kafka, Hazelcast, and Cassandra together and build a use case. This use case is based on telecoms data which is uniquely identified using phone numbers. Telecoms real-time packet data is entered into Kafka. The system has to store the total usage (bytes) per phone number into Hazelcast and persist the total usage into Cassandra and also persist each event into Cassandra.

Pseudo code:

- Create `CassandraBolt` which persists data in Cassandra.
- Create a bolt which reads values from Hazelcast on the basis of phone numbers and adds up with the current value. Also update the same entry back in Hazelcast.
- Create a topology to link the Kafka spout to the custom bolt mentioned in the previous step and then `CassandraBolt` to persist the total usage. Also link Kafka spout to `CassandraBolt` to persist each event.

Insert the code from the bundle:

```
package com.book.chapter7.diy;

Here we have the import files

import java.util.Date;
import java.util.Properties;
import java.util.concurrent.ThreadLocalRandom;

import org.apache.kafka.clients.producer.KafkaProducer;
import org.apache.kafka.clients.producer.ProducerRecord;
```

Code for generating data:

```
public class DataGenerator {
    public static void main(String args[]) {
    Properties properties = new Properties();
    properties.put("bootstrap.servers", "localhost:9092");
    properties.put("key.serializer",
    "org.apache.kafka.common.serialization.StringSerializer");
    properties.put("value.serializer",
    "org.apache.kafka.common.serialization.StringSerializer");
    properties.put("acks", "1");

    KafkaProducer<Integer, String> producer = new KafkaProducer<Integer,
    String>(properties);
```

```
    int counter =0;
    int nbrOfEventsRequired = Integer.parseInt(args[0]);
    while (counter<nbrOfEventsRequired) {
    StringBuffer stream = new StringBuffer();

    long phoneNumber = ThreadLocalRandom.current().nextLong(99999999501,
    99999999991);
    int bin = ThreadLocalRandom.current().nextInt(1000, 9999);
    int bout = ThreadLocalRandom.current().nextInt(1000, 9999);

    stream.append(phoneNumber);
    stream.append(",");
    stream.append(bin);
    stream.append(",");
    stream.append(bout);
    stream.append(",");
    stream.append(new Date(ThreadLocalRandom.current().nextLong()));

    System.out.println(stream.toString());
    ProducerRecord<Integer, String> data = new ProducerRecord<Integer,
    String>(
        "storm-diy", stream.toString());
        producer.send(data);
        counter++;
    }

    producer.close();
    }
}
```

To start Hazelcast server using the following code snipptet:

```
package com.book.chapter7.diy;

import com.hazelcast.core.Hazelcast;

public class HCServer {
    public static void main(String args[]) {
        Hazelcast.newHazelcastInstance();
    }
}
```

Data transfer object between bolts:

```
Sending data from the import java.io.Serializable

package com.book.chapter7.diy;

import java.io.Serializable;

public class PacketDetailDTO implements Serializable {

    private static final long serialVersionUID = 9148607866335518739L;
    private long phoneNumber;
    private int bin;
    private int bout;
    private int totalBytes;
    private String timestamp;

    public long getPhoneNumber() {
        return phoneNumber;
    }

    public void setPhoneNumber(long phoneNumber) {
        this.phoneNumber = phoneNumber;
    }

    public int getBin() {
        return bin;
    }

    public void setBin(int bin) {
        this.bin = bin;
    }
    public int getBout() {
        return bout;
    }

    public void setBout(int bout) {
        this.bout = bout;
    }

    public int getTotalBytes() {
        return totalBytes;
    }

    public void setTotalBytes(int totalBytes) {
        this.totalBytes = totalBytes;
    }
```

```
        public String getTimestamp() {
            return timestamp;
        }
        public void setTimestamp(String timestamp) {
            this.timestamp = timestamp;
        }
}
```

Parser and usage computation bolt.

In the code, we have the class map:

```
package com.book.chapter7.diy;

import java.util.Map;

import org.apache.storm.task.TopologyContext;
import org.apache.storm.topology.BasicOutputCollector;
import org.apache.storm.topology.OutputFieldsDeclarer;
import org.apache.storm.topology.base.BaseBasicBolt;
import org.apache.storm.tuple.Fields;
import org.apache.storm.tuple.Tuple;
import org.apache.storm.tuple.Values;

import com.hazelcast.client.HazelcastClient;
import com.hazelcast.client.config.ClientConfig;
import com.hazelcast.core.HazelcastInstance;
import com.hazelcast.core.IMap;

public class ParseAndUsageBolt extends BaseBasicBolt {

    private static final long serialVersionUID = 1271439619204966337L;
    HazelcastInstance client;
    IMap<String, PacketDetailDTO> usageMap;

@Override
public void prepare(Map stormConf, TopologyContext context) {
    ClientConfig clientConfig = new ClientConfig();
    clientConfig.getNetworkConfig().addAddress("127.0.0.1:5701");
    client = HazelcastClient.newHazelcastClient(clientConfig);
    usageMap = client.getMap("usage");
}

@Override
public void execute(Tuple input, BasicOutputCollector collector) {
    PacketDetailDTO packetDetailDTO = new PacketDetailDTO();
    String valueByField = input.getString(0);
    String[] split = valueByField.split(",");
```

```
long phoneNumber = Long.parseLong(split[0]);
PacketDetailDTO packetDetailDTOFromMap = usageMap.get(phoneNumber);
if (null == packetDetailDTOFromMap) {
    packetDetailDTOFromMap = new PacketDetailDTO();
}
packetDetailDTO.setPhoneNumber(phoneNumber);
int bin = Integer.parseInt(split[1]);
packetDetailDTO.setBin((packetDetailDTOFromMap.getBin() + bin));
int bout = Integer.parseInt(split[2]);
packetDetailDTO.setBout(packetDetailDTOFromMap.getBout() + bout);
packetDetailDTO.setTotalBytes(packetDetailDTOFromMap.getTotalBytes()
+ bin + bout);

usageMap.put(split[0], packetDetailDTO);

PacketDetailDTO tdrPacketDetailDTO = new PacketDetailDTO();
tdrPacketDetailDTO.setPhoneNumber(phoneNumber);
tdrPacketDetailDTO.setBin(bin);
tdrPacketDetailDTO.setBout(bout);
tdrPacketDetailDTO.setTimestamp(split[3]);

collector.emit("usagestream", new Values(packetDetailDTO));
collector.emit("tdrstream", new Values(tdrPacketDetailDTO));
}

@Override
public void cleanup() {
    client.shutdown();
}

@Override
public void declareOutputFields(OutputFieldsDeclarer declarer) {
    declarer.declareStream("usagestream", new Fields("usagestream"));
    declarer.declareStream("tdrstream", new Fields("tdrstream"));
}

}
```

Cassandra persistance bolt:

```
package com.book.chapter7.diy;

import java.util.Map;

import org.apache.storm.task.TopologyContext;
import org.apache.storm.topology.BasicOutputCollector;
import org.apache.storm.topology.OutputFieldsDeclarer;
import org.apache.storm.topology.base.BaseBasicBolt;
import org.apache.storm.tuple.Tuple;

import com.datastax.driver.core.Cluster;
import com.datastax.driver.core.Session;

public class TDRCassandraBolt extends BaseBasicBolt {
    private static final long serialVersionUID = 1L;
    private Cluster cluster;
    private Session session;
    private String hostname;
    private String keyspace;

    public TDRCassandraBolt(String hostname, String keyspace) {
        this.hostname = hostname;
        this.keyspace = keyspace;
    }

    @Override
    public void prepare(Map stormConf, TopologyContext context) {
        cluster = Cluster.builder().addContactPoint(hostname).build();
        session = cluster.connect(keyspace);
    }

    public void execute(Tuple input, BasicOutputCollector arg1) {
        PacketDetailDTO packetDetailDTO = (PacketDetailDTO)
        input.getValueByField("tdrstream");
        session.execute("INSERT INTO packet_tdr (phone_number, bin, bout,
        timestamp) VALUES ("
        + packetDetailDTO.getPhoneNumber()
        + ", "
        + packetDetailDTO.getBin()
        + ","
        + packetDetailDTO.getBout()
        + ",'" + packetDetailDTO.getTimestamp() + "')");
    }

    public void declareOutputFields(OutputFieldsDeclarer arg0) {
```

```
        }

        @Override
        public void cleanup() {
            session.close();
            cluster.close();
        }
    }
```

Code for `java.util.Map`: using persistence in Cassandra:

```java
package com.book.chapter7.diy;

import java.util.Map;

import org.apache.storm.task.TopologyContext;
import org.apache.storm.topology.BasicOutputCollector;
import org.apache.storm.topology.OutputFieldsDeclarer;
import org.apache.storm.topology.base.BaseBasicBolt;
import org.apache.storm.tuple.Tuple;

import com.datastax.driver.core.Cluster;
import com.datastax.driver.core.Session;

public class UsageCassandraBolt extends BaseBasicBolt {
    private static final long serialVersionUID = 1L;
    private Cluster cluster;
    private Session session;
    private String hostname;
    private String keyspace;

    public UsageCassandraBolt(String hostname, String keyspace) {
        this.hostname = hostname;
        this.keyspace = keyspace;
    }

    @Override
    public void prepare(Map stormConf, TopologyContext context) {
        cluster = Cluster.builder().addContactPoint(hostname).build();
        session = cluster.connect(keyspace);
    }

    public void execute(Tuple input, BasicOutputCollector arg1) {
        PacketDetailDTO packetDetailDTO = (PacketDetailDTO)
        input.getValueByField("usagestream");
        session.execute("INSERT INTO packet_usage (phone_number, bin, bout,
        total_bytes) VALUES ("
        + packetDetailDTO.getPhoneNumber()
```

```
            + ", "
            + packetDetailDTO.getBin()
            + ", "
            + packetDetailDTO.getBout()
            + ", " + packetDetailDTO.getTotalBytes() + ")");
    }

    public void declareOutputFields(OutputFieldsDeclarer arg0) {
    }

    @Override
    public void cleanup() {
        session.close();
        cluster.close();
    }
}
```

Topology builder binds spout and bolts:

```java
package com.book.chapter7.diy;

import java.util.UUID;

import org.apache.storm.Config;
import org.apache.storm.LocalCluster;
import org.apache.storm.kafka.BrokerHosts;
import org.apache.storm.kafka.KafkaSpout;
import org.apache.storm.kafka.SpoutConfig;
import org.apache.storm.kafka.StringScheme;
import org.apache.storm.kafka.ZkHosts;
import org.apache.storm.spout.SchemeAsMultiScheme;
import org.apache.storm.topology.TopologyBuilder;

public class TelecomProcessorTopology {
    public static void main(String[] args) {
        Config config = new Config();
        config.setNumWorkers(3);
        TopologyBuilder topologyBuilder = new TopologyBuilder();

        String zkConnString = "localhost:2181";
        String topicName = "storm-diy";

        BrokerHosts hosts = new ZkHosts(zkConnString);
        SpoutConfig spoutConfig = new SpoutConfig(hosts, topicName , "/" +
topicName, UUID.randomUUID().toString());
        spoutConfig.scheme = new SchemeAsMultiScheme(new StringScheme());
```

```
            KafkaSpout kafkaSpout = new KafkaSpout(spoutConfig);
            topologyBuilder.setSpout("spout", kafkaSpout, 1);
            topologyBuilder.setBolt("parser", new ParseAndUsageBolt(),
            1).shuffleGrouping("spout");
            topologyBuilder.setBolt("usageCassandra", new
            UsageCassandraBolt("localhost", "usage"),
            1).shuffleGrouping("parser", "usagestream");
            topologyBuilder.setBolt("tdrCassandra", new
            TDRCassandraBolt("localhost", "tdr"), 1).shuffleGrouping("parser",
            "tdrstream");

            LocalCluster cluster = new LocalCluster();
                    cluster.submitTopology("storm-diy", config,
            topologyBuilder.createTopology());
        }
    }
```

Summary

In this chapter, we explained all the possible sinks available with Storm. There is in-built integration available between Storm and the sinks but they are not mature enough to run on the required configuration. So in this chapter we used plain Java code to connect with any external tool for linkage. First we explained the integration of Storm and the latest version of Cassandra. Then we looked at in-memory databases which are required in all types of usecases related to Storm. We explained the integration of Storm and Hazelcast. After integration with Cassandra and Hazelcast, one more important integration was explained: the presentation layer. So we chose Elasticsearch with Grafana, and completed the example. In the end, we provided one problem to the reader so that the reader can think about and write the code using the same sinks that were explained in the initial part of the chapter.

8
Storm Trident

This is the chapter where we introduce you to DRPC and Storm Trident abstraction with respect to micro batching and equip you with some practical use cases implemented around them. The following are the list of components that will be covered in this chapter:

- State retention and the need for Trident
- Basic Storm Trident topology
- Trident internals
- Trident operations
- DRPC
- Do It Yourself

State retention and the need for Trident

Trident is a distributed real-time analytics framework. Trident maintains its state either internally for example, in-memory, or externally for example, Hazelcast, in a fault-tolerant way. It is similar to processing an event exactly once. Trident fits for micro batch processing use cases such as aggregation, filtration, and so on.

Let's take an example that explains how to achieve exactly-once semantics. Suppose that you're doing a count of how many people visited your blog and also storing the running count in a database. Now suppose you store a single value representing the count in the database, and every time you process a new tuple you increment the count.

Now, if failures happen, tuples will be replayed by Storm topology. Here the problem is whether or not the tuple has been processed and the count has already been updated in the database—if so, then you should not update it again or if the tuple did not process successfully then you have to update the count in the database or if the tuple processed but failed while updating the count in the database then you should update the database.

To achieve the exactly-once semantics which ensures that the tuple has been processed only once in the system, spout should provide the information to bolts/spouts. There are three types of spouts available with respect to fault-tolerance: transactional, non-transactional, and opaque transactional. Now, let's have a look at each type of spout.

Transactional spout

Let's have a look at how trident spout processes tuples and what the characteristics are:

- Trident processes tuples in small batches.
- Each batch has its own unique transaction ID
- Trident ensures every tuple is in batch so no tuples are skipped
- Batches with a given transaction id are always the same. If a batch is reprocessed, even then the batch would have the same transaction ID and the same set of tuples
- Tuples can't be part of more than one batch. Every batch would have a unique set of tuples

Using the following statement in code, we can define a transactional spout with Kafka:

```
TransactionalTridentKafkaSpout tr = new TransactionalTridentKafkaSpout(new
TridentKafkaConfig(new ZkHosts("localhost:9091"), "test"));
```

The `TransactionalTridentKafkaSpout` is available in the `storm-core` library which provides all the preceeding properties. Transactional spout is not fault tolerant in case spout is not able to get the same set of tuples due to unavailability of nodes. To overcome this problem, opaque transactional spout exists.

Opaque transactional Spout

An opaque transactional spout has the following property:

- Every tuple is successfully processed in exactly one batch. However, it's possible for a tuple to fail to process in one batch and then succeed to process in a later batch.

`OpaqueTridentKafkaSpout` is a spout that has this property and is fault-tolerant to losing Kafka nodes. Whenever it's time for `OpaqueTridentKafkaSpout` to emit a batch, it emits tuples starting from where the last batch finished emitting. This ensures that no tuple is ever skipped or successfully processed by multiple batches.

Using the following statement in code we can define an opaque transactional spout with Kafka:

```
OpaqueTridentKafkaSpout otks = new OpaqueTridentKafkaSpout(new
TridentKafkaConfig(new ZkHosts("localhost:9091"), "test"));
```

Basic Storm Trident topology

Here, in basic Storm Trident topology we will go through a word count example. More examples will be explained later in the chapter. This is the code for the example:

```
FixedBatchSpout spout = new FixedBatchSpout(new Fields("sentence"), 3,
new Values("this is simple example of trident topology"),
new Values("this example count same words"));
spout.setCycle(true); // Line 1
TridentTopology topology = new TridentTopology(); // Line 2
MemoryMapState.Factory stateFactory = new MemoryMapState.Factory(); // Line
3
topology.newStream("spout1", spout) // Line 4
.each(new Fields("sentence"), new Split(), new Fields("word")) // Line 5
.groupBy(new Fields("word")) // Line 6
.persistentAggregate(stateFactory, new Count(), new
Fields("count")).newValuesStream() // Line 7
.filter(new DisplayOutputFilter()) // Line 8
.parallelismHint(6); // Line 9
Config config = new Config(); // Line 10
config.setNumWorkers(3); // Line 11
LocalCluster cluster = new LocalCluster(); // Line 12
cluster.submitTopology("storm-trident-example", config, topology.build());
// Line 13
```

Start the program with spout in `Line 1`. `FixedBatchSpout` is available for testing purposes in code bundle. You can give a set of values that will be repeated in case `setCycle` is set to `True`. You can define `TransactionalTridentKafkaSpout`, which requires Zookeeper details to connect and a topic name. Another constructor is having the same parameters along with the client ID:

```
TransactionalTridentKafkaSpout spout = new
TransactionalTridentKafkaSpout(new TridentKafkaConfig(new
ZkHosts("localhost:9091"), "test"));
```

Create the `TridentTopology` object in `Line 2`, which needs to be submitted on the cluster.

Create an object of `MemoryMapState.Factory` in `Line 3`, which keeps data in memory along with maintaining states.

Set the spout in topology with its name as `spout1` in `Line 4`.

Now, perform an operation on each tuple in `Line 5`. Here, the `split` function needs to be executed for each tuple. Each method of topology has three arguments that is the input field's name from spout, the function to be executed for each tuple, and the output field's name. The implementation of the `split` method is as follows. Sentences are split on the basis of space:

```
class Split extends BaseFunction {
    public void execute(TridentTuple tuple, TridentCollector collector) {
        String sentence = tuple.getString(0);
        for (String word : sentence.split(" ")) {
            collector.emit(new Values(word));
        }
    }
}
```

 We will discuss function, filter, and aggregation operations in detail in the *Trident operations* section.

The `Line 6` is performing group by operation on tuples with name as `word`. It will group by all the tuples with the same word and create batches. It produces tuples with word and count.

The `persistentAggregate` performs aggregation as per the given function in Line 7. Also it keeps in memory to maintain state. It first reads from memory and then adds up the current values. After that it updates the in-memory cache to keep it updated. Here the function count is called up, which adds up the count of the same word. Implementation of the count is:

```
public class Count implements CombinerAggregator<Long> {
  @Override
  public Long init(TridentTuple tuple) {
    return 1L;
  }
  @Override
  public Long combine(Long val1, Long val2) {
    return val1 + val2;
  }
  @Override
  public Long zero() {
    return 0L;
  }
}
```

To display output, implement a custom filter to print the tuple values on the console. Line 8 is applying the filter. Implementation of the custom filter `DisplayOutputFilter` is:

```
public class DisplayOutputFilter implements Filter {
  @Override
  public void prepare(Map conf, TridentOperationContext context) {
  }
  @Override
  public void cleanup() {
  }
  @Override
  public boolean isKeep(TridentTuple tuple) {
    System.out.println(tuple.get(0)+":"+tuple.get(1));
    return true;
  }
}
```

Line 9 is setting parallelism and from line 10 to line 13 is creating a configure object and submitting the previously created topology on a local cluster.

The complete code is available in a code bundle named `BasicTridentTopology.java`.

Output is shown in the following screenshot:

```
example:2
is:1
simple:1
count:1
of:1
topology:1
trident:1
same:1
this:2
words:1
example:4
is:2
simple:2
of:2
topology:2
count:2
words:2
trident:2
same:2
this:4
```

Trident internals

Every Trident flow is a Storm flow. The concept of executors and workers is exactly the same as Storm. Trident topology is nothing but a Storm bolt. Trident operations such as spouts, each, and aggregations are actually implemented in Storm bolt.

Trident turns your topology into a dataflow (acyclic directed) graph that it uses to assign operations to bolts and then to assign those bolts to workers. It's smart enough to optimize that assignment: it combines operations into bolts so that, as much as possible, tuples are handed off with simple method cause and it arranges bolts among workers so that, as much as possible, tuples are handed off to local executors.

The actual spout of a Trident topology is called the **Master Batch Coordinator** (**MBC**). All it does is emit a tuple describing itself as batch 1 and then a tuple describing itself as batch 2, and so forth. Also deciding when to emit those batches, retry them, and so on, is quite exciting, but Storm doesn't know anything about all that. Those batch tuples go to the topology's spout coordinator. The spout coordinator understands the location and arrangement of records in the external source and ensures that each source record belongs uniquely to a successful Trident batch.

Trident operations

As we discussed earlier, Trident operations are Storm bolt implementation. We have a vast range of operations available in Trident. They can perform complex operations and aggregate with cache in memory. The following are operations available with Trident.

Functions

The following are characteristics of functions:

- Class has to extend `BaseFunction`
- This is a partition of the local operation that means no network transfer is involved and is applied to each batch partition independently
- It takes a set of inputs and emits zero or more output
- In output, it emits an output tuple including the original input tuple

Here is the example:

```
class PerformDiffFunction extends BaseFunction {
  @Override
  public void execute(TridentTuple tuple, TridentCollector collector) {
    int number1 = tuple.getInteger(0);
    int number2 = tuple.getInteger(1); if(number2>number1){
      collector.emit(new Values(number2-number1));
    }
  }
}
```

Input:

```
[1,2]
[3,4]
[7,3]
```

Output:

```
[1,2,1]
[3,4,1]
```

map and flatMap

The following are characteristics of the map function:

- This is one-to-one transformation of tuples
- Class has to implement MapFunction

Here is the example:

```
class UpperCase implements MapFunction {
  @Override
  public Values execute(TridentTuple input) {
    return new Values(input.getString(0).toUpperCase());
  }
}
```

Input:

```
[this is a simple example of trident topology]
```

Output:

```
[THIS IS A SIMPLE EXAMPLE OF TRIDENT TOPOLOGY]
```

The following are characteristics of the FlatMap function:

- This is one-to-many transformation for tuple
- It's flattening the resulting elements into a new stream
- The Class has to implement FlatMapFunction

Here is the example:

```
class SplitMapFunction implements FlatMapFunction {
  @Override
```

```
    public Iterable<Values> execute(TridentTuple input) {
      List<Values> valuesList = new ArrayList<>();
      for (String word : input.getString(0).split(" ")) {
        valuesList.add(new Values(word));
      }
      return valuesList;
    }
}
```

Input:

```
[this is s simple example of trident topology]
```

Output:

```
[this]
[is]
[simple]
[example]
[of]
[trident]
[topology]
[this]
[example]
[count]
[same]
[words]
```

peek

This is used to debug the tuples flowing between the operations. The following is the example using the previous functions:

```
topology.newStream("spout1", spout).flatMap(new SplitMapFunction())
.map(new UpperCase()).peek(
  new Consumer() {
    @Override
    public void accept(TridentTuple tuple) {
      System.out.print("[");
      for (int index = 0; index < tuple.size(); index++) {
        System.out.print(tuple.get(index));
        if (index < (tuple.size() - 1))
        System.out.print(",");
      }
      System.out.println("]");
    }
});
```

Filters

The following are characteristics of filter:

- Filters take in a tuple as input and decide whether or not to keep that tuple or not

Here is the example:

```
class MyFilter extends BaseFilter {
    public boolean isKeep(TridentTuple tuple) {
        return tuple.getInteger(0) == 1 &amp;&amp; tuple.getInteger(1) == 2;
    }
}
```

Input:

```
[1,2]
[3,4]
[7,3]
```

Output:

```
[1,2]
```

Windowing

In windowing, Trident tuples are processed within the same window and emit to the next operation. There are two types of window operations:

Tumbling window

Window with a fixed interval or count as processed at one time. One tuple is processed in only a single window. It is explained in the following screenshot:

```
| e1 e2 | e3 e4 e5 e6 | e7 e8 e9 |...
0          5             10          15      -> time
    w1          w2              w3
```

The e1, e2, e3 are events. 0, 5, 10, and 15 are windows of five seconds. w1, w2, and w3 are windows. Here, every event is part of only one window.

Sliding window

Windows with interval and after processing slide the window on the basis of time interval. One tuple is processed in more than one window. It is explained in the following screenshot:

```
........| e1 e2 | e3 e4 e5 e6 | e7 e8 e9 |...
-5       0       5              10        15    -> time
|<------- w1 -->|
    |<----------- w2 ----->|
        |<-------------- w3 ---->|
```

Here, windows are overlapping and one event can be part of more than one window. In the example of the `window` function, we will integrate the feed from Kafka and check the output on the console.

 The code is taken from `https://github.com/apache/storm/blob/v1.0.3/` `examples/storm-starter/src/jvm/org/apache/storm/starter/trident/` `TridentKafkaWordCount.java` but modified to work with Kafka and also added prints. You will find the complete code in the code bundle with the class name `TridentWindowingInmemoryStoreTopology`.

The following is the code snippet for understanding linking Storm Trident with Kafka:

```
TridentKafkaConfig config = new TridentKafkaConfig(new
ZkHosts("localhost:2181"), "test"); // line 1
config.scheme = new SchemeAsMultiScheme(new StringScheme()); // line 2
config.startOffsetTime = kafka.api.OffsetRequest.LatestTime();// line 3
TransactionalTridentKafkaSpout spout = new
TransactionalTridentKafkaSpout(config); // line 4
```

First create the object of `TridentKafaConfig`, which takes the ZooKeeper hostname and port with the topic name in `line 1`. Set the scheme as String for input in `line 2`. Also set the `startOffsetTime` to consider only the latest events in the topic instead of all events from starting in `line 3`. Create Trident Kafka spout using the configuration defined previously in `line 4`.

The following is the code snippet for understanding useing the window API available in Storm Trident:

```
topology.newStream("spout1", spout) // line 1
.each(new Fields("str"),new Split(), new Fields("word")) // line 2
.window(windowConfig, windowStore, new Fields("word"), new
CountAsAggregator(), new Fields("count")) // line 3
```

First, we will define the spout in line 1. We are using the Kafka spout that we created in the previous step. In line 2, split the input string separated by space and define the output as word for each event in spout. The following common window API is used for any supported windowing function:

```
public Stream window(WindowConfig windowConfig, WindowsStoreFactory
windowStoreFactory, Fields inputFields, Aggregator aggregator, Fields
functionFields)
```

The windowConfig can be any of the following:

- SlidingCountWindow.of(int windowCount, int slidingCount)
- SlidingDurationWindow.of(BaseWindowedBolt.Duration windowDuration, BaseWindowedBolt.Duration slidingDuration)
- TumblingCountWindow.of(int windowLength)
- TumblingDurationWindow.of(BaseWindowedBolt.Duration windowLength)

The windowStore can be any of the following. It is required to process the tuples and the aggregate of values:

- HBaseWindowStoreFactory
- InMemoryWindowsStoreFactory

For this example, we are using:

```
WindowsStoreFactory mapState = new InMemoryWindowsStoreFactory();
```

In line 3, apart from windowConfig and windowStore, the input field is used as word, output as count, and aggregation function as CountAsAggregator which calculates the count of tuples received in the window.

The following is for understanding output as per the window configuration:

- **Sliding count window**: It performs the operation after the sliding count of 10 in window of 100:

```
SlidingCountWindow.of(100, 10)
```

Input on the Kafka console is shown in the following screenshot:

```
1 2 3 4 5 6 7 8 9 10
1 2 3 4 5 6 7 8 9 10
1 2 3 4 5 6 7 8 9 10
1 2 3 4 5 6 7 8 9 10
1 2 3 4 5 6 7 8 9 10
1 2 3 4 5 6 7 8 9 10
1 2 3 4 5 6 7 8 9 10
1 2 3 4 5 6 7 8 9 10
1 2 3 4 5 6 7 8 9 10
1 2 3 4 5 6 7 8 9 10
```

Output is shown in the following screenshot:

```
[10]
[20]
[30]
[40]
[50]
[60]
[70]
[80]
[90]
[100]
```

- **Tumbling count window**: It performs the operation after window count of 100:

```
TumblingCountWindow.of(100)
```

Output is shown in the following screenshot:

```
[100]
```

- **Sliding duration window**: Window duration is six seconds and sliding duration is three seconds:

```
SlidingDurationWindow.of(new BaseWindowedBolt.Duration(6,
TimeUnit.SECONDS), new BaseWindowedBolt.Duration(3,
TimeUnit.SECONDS))
```

Output is shown in the following screenshot:

```
[20]
[60]
[50]
[50]
[51]
[32]
[61]
[50]
[32]
[22]
```

The output cannot be consistent as previously. It depends on the velocity of incoming data.

- **Tumbling duration window**: Window duration is three seconds:

```
TumblingDurationWindow.of(new BaseWindowedBolt.Duration(3,
TimeUnit.SECONDS))
```

Output is shown in the following screenshot:

```
[20]
[20]
[20]
[10]
[20]
[10]
[20]
```

The output cannot be consistent as previously. It depends on the velocity of incoming data.

Aggregation

Aggregation is an operation performed on a batch or partition or stream. Trident has three types of aggregation:

Aggregate

Each batch of the tuple is aggregated in isolation. In aggregates the process, initially tuples are repartitioned using global grouping. We will discuss grouping in the next section in detail:

```
stream.aggregate(new Count(), new Fields("count"))
```

The preceding statement will give the count of a batch.

Partition aggregate

Partition aggregate runs a function on each partition of a batch of tuples. The output of the partition aggregate contains a single field tuple. The following is the example:

```
stream.partitionAggregate(new Fields("b"), new Sum(), new Fields("sum"))
```

Let's say the input is as follows:

```
Partition 0:
["a", 1]
["b", 2]

Partition 1:
["a", 3]
["c", 8]

Partition 2:
["e", 1]
["d", 9]
["d", 10]
```

The output would be:

```
Partition 0:
[3]

Partition 1:
[11]

Partition 2:
[20]
```

Persistence aggregate

Persistent aggregate aggregates all tuples across all batches in the stream and stores the result in either memory or database. An example is shown in Basic Trident topology where we used in-memory storage to perform the count.

There are three different interfaces for performing aggregator:

Combiner aggregator

The following are the characteristics of the combiner aggregator:

- It returns a single field as output
- Partial aggregations before transferring tuples over the network
- It executes an `init` function for all tuples
- It executes an `combine` function for all tuples until a single value is left
- Interface available in package:

```
public interface CombinerAggregator<T> extends Serializable {
  T init(TridentTuple tuple);
  T combine(T val1, T val2);
  T zero();
}
```

Example:

```
public class Count implements CombinerAggregator<Long> {
  public Long init(TridentTuple tuple) {
    return 1L;
  }
  public Long combine(Long val1, Long val2) {
    return val1 + val2;
  }
  public Long zero() {
    return 0L;
  }
}
```

Reducer aggregator

The following are the characteristics of the reducer aggregator:

- It produces a single value
- It executes an init function only once to get the init value
- It executes an reduce function on all tuples
- It transfers all tuples over the network and then performs the reduce function
- Less optimized compared to the combiner aggregator
- Interface available in package:

```
public interface ReducerAggregator<T> extends Serializable {
  T init();
  T reduce(T curr, TridentTuple tuple);
}
```

Example:

```
public class Count implements ReducerAggregator<Long> {
  public Long init() {
    return 0L;
  }
  public Long reduce(Long curr, TridentTuple tuple) {
    return curr + 1;
  }
}
```

Aggregator

The following are the characteristics of aggregator:

- It emits any number of tuples with any number of fields.
- It executes the `init` method before processing the batch.
- It executes the aggregate method for each input tuple in the batch partition. This method can update the state and optionally emit tuples.
- It executes the complete method when all tuples for the batch partition have been processed by the aggregate method.
- Interface available in package:

```
public interface Aggregator<T> extends Operation {
    T init(Object batchId, TridentCollector collector);
    void aggregate(T state, TridentTuple tuple, TridentCollector
collector);
    void complete(T state, TridentCollector collector);
}
```

Example:

```
public class CountAgg extends BaseAggregator<CountState> {
  static class CountState {
    long count = 0;
  }
  public CountState init(Object batchId, TridentCollector collector) {
    return new CountState();
  }
  public void aggregate(CountState state, TridentTuple tuple,
TridentCollector collector) {
    state.count+=1;
  }
  public void complete(CountState state, TridentCollector collector) {
    collector.emit(new Values(state.count));
  }
}
```

Grouping

Grouping operation is an built-in operation of Storm Trident. It is performed by the groupBy function. It repartitions tuples using `partitionBy` and then within the partition it groups all the tuples that have the same group fields. Code example:

```
topology.newStream("spout", spout)
.each(new Fields("sentence"), new Split(), new Fields("word"))  .groupBy(new
Fields("word"))
.persistentAggregate(stateFactory, new Count(), new Fields("count"));
```

As per Storm Trident documentation, the group by function is explained using the following diagram:

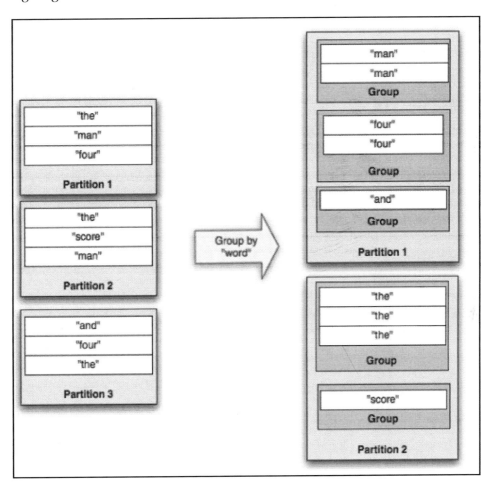

Merge and joins

The merge operation is used to merge more than one stream together. Code example:

```
topology.merge(stream1, stream2, stream3);
```

Another way to combine streams is using join. Let's take an example: stream1 has the fields (key, val1, val2) and stream2 has (x, val1). Now perform a join with stream1 and stream2 as follows:

```
topology.join(stream1, new Fields("key"), stream2, new Fields("x"), new
Fields("key", "a", "b", "c"));
```

The stream1 and stream2 are joined on the basis of key and x respectively. The output of the field is defined as key from stream1, val1, and val2 as a and b from stream1 again, val1 as c from stream2.

Input:

```
Stream 1:
[1, 2, 3]

Stream 2:
[1, 4]
```

Output:

```
[1, 2, 3, 4]
```

DRPC

Distributed Remote Produce Call (DRPC). It is computing very intense functionality on the fly using storm. It gives input as function name and corresponding arguments and the output is results for each of those function calls.

Code example DRPC client:

```
DRPCClient client = new DRPCClient("drpc.server.location", 3772);
System.out.println(client.execute("words", "cat dog the man"));
```

DRPC Storm code:

```
topology.newDRPCStream("words")
.each(new Fields("args"), new Split(), new Fields("word"))
.groupBy(new Fields("word"))
.stateQuery(wordCounts, new Fields("word"), new MapGet(), new
Fields("count"))
.aggregate(new Fields("count"), new Sum(), new Fields("sum"));
```

The program is explained in the following diagram:

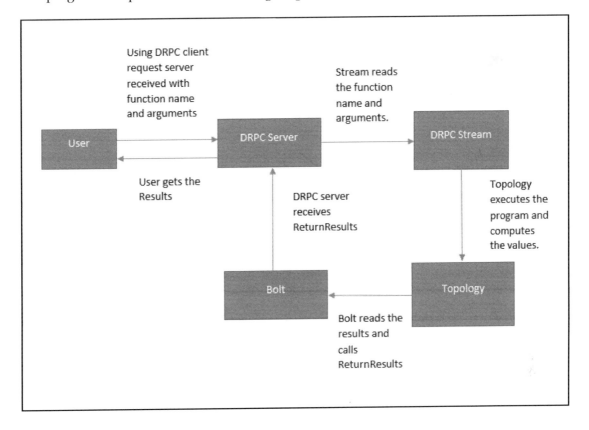

Do It Yourself

We will build a use case using filters, group by, and aggregators. The use case finds the top 10 devices that generate the maximum data in a batch. Here is the pseudo code:

- Write a data generator that will publish an event with fields such as phone number, bytes in and bytes out
- The data generator will publish events in Kafka
- Write a topology program:
    - To get the events from Kafka
    - Apply filter to exclude phone number to take part in top 10
    - Split event on the basis of comma
    - Perform group by operation to bring same phone numbers together
    - Perform aggregate and sum out bytes in and bytes out together
    - Now, apply assembly with the `FirstN` function which requires the field name and number elements to be calculated
    - And finally display it on the console

You will find the code in the code bundle for reference.

Program:

```
package com.book.chapter8.diy;
```

In the following code snippet, we have import files:

```
import org.apache.storm.Config;
import org.apache.storm.LocalCluster;
import org.apache.storm.kafka.StringScheme;
import org.apache.storm.kafka.ZkHosts;
import org.apache.storm.kafka.trident.TransactionalTridentKafkaSpout;
import org.apache.storm.kafka.trident.TridentKafkaConfig;
import org.apache.storm.spout.SchemeAsMultiScheme;
import org.apache.storm.trident.TridentTopology;
import org.apache.storm.trident.operation.BaseFilter;
import org.apache.storm.trident.operation.BaseFunction;
import org.apache.storm.trident.operation.TridentCollector;
import org.apache.storm.trident.operation.builtin.Debug;
import org.apache.storm.trident.operation.builtin.FirstN;
import org.apache.storm.trident.operation.builtin.Sum;
import org.apache.storm.trident.tuple.TridentTuple;
import org.apache.storm.tuple.Fields;
import org.apache.storm.tuple.Values;
```

Topology builder which binds spout and bolts

The basic class:

```
public class TridentDIY {
    public static void main(String args[]) {
        TridentKafkaConfig config = new TridentKafkaConfig(new ZkHosts(
            "localhost:2181"), "storm-trident-diy");
        config.scheme = new SchemeAsMultiScheme(new StringScheme());
        config.startOffsetTime = kafka.api.OffsetRequest.LatestTime();
        TransactionalTridentKafkaSpout spout = new
TransactionalTridentKafkaSpout(config);
        TridentTopology topology = new TridentTopology();
        topology.newStream("spout", spout).filter(new ExcludePhoneNumber())
                    .each(new Fields("str"), new DeviceInfoExtractor(),
new Fields("phone", "bytes"))
                    .groupBy(new Fields("phone"))
                    .aggregate(new Fields("bytes", "phone"), new Sum(),
new Fields("sum")).applyAssembly(new FirstN(10, "sum"))
.each(new Fields("phone", "sum"), new Debug());

Config config1 = new Config();
        config1.setNumWorkers(3);
        LocalCluster cluster = new LocalCluster();
        cluster.submitTopology("storm-trident-diy", config1,
topology.build());
    }
}
```

Filtering phone number events from stream

The class to format the data:

```
class ExcludePhoneNumber extends BaseFilter {
    private static final long serialVersionUID = 7961541061613235361L;

    public boolean isKeep(TridentTuple tuple) {
        return !tuple.get(0).toString().contains("9999999950");
    }
}
```

Extract device information from event in stream

In the following code, we code the way we present the data:

```java
class DeviceInfoExtractor extends BaseFunction {

    private static final long serialVersionUID = 4889855511293326495L;

    @Override
    public void execute(TridentTuple tuple, TridentCollector collector) {
        String event = tuple.getString(0);
        System.out.println(event);
        String[] splittedEvent = event.split(",");
        if(splittedEvent.length>1){
            long phoneNumber = Long.parseLong(splittedEvent[0]);
            int bin = Integer.parseInt(splittedEvent[1]);
            int bout = Integer.parseInt(splittedEvent[2]);
            int totalBytesTransferred = bin + bout;
            System.out.println(phoneNumber+":"+bin+":"+bout);
            collector.emit(new Values(phoneNumber, totalBytesTransferred));
        }
    }
}

package com.book.chapter8.diy;
```

Import files:

```java
import java.util.Date;
import java.util.Properties;
import java.util.concurrent.ThreadLocalRandom;

import org.apache.kafka.clients.producer.KafkaProducer;
import org.apache.kafka.clients.producer.ProducerRecord;
```

Class for data to generate:

```java
public class DataGenerator {
    public static void main(String args[]) {
        Properties properties = new Properties();
        properties.put("bootstrap.servers", "localhost:9092");
        properties.put("key.serializer",
"org.apache.kafka.common.serialization.StringSerializer");
        properties.put("value.serializer",
"org.apache.kafka.common.serialization.StringSerializer");
        properties.put("acks", "1");
```

```
            KafkaProducer<Integer, String> producer = new
    KafkaProducer<Integer, String>(properties);
            int counter =0;
            int nbrOfEventsRequired = Integer.parseInt(args[0]);
            while (counter<nbrOfEventsRequired) {
                    StringBuffer stream = new StringBuffer();
                    long phoneNumber =
    ThreadLocalRandom.current().nextLong(99999999501,
                            99999999601);
                    int bin = ThreadLocalRandom.current().nextInt(1000, 9999);
                    int bout = ThreadLocalRandom.current().nextInt(1000, 9999);
                    stream.append(phoneNumber);
                    stream.append(",");
                    stream.append(bin);
                    stream.append(",");
                    stream.append(bout);
                    stream.append(",");
                    stream.append(new
    Date(ThreadLocalRandom.current().nextLong()));

                    System.out.println(stream.toString());
                    ProducerRecord<Integer, String> data = new
    ProducerRecord<Integer, String>(
                            "storm-trident-diy", stream.toString());
                    producer.send(data);
                    counter++;
            }
            producer.close();
        }
    }
```

Summary

In this chapter, we explained what Trident state is and how it is maintained. After that we built basic trident topology explaining and acquainting the reader with writing basic trident topology. We have multiple operations available with trident, so we explained all possible operations with examples. We also explained how trident works. We explained about the DRPC way of calling in trident and its processing. In the end, we gave the user a problem to solve with operations such as `filter`, `group by`, and `top n`.

9
Working with Spark

This is the chapter where we introduce our readers to Spark engine. We will introduce the fundamentals of spark architecture and make them understand the need for and utility of using spark as an option for practical use cases.

We will cover the following topics:

- Spark overview
- Distinct advantages of Spark
- Spark – use cases
- Spark architecture - working inside the engine
- Spark pragmatic concepts
- Spark 2.x - advent of data frames and datasets

Spark overview

Apache Spark is a highly distributed compute engine, which comes with promises of speed and reliability for the computations. As a framework it's based on Hadoop, but it's further enhanced to perform in memory computations to cater to interactive queries and near real-time stream processing. The parallel processing clustering and in-memory processing offer Spark an edge in terms of performance and reliability. Today Apache Spark is known for its proven salient features:

- **Speed and efficiency**: While it runs off traditional disk-based HDFS, it has 100x higher speed, because of in-memory computations and savings on disk I/O. It saves the intermediate results in memory, thus saving the overall execution time.

- **Extensibility and compatibility**: It has a variety of interaction APIs for developers to choose from. It comes out of the box with Java, Scala, and Python APIs.
- **Analytics and ML**: It provides robust support for all machine learning and graph algorithms. In fact, now it's becoming the top choice among developers for big data implementation for complex data science and artificial intelligence models.

Spark framework and schedulers

The following diagram captures the various components of the Spark framework and the variety of scheduling modes in which it could be deployed:

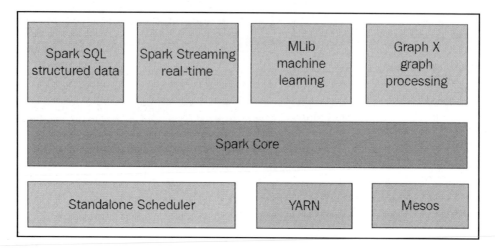

The preceding diagram has all the basic components of the Spark ecosystem, though over a period of time some have evolved/deprecated, which we will get the users acquainted with in due course. These are the basic components of the Spark framework:

- **Spark core**: As the name suggests, this is the core control unit of Spark framework. It predominantly handles the scheduling and management of tasks. These using a spark abstraction called **resilient distributed dataset (RDDs)**. RDD is the basic data abstraction unit in Spark and, shall be discussed in detail in the following sections.

- **Spark SQL**: This module of Spark is typically designed for data engineers who are familiar with using SQL on structured datasets of Oracle, SQL Server, MySQL, and so on. It supports hive and one can easily query data using HiveQL—Hive Query Language—which is very similar to SQL. The Spark SQL also interfaces with popular connectors like JDBC and ODBC that let the developers integrate it with popular databases and other data marts and BI and visualization tools.

- **Spark streaming**: This is the Spark module that supports processing on real-time/near real-time streaming data. It integrates seamlessly to ingestion pipelines like Kafka, RabbitMQ, Flume, and so on. This module is built for scalable and fault tolerant, high speed processing.

- **Spark MLLib**: This module for Spark is predominantly an implementation of commonly used data science statistical and machine learning algorithms. It's a highly scalable, distributed, and fault tolerant module that provides implicit implementations on classification, component analysis, clustering and regression, and so on.

- **GraphX**: GraphX was an independent project at Berkley research center, but that was later donated to Spark and thus became part of the Apache Spark framework. It is basically the module that supports graph computation and analysis of a large volume of data. It supports Pregel API and a wide variety of graphing algorithms.

- **Spark R**: This is one of the late added modules of spark and it was predominantly designed as a tool for data scientists. The data analysts and scientists have been widely using R Studio as a model designing tool, but that provides them with a limited capability single node tool that can only cater to a subset of the data sample. These models later require a lot of rework and redesign in terms of logic and optimization to execute on a wider set of data. Spark R is an attempt to bridge this gap; it's a lightweight framework that leverages Spark's capabilities and lets the data scientists execute the R model in distributed mode over a wider set of data on the Spark engine.

The following diagram quickly captures the synopsis of the preliminary functions of various spark components:

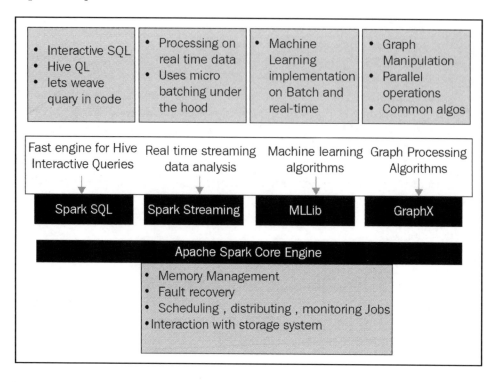

Now that we understand the basic modules and components of spark framework, let's have a closer look at the orchestration mechanism and options for Spark. There are three ways in which spark can be deployed and orchestrated. This is captured in the following diagram and is described in the following section:

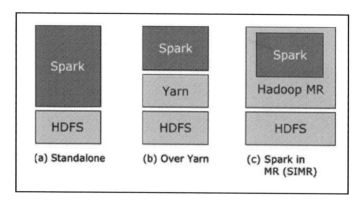

It is described as follows:

- **Standalone**: In this kind of Spark deployment, Spark is deployed on top of HDFS. There is quota allocated to Spark on HDFS and the Spark jobs co-execute with other MapReduce jobs executing on the same setup of Hadoop Yarn.
- **Hadoop Yarn**: This kind of deployment doesn't require any pre-installation, and Spark is integrated atop of the Hadoop eco-system - all jobs and spark components run on top of the Hadoop eco-system.
- **Spark in MapReduce (SIMR)**: We have all been using and talking about Spark on Yarn, but one of the practical challenges people have been struggling with for a while is running Spark jobs on Hadoop clusters with version V1. It was really cumbersome and required administrative rights to execute spark jobs on Hadoop V1 clusters. SIMR has been jointly developed by Berkley Analytics lab, so that any user with access to HDFS and MapReduce on Hadoop V1 cluster can submit and execute spark jobs without admin rights or Spark/Scala setup.

Distinct advantages of Spark

Now that we understand the Spark components, let's move to the next step to understand what the key advantages of spark are for distributed, fault tolerant processing over its peers in this section. We will also touch upon the situations where Spark might not be the best choice for the solution:

- **High performance**: This is the key feature responsible for the success of Spark, the high performance in data processing over HDFS. As we have seen in the previous section, Spark leverages its framework over HDFS and the Yarn eco-system, but offers up to 10x faster performance; this makes it a better choice over map-reduce. Spark achieves this performance enhancement by limiting the use of latency intensive disk I/O and leveraging over it in memory compute capability.
- **Robust and dynamic**: Apache Spark is robust in its out-of-the-box implementation and it comes with over 80+ operations. It's built in Scala and has interfacing APIs in Java, Python, and so on. The entire combination of choice of base and peripheral technologies makes it highly extensible for any kind of custom implementation.

- **In-memory computation**: The in-memory compute capability is the crux to the speed and efficiency of the Spark engine. It saves overall processing time by saving time in writing to disk, it uses a pragmatic abstraction RDD, and it stores most of the computes in memory. It uses the **Directed Acyclic Graph (DAG)** engine for in-memory computation and execution flow orchestration.

- **Reusable**: The RDD abstraction helps the programmers develop code in spark in a manner that is reusable for batch, hybrid, and real-time stream processing with a few tweaks.

- **Fault tolerant**: The Spark RDD's are the basic programming abstraction of Spark framework and they are resilient not only in name, but in nature as well. They have been designed to handle the failures of nodes within the cluster during the computation without any data loss. While RDD's are designed to handle the failures, another notable aspect is that Spark leverages HDFS/Yarn for its basic framework, thus the Hadoop resilience in terms of stable storage is inherent to it.

- **Near Real-time stream processing**: Spark streaming module is designed to handle super-fast computation and analysis on top of streaming data to deliver insights and actionable insights in realtime. This is definitely an edge over Hadoop's MapReduce, wherein we had to wait for long batch cycles to get the results.

- **Lazy evaluation**: The execution model in Spark by its nature is lazy and all transformations applied to an RDD don't yield immediate results—instead another RDD is formed. The actual execution happens when we issue an action. This model helps a lot in terms of making the total execution efficient in terms of time.

- **Active and extending community**: The project Spark was initiated in 2009 as part of **Berkley's Data Analytics System (BDAS)**. Developers from more than 50 companies joined hands in its making. The community is ever-expanding and plays an essential part in spark's adoption by the industry.

- **Complex analytics**: It's a system made and designed to handle complex analytics jobs on top of both historic batch and streaming real-time data.

- **Integration with Hadoop**: This is another cost-efficient and distinct advantage of Spark. Its integration with Hadoop makes its adoption so easy by the industry, as it can leverage and sit upon the existing Hadoop cluster and provide for lightning fast computations in a fail-safe, scale mode.

The following diagram conclusively captures all the advantages of Spark:

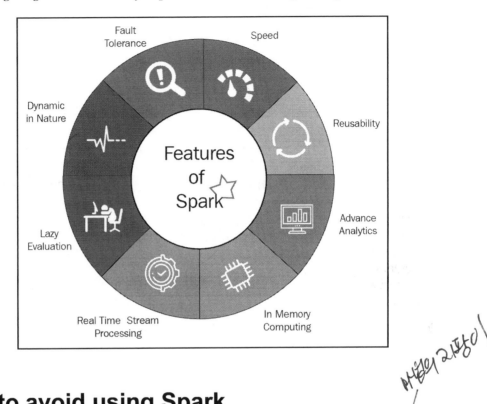

When to avoid using Spark

We have said so much about Spark and its distinct features, I really don't want our readers to believe that it's a one solution fits all kind of tool and it comes with a magic wand to solve all our woes. Well, there are situations when spark should be avoided and a few common ones are listed as follows:

- **No real-time and event Windowing**: Spark doesn't do real-time processing, in fact it plays on micro batching that essentially gives an illusion of NRT. So what it actually does is it creates micro batches out of the streaming events and instead of executing the processing logic on one big batch, it executes it on a micro batch and thus results arrive very close to realtime. There is a big trade off to this approach, which spark can't execute on record level/event level processing assertions as reducing the batch size has a derogating effect on the overall performance.

- **Small file and tiny partitions**: Spark, if used in conjunction to Hadoop for NRT, can run into this situation. It largely depends on the size of the micro-batch we are using for over execution. Hadoop is designed for handling large/very large file blocks, while in spark realtime combination, we end up creating a very large number of files that are very small in size. The maintenance with respect to file read/write handlers and other OS operations results in degrading the solution performance.

- **No filesystem**: This is a known fact, though it can be taken as flexibility that Spark can be plugged to any filesystem—Hadoop/cloud, and so on.

- **Memory is more expensive than disk**: Spark relies on in-memory computation and thus is faster that Hadoop—MapReduce, which uses disk operation for this. But the side effect is the cost, as memory cost is higher than disk. So the performance of Spark comes with a trade-off of additional cost to be spent in procuring memory along with disk.

- **Latency**: Spark provides lower latency than Hadoop, but it's still higher than the newer kids like Flink.

- **Back pressure handling**: The back-pressure handling mechanism is not built in; it's handled manually/built by the developer.

The following diagram captures them all in a diagrammatic representation, along with a few others like:

- Lack of optimization hints
- Iterative nature of data processing
- Less number of data science algorithms in out-of-the-box implementation

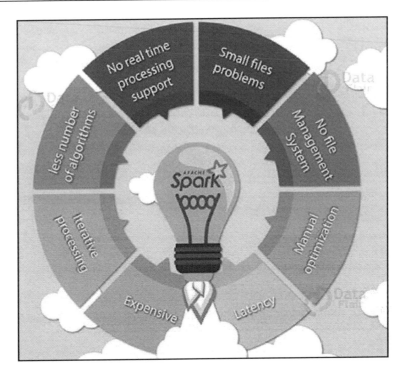

Now that we clearly understand all the salient features of Spark, including the ones that are not so sparkling, let's move to the next section that talks about some of the use cases where Spark is the best choice in terms of analytical framework

Spark – use cases

This section is dedicated to walking the users through distinct real-life uses cases where spark is the best and obvious choice for analytical processing in the solution:

- Financial domain:
    - **Fraud detection**: A very important use case to all of us as credit card users, here the real-time streaming data is mapped to your persona and historical usage records through a series of complex data science prediction algorithms to choose a fraudulent from a seemingly fraudulent card transaction. In accordance, further action like allowing the payment, calling for mobile verification, blocking the transaction, and so on are taken into account.

- **Customer 360 churn and recommendation (cross-sell/up-sell)**: All financial institutes have hordes of data, but they struggle with maintenance aspects. Today the need of the hour is unified customer personification and correlation of all a customer's actions in realtime to further enrich data. This unified personification is being done very effectively in large institutions using Spark and further it helps in behavioral data science modeling to predict churn and provide recommendations using cross sell and up sell based on customer profiling and personification.
- **Real-time monitoring (better client service)**: Real-time monitoring of customer activities across all channels helps in personification and recommendation. But it also helps in monitoring client activities and identifies issues and breaches if any. For instance, the same client can't use an ATM physically 100 miles apart within a span of 30 minutes.

- E-commerce:

  - **Partnership and prediction**: Lot of companies are using spark-based analytics to predict the market and trend analysis and build their partner base accordingly
  - **Alibaba**: It runs some of the largest analytical spark jobs over hundreds of petabytes of data to perform extraction of text from images, merchant data ETL, and machine learning models on top of the same to analyze, predict, plot, and recommend.
  - **Graphing, analytics, ETL, integration**: It does it all for eBay.

- Health care:

  - **Wearable devices**: The industry is better equipped to provide clinical diagnosis based on Spark recommendations using real-time streaming data and past medical history of the patients. It also takes other dimensions such as nationality, regional eating habits, any epidemic outbreak in the region, weather, temperature, and so on into consideration.

- Media and entertainment:

  - **Conviva**: Provides for the best quality streaming service by removing the screen buffering, which is managed by learning and handling network issues in realtime without impacting the service quality.

- **Netflix**: Provides online recommendations using advance analytical algorithms implemented and running in spark. It uses a very high degree of personalization and personification based on activity as a user of the Netflix system.

- Travel domain:
    - **Personalized recommendations (TripAdvisor)**
    - **NLP and Spark for recommendations (OpenTable)**

Spark architecture - working inside the engine

We have looked at the components of spark framework, its advantages/disadvantages, and the scenarios where it best fits in solution design. In the following section, we will delve deeper into the internals of Spark, its architectural abstractions, and workings. Spark works in a master salve model and the following diagram shows the layered architecture for it:

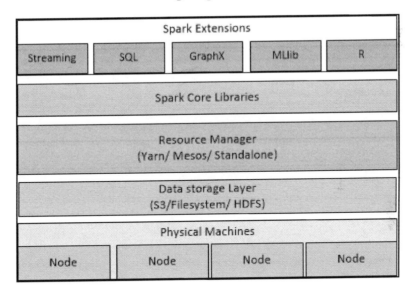

If we start bottom up from the layered architecture depicted in the preceding diagram:

- The physical machines or the nodes are abstracted by a data storage layer (that could a HDFS/distributed file system/AWS S3). This data storage layer provides the APIs for storage and retrieval of final/intermediate data sets generated during the execution.
- The resource manager layer on top of the data storage obfuscates the underlying storage and resource orchestration from spark set up and execution model, thus providing the users a spark setup that could leverage any of the available resource managers, such as Yarn, Mesos, or Spark standalone/local.
- On top of this layer we have the Spark core and Spark extensions, each of which we already discussed and touched upon in the previous section.

Now that we have understood the layer abstraction of spark framework over the raw physical hardware, the next step is to have a look at spark with a different perspective, that is, its execution model. The following diagram captures the execution components under various nodes in a spark cluster:

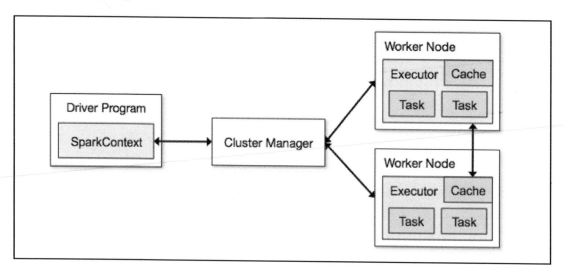

Image referenced from http://spark.apache.org/docs/1.3.0/cluster-overview.html

As evident from the preceding diagram, the key physical components of the Spark cluster are:

- Master or the driver node
- Worker or the executor nodes
- Cluster manager

All the preceding three are vital ingredients essential to the execution of any Spark application job. All components work as their name suggests: the **driver node** hosts the spark context where the main driver program runs in the spark cluster, while the **cluster manager** is basically the resource managing component of the spark cluster and it could be either Spark—standalone resource manager, Yarn-based resource manager, or Mesos-based resource manager. It predominantly handles the orchestration and management of underlying resources of the cluster for application execution in a manner that's agnostic to the overall implementation. Spark **worker nodes** are actually the nodes where the executors and tasks are spawned and the spark job actually executes.

Let's look a little closer at each of these components.

What is a driver in a Spark cluster?

- This is the main process that executes under the master/driver node
- It is the entry point for the Spark Shell
- This is where the Spark context is created
- The RDD is translated to execution DAG on the driver Spark context
- All tasks are scheduled and controlled by the driver during their execution
- All the metadata for RDD and their lineage is managed by the driver
- It brings the Spark webUI

What is the executor in a Spark cluster?

- This is the process within the slave/worker nodes where the spark job tasks are created and executed
- It reads/writes data from external sources
- All data processing and logic execution is performed here

What is Spark application and its working components?

It's a single instance of Spark context that has data and computation logic. It can schedule a series of parallel/sequential jobs for execution.

- **Job**: It refers to a Spark Job, which is a complete autonomous set of transformations that runs on RDD; it finishes its execution with an action. A job is triggered by the driver application.
- **Stage**: It's a group of transformations that are sequenced to be executed as a pipeline over a single worker.
- **Task**: It's the execution of stage over a single data partition. This is a basic unit of scheduling in spark.

Spark pragmatic concepts

You know what appeals the most to us developers? The ability to tap into the framework and the flexibility to extend it as per our needs. In today's world of abstraction and decoupling, this is taken care of using a variety of APIs that come out of the box.

We have talked enough about the latency issue the big data world was struggling with before Spark came and took the performance to the next level. Let's have a closer look to understand this latency problem a little better. The following diagram captures the execution of typical Hadoop processes and its intermediate steps:

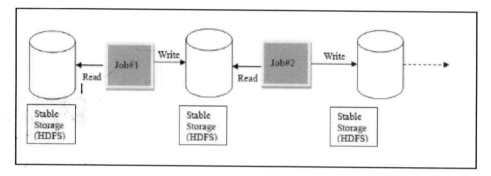

Well, as depicted, Hadoop ecosystem leverages HDFS (a disk-based distributed stable storage) extensively to store the intermediate processing results:

- **Job #1**: This reads the data for processing from HDFS and writes its results to HDFS
- **Job #2**: This reads the interim processing results of job 1 from HDFS, processes, and writes the outcome to HDFS

While HDFS is a fault tolerant and persistent store, any disk-based read/write operation is very expensive in terms of overall latency. Do remember the serialization and de-serialization, and the distributed nature of HDFS adds a network latency aspect as well to the disk read-write latency.

So while the solution is robust, all these latent delays add to the total turnaround time of the job and delay the final processing outcome.

The following diagram recaptures the same scenario as previously in wake of memory resident intermediate storage:

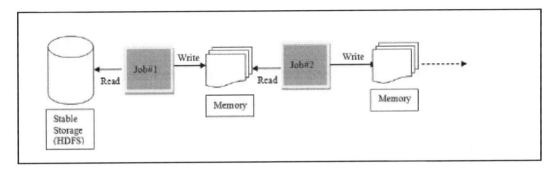

The noticeable difference is that job 1 writes the interim results in-memory, while job 2 reads these interim results for further processing from memory, thus saving time on disk I/O operations.

So, what's the magic that Spark does? Well, it quotes to provide faster results even while it utilizes HDFS. The magic is in-memory computations and the abstraction is a **Resilient Distributed Dataset (RDD)**.

RDD is the fundamental distinct feature and core of all spark computations. As a concept, it was independent research work at Berkley University, which was first implemented and adopted in Spark. If I have to define RDD in a nutshell I would say it is an abstraction that exhibits all features of Hadoop, but exists in memory—not on disk.

It's a distributed, fault tolerant, in-memory representation of data (immutable) that can be further processed in a parallel, distributed manner across executors scattered over various worker nodes in a spark cluster.

You may want to refer to the original research paper by *Matei Zaharia* about the RDD concept at https://cs.stanford.edu/~matei/papers/2012/nsdi_spark.pdf.

RDD – the name says it all

Resilient—that means RDDs are fault tolerant—now the question is, if they are in-memory, how can they recover from the failures unless they are persisted, which brings back the disk latency? Well let me help you all here—the answer is RDD lineage that helps in the re-computation of missing/damaged partition data in the event of any failures.

 RDD lineage is actually an RDD operator/dependency graph that captures the logical execution plan of all transformations applied to parent RDD, so that under event of failure the entire graph/subgraph could be recomputed to regenerate the corrupt RDD.

Distributed—well an RDD data resides in-memory across the different worker nodes in the cluster.

Dataset—well it's a collection of partitioned data with primitive values/tuples.

The following is a list of a few more significant features of RDD:

- **In-memory**: An RDD resides in memory as long as possible to provide faster access and low latency computation.
- **Immutable**: An RDD is read-only when an operation is applied and a new RDD is generated as a result of the transformation.
- **Lazy evaluation**: It supports two kinds of operations: the transformations (the ones that generate another RDD) and actions (they are actually the triggers and return values), but all processes or transformations are executed in lazy mode only when an action is executed.
- **Partitioned**: The data within an RDD is logically partitioned across multiple nodes in the cluster. Placement preferences can be defined to compute the partitions.
- **Handle unstructured data**: This is designed to handle unstructured data such as text/media stream, and so on.

Spark 2.x – advent of data frames and datasets

With Spark 2.x we have two new spark computational abstractions:

- **Data frames**: These are distributed, resilient, fault tolerant in-memory data structures that are capable of handling only structured data, which means they are designed to manage data that can be segregated in fixed typed columns. Though it may sound like a limitation with respect to RDD, which can handle any type of unstructured data, in practical terms this structured abstraction over the data makes it very easy to manipulate and work over a large volume of structured data, the way we used to with RDBMS.
- **Datasets**: It's an extension of the Spark data frame. It's a type safe object-oriented interface. For the sake of simplicity, one could say that data frames are actually an un-typed dataset. This newest API in spark pragmatic abstraction actually leverages features of tungsten in-memory encoding and catalysts optimizer.

Summary

In this chapter, we introduced the readers to Apache Spark compute engine, and we talked about the various components of Spark framework and its schedulers. We touched upon the advantages that provide edge to spark as a scalable, high performing compute engine. The users were also acquainted with the not-so sparkling features of Spark—when it's not the best fit to be used. We walked the users through some practical realtime industry wide use cases. Next we got into the layered architecture of Spark and its internal working across the cluster. In the end we touched upon the pragmatic concepts of Spark: RDD, DataFrame, and datasets.

The next chapter will touch upon the spark APIs and execution of all components through working code blocks.

10
Working with Spark Operations

This is the chapter where we introduce our readers to Spark actions, transformations, and shared variables. We will introduce the fundamentals of Spark Operations and explain the need for and utility of using Spark as an option for practical use cases. We'll look at:

- Spark – packaging and API
- RDD Pragmatic exploration
- Shared variables – broadcast variables and accumulators

Spark – packaging and API

Now that the readers have been well acquainted with the architecture and basic data flow of Spark, in the following section we will take the journey to the next step and get the users acquainted with the programming paradigms and APIs that are used frequently to build varied custom solutions around Spark.

As we know by now, the Spark framework is developed in Scala, but it provides a facility for developers to interact, develop, and customize the framework using Scala, Python, and Java APIs too. For the context of this discussion, we will limit our learning to Scala and Java APIs.

Spark APIs can be categorized into two broad segments:

- Spark core
- Spark extensions

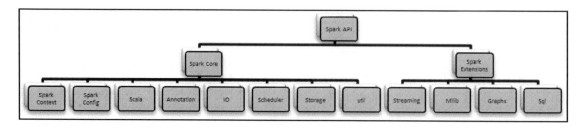

As depicted in the preceding diagram, at high level, the Spark codebase is divided into two packages:

- **Spark extensions**: All API's for the particular extension are packaged in their own package structure. For example, all API's for Spark Streaming are packaged in the `org.apache.spark.streaming.*` package and the same packaging structure goes for other extensions: Spark MLlib—`org.apache.spark.mllib.*`, Spark SQL—`org.apcahe.spark.sql.*`, and Spark GraphX—`org.apache.spark.graphx.*`.

     For more information, refer to `http://tinyurl.com/q2wgar8` for Scala APIs and `http://tinyurl.com/nc4qu5l` for Java API's.

- **Spark core**: Spark core is the heart of Spark and it provides two basic components: `SparkContext` and `SparkConfig`. Both of these components are used by each and every standard or customized Spark job or Spark library and extension. Context and config is not a new term/concept and it has more or less now become a standard architectural pattern. By definition, a context is an entry point of the application that provides the access to various resources/features exposed by the framework while the config contains the application configurations, which helps in defining the environment of the application.

As a developer you will get to work a lot with Spark core, so let's take a look at the details of Scala API's exposed under the Spark core package of the Spark Framework.

- `org.apache.spark`: This is the basic package of the Spark core API, and it generally encapsulates the classes, providing functionality for:
  - Creation of Spark jobs on clusters
  - Distribution and orchestration of Spark jobs on clusters
  - Submitting the Spark jobs on clusters

- `org.apache.spark.SparkContext`: This is the first item you will see in any Spark job/program. This is the entry point of the Spark application and the context that provides a pathway to developers to access and use all the other features provided by the Spark Framework to develop and encode the business logic driven application. This provides the execution handle for the Spark job and even the references to the Spark extensions. A note worthy aspect is that it's immutable and only one Spark context can be instantiated per JVM.

- `org.apache.spark.rdd.RDD.scala`: This package holds the API's pertaining to the operation that can be executed in a parallel and distributed manner using the Spark pragmatic data unit RDD over the distributed Spark compute engine. `SparkContext` provides access to various methods that can be used to load the data from the HDFS/filesystem/Scala collection to create an RDD. This package holds various operational contexts for RDD such as map, join, filter, and even persist. It also has some specialized classes that come in very handy in certain specific scenarios, such as:
  - **PairRDDFunctions**: It's useful when working with key value data
  - **SequenceFileRDDFunctions**: A great aide for handling Hadoop sequence files
  - **DoubelRDDFunctions**: Functions for working with RDD of double data

- `org.apache.spark.broadcast`: Once you start programming in Spark, this will be one of the most frequently used packages of the framework, second only to RDD and `SparkContext`. It encapsulates the APIs for sharing the variables across the Spark jobs in a cluster. By nature, Spark is used to process humongous amount of data, thus these variables we are talking about broadcasting would be of huge size, and the mechanism of exchange and broadcast needs to be smart and efficient so that information is passed on without jeopardizing the performance and entire job execution. There are two broadcast implementations in Spark:

    - **HttpBroadcast**: As the name suggests, this implementation relies on an `HTTPServer` mechanism to fetch and retrieve the data where the server itself runs at the Spark driver location. The data is being stored in the Executor and BlockManager.

    - **TorrentBroadcast**: This is the default broadcast implementation of Spark. Here the broadcast mechanism fetches the data in chunks from the Executor/driver and is maintained in its own BlockManager. In principle, it uses the same mechanism as BitTorrent to ensure the driver isn't bottlenecking the entire broadcast pipeline.

- `org.apache.spark.io`: This provides implementation of various compression libraries, used at block storage level. This whole package is marked as `DeveloperAPI`, so it can be extended and custom implementation can be provided by the developers. By default, it provides three implementations: LZ4, LZF, and Snappy.

- `org.apache.spark.scheduler`: This provides various scheduler libraries that help in job scheduling, tracking, and monitoring. It defines the **directed acyclic graph (DAG)** scheduler `http://en.wikipedia.org/wiki/Directed_acyclic_graph`. Spark DAG scheduler defines the stage oriented scheduling where it keeps track of the completion of each RDD and the output of each stage and then computes the DAG, which is further submitted to the underlying `org.apache.spark.scheduler.TaskScheduler` that executes them on the cluster.

- `org.apache.spark.storage`: Provides APIs for structuring, managing, and finally persisting the data stored in RDD within blocks. It also keeps track of data and ensures it is either stored in memory or, if the memory is full, it is flushed to an underlying persistent storage area.
- `org.apache.spark.util`: Utility classes for performing common functions across the Spark APIs. For example, it defines `MutablePair`, which can be used as an alternative to Scala's Tuple2 with the difference that `MutablePair` is updatable while Scala's Tuple2 is not. It helps in optimizing memory and minimizing object allocations.

RDD pragmatic exploration

We have read and understood well that RDDs are an immutable, distributed collection of object values used as a unit of abstraction in Spark Framework. There are two ways RDDs can be created:

- Loading external dataset
- Distributing a list/set/collection of objects in their driver program

Now let's create some simple programs to create and use RDDs:

```
tmpadmin@IMPETUS-NL276:~/setup/spark-2.1.1-bin-hadoop2.7$ ./bin/spark-shell
Using Spark's default log4j profile: org/apache/spark/log4j-defaults.properties
Setting default log level to "WARN".
To adjust logging level use sc.setLogLevel(newLevel). For SparkR, use setLogLevel(newLevel).
17/08/20 03:21:07 WARN NativeCodeLoader: Unable to load native-hadoop library for your platform... using builtin-java classes where applicable
17/08/20 03:21:08 WARN Utils: Your hostname, IMPETUS-NL276 resolves to a loopback address: 127.0.1.1; using 192.168.1.38 instead (on interface wlan0)
17/08/20 03:21:08 WARN Utils: Set SPARK_LOCAL_IP if you need to bind to another address
17/08/20 03:21:16 WARN ObjectStore: Failed to get database global_temp, returning NoSuchObjectException
Spark context Web UI available at http://192.168.1.38:4040
Spark context available as 'sc' (master = local[*], app id = local-1503179469035).
Spark session available as 'spark'.
Welcome to


      ____              __
     / __/__  ___ _____/ /__
    _\ \/ _ \/ _ `/ __/  '_/
   /___/ .__/\_,_/_/ /_/\_\   version 2.1.1
      /_/

Using Scala version 2.11.8 (Java HotSpot(TM) 64-Bit Server VM, Java 1.8.0_111)
Type in expressions to have them evaluated.
Type :help for more information.

scala> val inputfile = sc.textFile("input.txt")
inputfile: org.apache.spark.rdd.RDD[String] = input.txt MapPartitionsRDD[1] at textFile at <console>:24
```

The preceding screenshot captures quick steps to create an RDD on Spark Shell. Here are the specific commands and further transformational outputs for this:

```
Scala> val inputfile = sc.textFile("input.txt")
```

The preceding command reads the file called `input.txt` from the specified absolute location and a new RDD is created under the name `inputfile`. In the preceding snippet we have not specified the entire path, thus the framework would assume that the file exists under the current location.

Once the RDD is created and the data from the said input file is loaded into it, let's put it to use to count the number of words in the file. To achieve this, we can execute the following steps:

1. Let's split the file into words, in the form of a flatMap. We split using the space " " character.
2. Create a key value pair by reading each word. The value will be "1" for all words.
3. Run a reducer cycle and add the similar keys.

Well the beauty of Scala is that it compresses all the preceding steps into a single line of execution as follows:

```
Scala> val counts = inputfile.flatMap(line => line.split(" ")).map(word =>
(word, 1)).reduceByKey(_+_);
```

Here I'll quickly explain the break-down of the preceding command:

- `inputfile.flatMap(line => line.split(" "))`: Here we create the flatMap of words by splitting over space
- `map(word => (word, 1))`: Using the flatMap we created previously, we map the words and value "1"
- `(reduceByKey(_+_))`: The reducer adds the values of similar keys

Deed done, well yes and no. We have said RDDs are lazy in execution in the previous section, now you'll actually experience this. We have achieved the word count transformation previously, but the output is yet to be generated, and you will see none until there is a Spark action.

So now let's apply an action and persist the output to disk. Here, the following command persists the new RDD counts to disk under folder output:

```
Scala> counts.saveAsTextFile("output")
```

You need to look into the output folder under the current path to see the persisted/saved data of the counts RDD—in the following screenshot we have the current figure:

In the following screenshot, we have the result of the query:

```
(unpacked,1)
(Manager,1)
(to,13)
(follow,2)
(location.,1)
(more,3)
(Flash(R),1)
(directories,1)
(see,3)
(of,6)
(player,1)
(usr/*,1)
(An,1)
(Your,1)
(binary,1)
(Player,7)
(directory,1)
(prompts,2)
(investigate,1)
(where,1)
(and,13)
(Player.,1)
(generate,1)
(system,1)
```

You may also want to have a look at the job details form web console at:

```
http://localhost:4040/jobs/
```

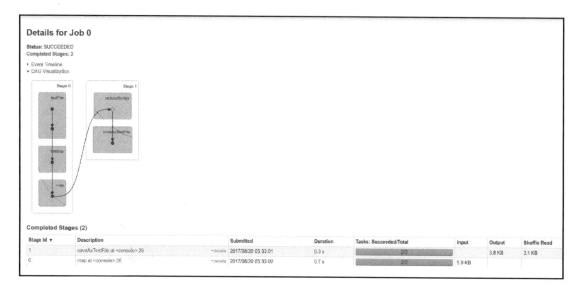

Before getting unto Scala programming, let's have a quick look at Spark transformation and actions ref at https://spark.apache.org/docs/latest/rdd-programming-guide. html#transformations.

Transformations

Spark transformations are basically the operations that take an RDD as an input and produce one or more RDD as output. All transformations are lazy in nature, while the logical execution plans in the form of direction acyclic graph /DAGs are built actual execution happens only when an action is called.

The transformations can be qualified as narrow transformations and wide transformations.

Narrow transformations	Wide transformations
Narrow transformations are where data from a single partition in child RDD is computed using data from a single partition of parent RDD. The examples are map(), filter().	Wide transformations are where records in a single partition in child RDD can be computed using data across parent RDD partitions. The examples are GroupBy(), ReduceBy(), and so on.

The Narrow transformation operates in a manner that all the elements that are required in the computational process are stored in a single partition of the parent RDD.	The wide transformation operates on the elements or data records that are stored across the partitions within the parent RDD.

Transformation	Meaning
map(*func*)	Return a new distributed dataset formed by passing each element of the source through a function *func*.
filter(*func*)	Return a new dataset formed by selecting those elements of the source on which *func* returns true.
flatMap(*func*)	Similar to map, but each input item can be mapped to 0 or more output items (so *func* should return a Seq rather than a single item).
mapPartitions(*func*)	Similar to map, but runs separately on each partition (block) of the RDD, so *func* must be of type Iterator<T> => Iterator<U> when running on an RDD of type T.
mapPartitionsWithIndex(*func*)	Similar to mapPartitions, but also provides *func* with an integer value representing the index of the partition, so *func* must be of type (Int, Iterator<T>) => Iterator<U> when running on an RDD of type T.
sample(*withReplacement, fraction, seed*)	Sample a fraction *fraction* of the data, with or without replacement, using a given random number generator seed.
union(*otherDataset*)	Return a new dataset that contains the union of the elements in the source dataset and the argument.
intersection(*otherDataset*)	Return a new RDD that contains the intersection of elements in the source dataset and the argument.
distinct([*numTasks*]))	Return a new dataset that contains the distinct elements of the source dataset.
groupByKey([*numTasks*])	When called on a dataset of (K, V) pairs, returns a dataset of (K, Iterable<V>) pairs. **Note:** If you are grouping in order to perform an aggregation (such as a sum or average) over each key, using reduceByKey or aggregateByKey will yield much better performance. **Note:** By default, the level of parallelism in the output depends on the number of partitions of the parent RDD. You can pass an optional numTasks argument to set a different number of tasks.
reduceByKey(*func, [numTasks]*)	When called on a dataset of (K, V) pairs, returns a dataset of (K, V) pairs where the values for each key are aggregated using the given reduce function *func*, which must be of type (V,V) => V. Like in groupByKey, the number of reduce tasks is configurable through an optional second argument.

aggregateByKey(*zeroValue*)(*seqOp, combOp,* [*numTasks*])	When called on a dataset of (K, V) pairs, returns a dataset of (K, U) pairs where the values for each key are aggregated using the given combine functions and a neutral "zero" value. Allows an aggregated value type that is different than the input value type, while avoiding unnecessary allocations. Like in `groupByKey`, the number of reduce tasks is configurable through an optional second argument.
sortByKey([*ascending*], [*numTasks*])	When called on a dataset of (K, V) pairs where K implements Ordered, returns a dataset of (K, V) pairs sorted by keys in ascending or descending order, as specified in the boolean `ascending` argument.
join(*otherDataset,* [*numTasks*])	When called on datasets of type (K, V) and (K, W), returns a dataset of (K, (V, W)) pairs with all pairs of elements for each key. Outer joins are supported through `leftOuterJoin`, `rightOuterJoin`, and `fullOuterJoin`.
cogroup(*otherDataset,* [*numTasks*])	When called on datasets of type (K, V) and (K, W), returns a dataset of (K, (Iterable<V>, Iterable<W>)) tuples. This operation is also called `groupWith`.
cartesian(*otherDataset*)	When called on datasets of types T and U, returns a dataset of (T, U) pairs (all pairs of elements).
pipe(*command,* [*envVars*])	Pipe each partition of the RDD through a shell command, e.g. a Perl or bash script. RDD elements are written to the process's stdin and lines output to its stdout are returned as an RDD of strings.
coalesce(*numPartitions*)	Decrease the number of partitions in the RDD to numPartitions. Useful for running operations more efficiently after filtering down a large dataset.
repartition(*numPartitions*)	Reshuffle the data in the RDD randomly to create either more or fewer partitions and balance it across them. This always shuffles all data over the network.
repartitionAndSortWithinPartitions(*partitioner*)	Repartition the RDD according to the given partitioner and, within each resulting partition, sort records by their keys. This is more efficient than calling `repartition` and then sorting within each partition because it can push the sorting down into the shuffle machinery.

This is the classification of transformation:

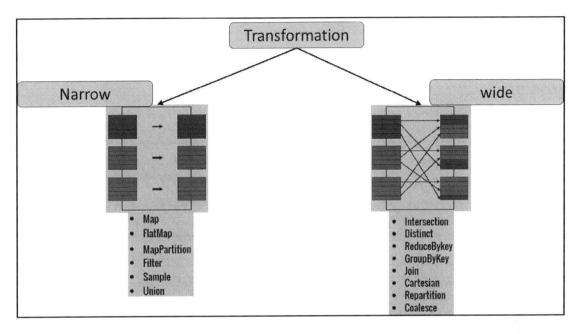

The following section captures the code snippets highlighting the usage of various transformation operations:

- Map: The following code reads a file called map_spark_test.txt and maps each line of the file to its length and prints it:

```
import org.apache.spark.SparkContext
import org.apache.spark.SparkConf
import org.apache.spark.sql.SparkSession
object  mapOperationTest{
def main(args: Array[String]) = {
    val sparkSession =
SparkSession.builder.appName("myMapExample").master("local").ge
tOrCreate()
    val fileTobeMapped = sparkSession.read.textFile("my
_spark_test.txt").rdd
    val fileMap = fileTobeMapped.map(line =>
(line,line.length))
    fileMap.foreach(println)
    }
}
```

- `flatMap operation()`: The Map and `flatMap` operations are similar because they both apply to every element from the input RDD, but they differ in a manner because where map returns a single element, `flatMap` can return multiple elements.

    In the following code snippet, the operation `flatMap` is executed to split each word on each line of the input file:

    ```
    val fileTobeMapped =
    spark.read.textFile("my_spark_test.txt").rdd
    val flatmapFile = fileTobeMapped.flatMap(lines => lines.split("
    "))
    flatmapFile.foreach(println)
    ```

- **Filter operation**: It returns only the elements from the parent RDD that satisfy the criteria mentioned in the filter. The following snippet counts the number of lines that have the word `spark` in them:

    ```
    val fileTobeMapped = spark.read.textFile("my_spark_test.txt
    ").rdd
    val flatmapFile = fileTobeMapped.flatMap(lines => lines.split("
    ")).filter(value => value=="spark")
    println(flatmapFile.count())
    ```

- `union`: This transformation accepts two or more RDDs of the same type and outputs an RDD containing elements of both the RDDs.

    In the following snippet, the three RDDs are merged and the resulting output RDD is printed:

    ```
    val rddA =
    spark.sparkContext.parallelize(Seq((2,"JAN",2017),(7,"NOV",2015
    ),(16,"FEB",2015)))
    val rddB =
    spark.sparkContext.parallelize(Seq((6,"DEC",2015),(18,"SEP",201
    6)))
    val rddC =
    spark.sparkContext.parallelize(Seq((7,"DEC",2012),(17,"MAY",201
    6)))
    val rddD = rddA.union(rddB).union(rddC)
    rddD.foreach(Println)
    ```

- `intersection`: An operation that runs between the same types of two or more RDDs to return the elements that are common among all the participating RDDs:

```
val rddA =
spark.sparkContext.parallelize(Seq((2,"JAN",2017),(4,"NOV",2015
, (17,"FEB",2015))))
val rddB=
spark.sparkContext.parallelize(Seq((5,"DEC",2015),(2,"JAN",2017
)))
val comman = rddA.intersection(rddB)
comman.foreach(Println)
```

- `distinct`: This transformation helps in removing duplicates from the parent RDD:

```
val rddA =
park.sparkContext.parallelize(Seq((2,"JAN",2017),(4,"NOV",2015)
, (17,"FEB",2015),(3,"NOV",2015)))
val result = rddA.distinct()
println(result.collect().mkString(", "))
```

- `groupByKey()`: This transformation, when applied over a key value dataset, leads to the shuffling of data according to the key. This is a very network intensive operation and caching and disk persistence should be taken care of to make it effective (read about persistence at `https://spark.apache.org/docs/latest/rdd-programming-guide.html#rdd-persistence`).

    The following snippet groups the numbers in accordance with the alphabet, where the alphabet serves as key and numbers are values. The function collect returns it as an array:

```
val mydata =
spark.sparkContext.parallelize(Array(('k',5),('s',3),('s',4),('
p',7),('p',5),('t',8),('k',6)),3)
val group = mydata.groupByKey().collect()
group.foreach(println)
```

- `reduceByKey()`: This operation works on a key value based dataset, where the values to the same key are mapped and grouped together, on the same machine not across the network, before the data is shuffled:

```
val myWordList =
Array("one","two","two","four","five","six","six","eight","nine
","ten")
val myWordList = spark.sparkContext.parallelize(words).map(w =>
(w,1)).reduceByKey(_+_)
myWordList.foreach(println)
```

- `sortByKey()`: The operation is applicable on key value pair based data wherein the values are arranged in the sorting order of the key:

```
val myMarkList =
spark.sparkContext.parallelize(Seq(("maths",52),
("english",75), ("science",82), ("computer",65), ("maths",85)))
val mySortedMarkList = myMarkList.sortByKey()
mySortedMarkList.foreach(println)
```

- `join()`: It's precisely a transformation that is analogous to the join in databases. In Spark it operates on paired RDDs , in which each element is a tuple—the first element is key, the second is value . The join operation takes up two input RDDs and joins them on the basis of the key, and the output RDD is generated:

```
val rddA =
spark.sparkContext.parallelize(Array(('A',1),('B',2),('C',3)))
val rddB
=spark.sparkContext.parallelize(Array(('A',4),('A',6),('B',7),(
'C',3),('C',8)))
val result = rddA.join(rddB)
println(result.collect().mkString(","))
```

- `coalesce()`: This is a very useful operation and it is generally used to reduce the shuffling of data across the nodes in Spark clusters by controlling the number of partitions defined for the dataset. The data would be distributed on a number of nodes based on the number of partitions defined under the coalesce operation.

  In the following code snippet, the data from `rddA` would be distributed only in two nodes in two partitions, even if the Spark cluster has six nodes in all:

```
val rddA =
spark.sparkContext.parallelize(Array("jan","feb","mar","april",
"may","jun"),3)
val myResult = rddA.coalesce(2)
myResult.foreach(println)
```

Actions

In a nutshell, it can be said that actions actually execute the transformations on real data to generate the output. Actions send the data from the executor to the driver. Following is capture of actions that return values (from: `https://spark.apache.org/docs/latest/rdd-programming-guide.html#actions`):

Action	Meaning
reduce(*func*)	Aggregate the elements of the dataset using a function *func* (which takes two arguments and returns one). The function should be commutative and associative so that it can be computed correctly in parallel.
collect()	Return all the elements of the dataset as an array at the driver program. This is usually useful after a filter or other operation that returns a sufficiently small subset of the data.
count()	Return the number of elements in the dataset.
first()	Return the first element of the dataset (similar to take(1)).
take(*n*)	Return an array with the first *n* elements of the dataset.
takeSample(*withReplacement, num, [seed]*)	Return an array with a random sample of *num* elements of the dataset, with or without replacement, optionally pre-specifying a random number generator seed.
takeOrdered(*n, [ordering]*)	Return the first *n* elements of the RDD using either their natural order or a custom comparator.
saveAsTextFile(*path*)	Write the elements of the dataset as a text file (or set of text files) in a given directory in the local filesystem, HDFS or any other Hadoop-supported file system. Spark will call toString on each element to convert it to a line of text in the file.
saveAsSequenceFile(*path*) (Java and Scala)	Write the elements of the dataset as a Hadoop SequenceFile in a given path in the local filesystem, HDFS or any other Hadoop-supported file system. This is available on RDDs of key-value pairs that implement Hadoop's Writable interface. In Scala, it is also available on types that are implicitly convertible to Writable (Spark includes conversions for basic types like Int, Double, String, etc).
saveAsObjectFile(*path*) (Java and Scala)	Write the elements of the dataset in a simple format using Java serialization, which can then be loaded using `SparkContext.objectFile()`.
countByKey()	Only available on RDDs of type (K, V). Returns a hashmap of (K, Int) pairs with the count of each key.
foreach(*func*)	Run a function *func* on each element of the dataset. This is usually done for side effects such as updating an Accumulator or interacting with external storage systems. **Note**: modifying variables other than Accumulators outside of the `foreach()` may result in undefined behavior. See Understanding closures for more details.

Let us look at some code snippets to see actions executing actually in action:

- `count ()`: As the name suggests, this operation counts and gives you the number of elements in an RDD. We used the count action in the preceding filter example where we counted the number of words in each line of the file being read.
- `collect ()`: The collect operation does what its name precisely denotes, it returns all the data from the RDD to the driver program. Due to the nature of this operation, one is suggested to use it carefully because it copies the data to the driver, thus all the data should fit into the node where the driver is executing.

  In the following snippet, the two RDDs are joined based on the alphabet keys and then the resulting RDD is returned to the driver program where the joined values are held as an array against the keys:

  ```
  val rddA =
  spark.sparkContext.parallelize(Array(('A',1),('b',2),('c',3)))
  val rddB
  =spark.sparkContext.parallelize(Array(('A',4),('A',6),('b',7),(
  'c',3),('c',8)))
  val resultRDD = rddA.join(rddB)
  println(result.collect().mkString(","))
  ```

- `top ()`: This operation returns the top element from the RDD wherein the ordering is maintained and preserved. It's good for sampling—the following snippet returns the top three records from the file based on its default ordering:

  ```
  val fileTobeMapped =
  spark.read.textFile("my_spark_test.txt").rdd
  val mapFile = fileTobeMapped.map(line => (line,line.length))
  val result = mapFile.top(3)
  result.foreach(println)
  ```

- `countByValue ()`: This operation returns the count of the number of times an element occurs in the input RDD. Its output is in the form of a key-value pair where the key is the element and the value represents its count:

  ```
  val fileTobeMapped = spark.read.textFile("my_spark_test.txt
  ").rdd
  val result= fileTobeMapped.map(line =>
  (line,line.length)).countByValue()
  result.foreach(println)
  ```

- `reduce()`: This operation takes up two elements from the input RDD; the type of the output remains the same as the input RDD—the result of the operation could be count or addition, depending upon the arguments that are passed. In terms of execution this action can be associative and commutative.

  The following snippet sums up the elements of the input RDD:

  ```
  val rddA =
  spark.sparkContext.parallelize(List(20,32,45,62,8,5))
  val sum = rddA.reduce(_+_)
  println(sum)
  ```

- `foreach()`: This action works precisely in the manner suggested by its name—the operation is applied to each element of the RDD being operated upon.

  In the following snippet, the `rddA` is grouped based on the key (alphabet), the transformation is executed using the collect operation, and the open `println` function is applied over each element of `myGroupedRdd` to print the elements on the console:

  ```
  val rddA =
  spark.sparkContext.parallelize(Array(('k',5),('s',3),('s',4),('
  p',7),('p',5),('t',8),('k',6)),3)
  val myGroupRdd = data.groupByKey().collect()
  myGroupRdd.foreach(println)
  ```

Shared variables – broadcast variables and accumulators

While working in distributed compute programs and modules, where the code executes on different nodes and/or different workers, a lot of time a need arises to share data across the execution units in the distributed execution setup. Thus Spark has the concept of shared variables. The shared variables are used to share information between the parallel executing tasks across various workers or the tasks and the drivers. Spark supports two types of shared variable:

- Broadcast variables
- Accumulators

In the following sections, we will look at these two types of Spark variables, both conceptually and pragmatically.

Broadcast variables

These are the variables that the programmer intends to share to all execution units throughout the cluster. Though they sound very simple to work with, there are a few aspects the programmers need to be cognizant of while working with broadcast variables: they need to be able to fit in the memory of each node in the cluster—they are like local read-only dictionary/index for each node, thus they can't be huge in size, and all nodes share same values thus they are read-only by design. Say, for instance, we have a dictionary for spell check, we would want each node to have the same copy.

So to summarize, here are the major caveats/features of the design and usage of broadcast variables:

- They are immutable
- They are distributed across the cluster (worker and driver)
- They have to fit into the memory

They are a great use for static or lookup tables or metadata where each node has its shared copy and data doesn't need to be shipped to each node—thus saving a lot on network I/O.

The following screenshot captures the on-prompt declaration and usage of broadcast variables: containing values 1, 2, and 3:

```scala
scala> val broadcastVar = sc.broadcast(Array(1, 2, 3))
broadcastVar: org.apache.spark.broadcast.Broadcast[Array[Int]] =
    Broadcast(0)

scala> broadcastVar.value
res0: Array[Int] = Array(1, 2, 3)
```

The next section captures a small code example to demonstrate the usage of the same in Scala code. The following is a CSV capturing the names of some states from India:

```
Uttar Pradesh, Delhi, Haryana, Punjab, Rajasthan, Himachal Pradesh,
Maharashtra, Tamilnadu, Telangana
```

Next, let's have this loaded into the map from disk and then convert it to a broadcast variable:

```
def loadCSVFile( filename: String): Option[Map[String, String]]
    val states= Map[String, String]()
    Try {
    val bufferedSource = Source.fromFile(filename)
    for(line <- bufferedSource.getLines) {
        val Array(state, capital) = line.split(","),map(_.trim)
        states +=state -> capital
    }
    bufferedSource.close()
    return Some(states)
    }.toOption
}
```

As in the next step, we will convert this map into a broadcast variable.

In the preceding snippet, we load our state name file and convert it to a map that is broadcasted as statesCache. Then we create a stateRDD from the keys of the map states and we have a method called searchStateDetails that searches for states from a particular alphabet specified by the user and returns its details such as capital and so on.

In this mechanism, we don't need to send over the state CSV to each node and executor every time the search operation is performed.

In the following snippet, one can see the entire source code for the example quoted previously:

```
import org.apache.spark.{ SparkContext, SparkConf }
import org.apache.spark.rdd.RDD
import org.apache.spark.broadcast.Broadcast

import scala.io.Source
import scala.util.{ Try, Success, Failure }
import scala.collection.mutable.Map


object TestBroadcastVariables {
    def main(args: Array[String]): Unit = {

        loadCSVFile("/myData/states.csv") match {
            case Some(states) => {
                val sc = new SparkContext(new SparkConf()
                .setAppName("MyBroadcastVariablesJob"))

                val statesCache = sc.broadcast(states)
```

```
        val statesRDD = sc.parallelize(states.keys.toList)

        // happy case...
        val happyCaseRDD = searchStateDetails(statesRDD,
statesCache, "P")
        println(">>>> Search results of states starting with 'P': "
+ happyCaseRDD.count())
        happyCaseRDD.foreach(entry => println("State:" + entry._1 +
", Capital:" + entry._2))

        // non-happy case...
        val nonHappyCaseRDD = searchStateDetails(statesRDD,
statesCache, "Yz")
        println(">>>> Search results of states starting with 'Yz':
" + nonHappyCaseRDD.count())
        nonHappyCaseRDD.foreach(entry => println("State:" +
entry._1 + ", Capital:" + entry._2))
        }
      case None => println("Error loading file...")
    }
  }

def searchStateDetails(statesRDD: RDD[String], stateCache:
Broadcast[Map[String, String]],
    searchToken: String): RDD[(String, String)] = {
      statesRDD.filter(_.startsWith(searchToken))
      .map(country => (state, stateCache.value(state)))
  }
def loadCSVFile(filename: String): Option[Map[String, String]] = {
    val countries = Map[String, String]()
    Try {
      val bufferedSource = Source.fromFile(filename)

      for (line <- bufferedSource.getLines) {
      val Array(state, capital) = line.split(",").map(_.trim)
      states += state -> capital
      }
    bufferedSource.close()
    return Some(states)

    }.toOption
  }
}
```

Accumulators

This is the second method of sharing values/data across different nodes and/or drivers in a Spark job. As is evident from the name of this variable, accumulators are used for counting or accumulating the values. They are the answer to MapReduces counters, and they are different from broadcast variables because they are mutable—the value of an accumulator can change, while the jobs can change the value of an accumulator, but only the driver program can read its value. They work as a great aide for data aggregation and counting across distributed workers of Spark.

Let's assume there is a purchase log for a Walmart store and we need to write a Spark job to detect the count of each type of bad records out of the log. The following snippet will help in attaining this.

```
def main(args: Array[String]): Unit = {

val tnxt = new SparkContext(new SparkConf().setAppName("SaleAnalysisJob"))

val badtnxts = tnxt.accumulator(0, "Bad Transaction")
val zeroValuetnxt= tnxt.accumulator(0, "Zero Value Transaction")
val missingFieldstnxt = tnxt.accumulator(0, "Missing Fields Transaction")
val blankLinesTnxt = tnxt.accumulator(0, "Blank Lines Transaction")

ctx.textFile("file:/mydata/sales.log", 4)
    .foreach { line =>
        if (line.length() == 0) blankLines += 1
        else if (line.contains("Bad Transaction")) badtnxts+= 1
        else {
        val fields = line.split("\t")
        if (fields.length != 4) missingFieldstnxt+= 1
        else if (fields(3).toFloat == 0) zeroValuetnxt += 1
        }
}
println("Sales Log Analysis Counters:")
println(s"\tBad Transactions=${ badtnxts.value}")
println(s"\tZero Value Sales=${ zeroValuetnxt.value}")
println(s"\tMissing Fields Transactions=${ missingFieldstnxt.value}")
println(s"\tBlank Lines Transactions=${ blankLines.value}")
```

Summary

In this chapter, we introduced the readers to Apache Spark APIs and its organization. We discussed the concept of transformation and actions in theory and with examples. We took the users through the arena of shared variables: broadcast variables and accumulators. The next chapter is dedicated to Spark Streaming.

11
Spark Streaming

This is the chapter where we introduce our readers to Spark Streaming, the architecture and the concept of microbatching. We will look at the various components of a streaming application and the internals of a streaming application integrated with myriad input sources. We will also do some practical hands-on exercises to illustrate the execution of streaming applications in action. We will explore and learn about Spark Streaming under the following topics:

- Spark Streaming concepts
- Spark Streaming - introduction and architecture
- Packaging structure of Spark Streaming
- Connecting Kafka to Spark Streaming

Spark Streaming concepts

The Spark framework and all its extensions together provide one universal solution to handle all enterprise data needs from batch to analytics to real time. To be able to handle the real-time data processing, the framework should be capable of processing unbounded streams of data as close to the time of occurrence of the event as possible. This capability is provided by virtue of microbatching and stream processing under the Spark Streaming extension of the Spark framework.

In very simple terms, we can understand that a data stream is an unbounded sequence of data that is being generated in real-time continuously. Now to be able to process these continuously arriving data streams, various frameworks handle them as follows:

- Distinct discrete events that are processed individually
- Microbatching the individual events into very small-sized batches that are processed as a single unit

Spark provides this streaming API as an extension to its core API which is a scalable, low latency, high throughput, and fault tolerant framework to process live incoming streaming data using the microbatching principle.

Some use cases where solutions based on the Spark framework for real-time processing will come in handy:

- Monitoring infrastructure, applications, or processes
- Fraud detection
- Marketing and advertising
- Internet of Things

The following screenshot captures some of the statistics in terms of the rate at which live data is generated at every moment around the world. All the scenarios depicted in the following screenshot are apt to be captured as a Spark Stream processing use case:

Spark Streaming - introduction and architecture

Spark Streaming is a very useful extension to the Spark core API that's being widely used to process incoming streaming data in real-time or close to real-time as in **near real-time (NRT)**. This API extension has all the core Spark features in terms of highly distributed, scalable, fault tolerant, and high throughput, low latency processing.

The following diagram captures how Spark Streaming works in close conjunction with the Spark execution engine to process real-time data streams:

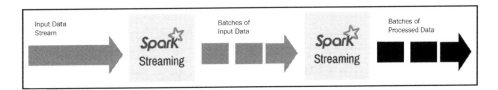

Spark Streaming works on microbatching based architecture --we can envision it as an extension to the core Spark architecture where the framework performs real-time processing by actually clubbing the incoming events from the stream into deterministic batches. Each batch is of the same size, and the live data is collected and stacked into these deterministically sized microbatches for processing.

Under the Spark framework, the size of each microbatch is determined using the batch duration defined by the user. In order to understand it better, let us take an example of an application receiving live/streaming data of 20 events per second and the batch duration provided by the user is 2 seconds. Now our Spark Streaming will continuously consume the data as it arrives but it will create the microbatches of data received at the end of every 2 seconds (each batch will consists of 40 events) and submit this to the user-defined jobs for further processing.

One important aspect that developers need to be cognizant of is that the batch size/duration and process latency for the overall execution cycle from the time of occurrence of the event to the arrival of the results is inversely proportional to each other. The size of the batches is usually defined based on the following two criteria:

- Performance and optimization
- Latency acceptable by the business/use case requirements

These microbatches are referred to as **Discretized Stream (DStream)** in Spark Streaming, which is just a series of **Resilient Distributed Datasets (RDDs)**.

Here we will get our readers acquainted with the key aspects where the Spark Streaming architecture differs from the traditional stream processing architecture and the benefits of this microbatching based processing abstraction over traditional event-based processing systems. This walk through of differences will in turn get the readers acquainted with the internal nitty-gritty of Spark Streaming architecture and design.

Traditional streaming systems are generally event-based and the data is processed by various operators in the system as it arrives. Each execution unit in the distributed setup operates by processing one record at a time, as shown in the following diagram:

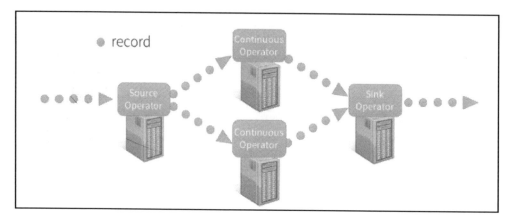

The preceding diagram captures the typical model where one record at a time is picked up from the source and propagated to the worker nodes, where it's operated on by processing workers record by record and the sink dumps it to the stable storage or downstream for further processing.

Before we move on, it's very important to touch base upon the key differences between Storm as a stream processing engine versus Spark as a streaming platform.

The following table clearly captures and articulates the various features of both of these top streaming platforms:

Feature	Apache Storm/Trident	Spark Streaming
Programming Languages	Java Clojure Scala	Java Scala
Reliability	Supports "exactly once" processing mode. Can be used in other modes like "at least once" processing & "at most once" processing mode as well.	Supports only "exactly once" processing mode.
Stream Sources	Spout	HDFS
Stream Primitives	Tuple, Partition	DStream
Persistence	MapState	Per RDD
State management	Supported	Supported
Resource Management	Yarn, Mesos	Yarn, Mesos
Provisioning	Apache Ambari	Basic monitoring using ganglia [3]
Messaging	ZeroMQ, Netty	Netty, Akka

The fundamental difference between these two frameworks is that Storm performs task parallel computation, while the Spark platform performs data parallel computing, as follows:

- **Task parallel**: This form of parallelism covers the execution of tasks/program units across multiple processors/worker threads on the same or multiple machines. It focuses on executing different operations in parallel to fully utilize the available computing resources in the form of processors and memory.
- **Data parallel**: This form of parallelism focuses on the distribution of datasets across the multiple computation programs. In this form, the same operations are performed on different parallel computing processors on the distributed data subset.

Both Storm Trident and Spark offer streaming and microbatch functionality constrained by time-based windows. Though similar in functional characteristics, they differ in the implementation semantics and which of the frameworks should be chosen for an application/problem statement depends upon the requirements. The following table articulates some ground rules:

Situation	Choice of Framework
Strictly Low latency	Storm can provide better latency with fewer restrictions than Spark streaming.
Low development cost	With Spark, the same code base can be used for batch processing and stream processing. But with storm, it is not possible.
Message Delivery Guarantee	Both Apache Storm (trident) and Spark Streaming offer "exactly once" processing mode.
Fault Tolerance	Both frameworks are relatively fault tolerant to the same extent. In Apache Storm/Trident, if a process fails, the supervisor process will restart it automatically as state management is handled through ZooKeeper. Spark handles restarting workers via the resource manager which can be YARN, Mesos, or its standalone manager.

Based on previous points, here are some final considerations:

- **Latency**: While Storm can offer sub-second level latency with ease, that's not an easy point of contention for Spark Streaming, which essentially is not a streaming platform but a microbatching one.
- **Total cost of ownership (TCO)**: This is a very important consideration for any application. If an application needs a similar solution for batch and real-time, then Spark has an advantage, as the same application code base can be utilized, thus saving the development cost. The same is not the case in Storm though as its dramatically different in implementation from **MapReduce**/batch applications.
- **Message delivery**: The exactly once semantic is the default expectation in Spark, while Storm offers at least once and exactly once. Achieving the latter is actually a little tricky in Storm.

The following diagram depicts various architecture components, such as **Input Data Streams**, **Output Data Streams/Stores,** and others. These components have a pivotal role and their own life cycle during the execution of a Spark Streaming program:

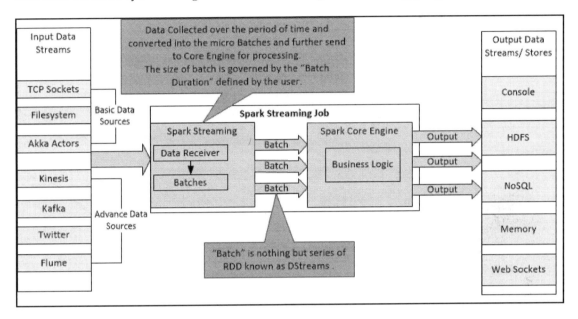

Let's take a look at the following components depicted in the preceding diagram:

- **Input Data Streams:** This defines the input data sources, essentially the sources that are emitting the live/streaming data at a very high frequency (seconds, milliseconds). These sources can be a raw socket, filesystem, or even highly scalable queuing products, such as Kafka. A Spark Streaming job connects to the input data sources using various available connectors. These connectors may be available with the Spark distribution itself or we may have to download it separately and configure it in our Spark Streaming job. These input streams are also referred to as **Input DStreams**. Based on the availability of the connectors, input data sources are divided into the following categories:
  - **Basic Data Sources:** The connectors and all of their dependencies for the basic data sources are packaged and shipped with the standard distribution of Spark. We do not have to download any other package to make them work.

- **Advanced Data Sources**: The connectors and the dependencies required by these connectors are not available with the standard distribution of Spark. This is simply to avoid the complexity and the version conflicts. We need to download and configure the dependencies for these connectors separately or provide them as dependencies in Maven scripts, as instructed in the integration guidelines for each of the following data sources:
    - **Kafka**: http://tinyurl.com/oew96sg
    - **Flume**: http://tinyurl.com/o4ntmdz
    - **Kinesis**: http://tinyurl.com/pdhtgu3
- Refer to http://tinyurl.com/psmtpco for the list of available advanced data sources.

 The Spark community also provides various other connectors which can be directly downloaded from http://spark-packages.org or refer to http://tinyurl.com/okrd34e for developing our custom connectors.

- **Spark Streaming Job**: This is the custom job developed by the user for consumption and processing of the data feeds in NRT. It has the following components:
    - **Data Receiver**: This is a receiver that is dedicated to receiving/consuming the data produced by the data source. Every data source has its own receiver and cannot be generalized or be common across the varied kinds of data sources.
    - **Batches**: Batches are the collection of messages that are received over the period of time by the receiver. Every batch has a specific number of messages or data collected in a specific time interval (batch window) provided by the user. These microbatches are just a series of RDDs known as **DStreams - Discretized Streams**.

- **Discretized Streams**: Also called DStreams, this is a new stream processing model in which computations are structured as a series of stateless, deterministic batch computations at small-time intervals. This new stream processing model enables powerful recovery mechanisms (similar to those in batch systems) and out-performs replication and upstream backup. It extends and leverages the concepts of resilient distributed datasets and creates a series of RDDs (of the same type) in one single DStream, which is processed and computed at a user-defined time interval (batch duration). DStreams can be created from input data streams that are connected to varied data sources, such as sockets, filesystems, and many more, or it can be created by applying high-level operations on other DStreams (similar to the RDDs). There can be multiple DStreams per Spark Streaming context and each DStream contains a series of RDDs. Each RDD is the snapshot of the data received at a particular point in time from the receiver. Refer to `http://tinyurl.com/nnw4xvk` for more information on DStreams.

- **Streaming context**: Spark Streaming extends the Spark Context and provides a new context, Streaming context, for accessing all functionality and features of Spark Streaming. It is the main entry of point and provides methods for initializing DStreams from various input data sources. Refer to `http://tinyurl.com/p5z68gn` for more information on Streaming Context.

- **Spark Core Engine**: The core engine receives the input in the form of RDDs and further processes as per the user-defined business logic and finally sends it to the associated **Output Data Streams/Stores**.

- **Output Data Streams/Stores**: The final output of each processed batch is sent to the output streams for further processing. These data output streams can be of varied types, ranging from a raw filesystem, WebSockets, NoSQL, and many more.

Packaging structure of Spark Streaming

In this section, we will discuss the various APIs and operations exposed by Spark Streaming.

Spark Streaming APIs

All Spark Streaming classes are packaged in the `org.apache.spark.streaming.*` package. Spark Streaming defines two core classes which also provide access to all Spark Streaming functionality, such as `StreamingContext.scala` and `DStream.scala`.

Let's examine the following functions and roles performed by these classes:

- `org.apache.spark.streaming.StreamingContext`: This is an entry point to Spark Streaming functionality. It defines methods for creating the objects of `DStream.scala` and also for starting and stopping the Spark Streaming jobs.

- `org.apache.spark.streaming.dstream.DStream.scala`: DStreams, or discretized streams, provide the basic abstraction for Spark Streaming. They provide the sequence of RDDs created from the live data for transforming the existing DStreams. This class defines the global operations that can be performed on all DStreams and a few specific operations that can be applied on specific types of DStreams.

Apart from the preceding defined classes, Spark Streaming also defines various subpackages for exposing functionality for various types of input receivers, as follows:

- `org.apache.spark.streaming.kinesis.*`: This package provides classes for consuming input data from Kinesis (`http://aws.amazon.com/kinesis/`)

- `org.apache.spark.streaming.flume.*`: This package provides classes for consuming input data from Flume (`https://flume.apache.org/`)

- `org.apache.spark.streaming.kafka.*`: This package provides classes for consuming input data from Kafka (`http://kafka.apache.org/`)

- `org.apache.spark.streaming.zeromq.*`: This package provides classes for consuming input data from ZeroMQ (`http://zeromq.org/`)

- `org.apache.spark.streaming.twitter.*`: This package provides classes for consuming input data from Twitter feeds using Twitter4J (`http://twitter4j.org`)

For more information on Spark Streaming APIs, refer to the following links:

Scala API's — `http://tinyurl.com/qz5bvvb`
Java API's — `http://tinyurl.com/nh9wu9d`

Spark Streaming operations

Spark provides various operations that can be performed over DStreams. All operations are categorized into transformation and output operations. Let us discuss both these operations:

- **Transformation operations**: Transformations are those operations that help with modification or change the structure of data in input streams. They are similar and support almost all transformation operations provided by RDDs; for example, `map()`, `flatmap()`, `union()`, and many more. Refer to the DStream API at `http://tinyurl.com/znfgb8a` for a complete list of transformation operations supported on **input streams**. Apart from the regular transformation operations, as defined by DStreams and similar to RDD, DStreams provide a few special transformation operations on streaming data. Let us discuss these operations:
  - **Windowing operations**: Windowing is a special type of operation that is provided only by DStreams. Windowing operations group all the records from a sliding window of past time intervals into one RDD. They provide the functionality for defining the scope of data which needs to be analyzed and processed. The DStream API also provides the functionality of incremental aggregation or processing on sliding windows, where we can compute an aggregate such as a count or max over a sliding window. There are a variety of windowing operations provided by the DStreams API. All methods in `DStream.scala` prefixed with `Window` provide incremental aggregations such as `countByWindow`, `reduceByWindow`, and many more.
  - **Transform operations**: Transform operations, such as `transform(....)` or `transformWith(...)`, are special types of operations that provide the flexibility to perform arbitrary RDD to RDD operations. Essentially, they help in performing any RDD operation that is not provided/exposed by the DStream API. This method is also used to merge the two Spark worlds, the batch and the streaming one. We can create RDDs using batch processes and merge with RDDs created using Spark Streaming. It helps in code reusability across Spark batches and streaming, where we may have written functions in Spark batch applications that we now want to use in our Spark Streaming application.

- **UpdateStateByKey operation**: Another special operation exposed by the DStream API for stateful processing, where the state, once computed, is continuously updated with new information. Let us take an example of web server logs where we need to compute the running count of all GET or POST requests served by the web server. This type of functionality can be achieved by leveraging the updateStateByKey operation.

 Refer to http://tinyurl.com/zh2w6k6 for more information on the various transformation operations provided by Spark Streaming.

- **Output operations**: Output operations are those operations that help in processing the final output produced by applying various transformations. It may be simply printing on the console or persisting in cache or any external systems, such as NoSQL databases. Output operations are similar to the actions defined by RDDs and trigger all the transformations as defined by the user on DStreams (again similar to RDDs). As of Spark 1.5.1, the following output operations are supported on DStreams:
    - print(): This is one of the most common operations used by the developers for debugging their jobs. It prints the first 10 elements of every batch of data in a DStream on the console of the driver node running the streaming application.
    - saveAsTextFiles(prefix, suffix): This persists the content of DStreams as text files. The filename of each batch is generated by appending a prefix and suffix.
    - saveAsObjectFiles(prefix, suffix): This persists the content of DStreams as sequence files of serialized Java objects. The filename of each batch is generated by appending a prefix and suffix.
    - saveAsHadoopFiles(prefix, suffix): This persists the content of DStreams as Hadoop files. The filename of each batch is generated by appending a prefix and suffix.

- `foreachRDD(func)`: This is one of the most important, widely used, and generic functions for processing the output. It applies the given function `func` to each RDD generated from the stream. This operation can used for writing custom business logic for persisting the output in external systems such as saving to NoSQL databases or writing to web sockets. It is important to note that this function is executed by the driver node running the streaming application.

In this section, we have discussed the high level architecture, components, and packaging structure of Spark Streaming. We also talked about the various transformation and output operations as provided by the DStreams API. Let us move forward and code our first Spark Streaming job.

Connecting Kafka to Spark Streaming

The following section walks you through a program that reads the streaming data off the Kafka topic and counts the words. The aspects that will be captured in the following code are as follows:

- Kafka-Spark Streaming integration
- Creating and consuming from DStreams in Spark
- See the streaming application reading from an infinite unbounded stream to generate results

Let's take a look at the following code:

```
package com.example.spark;
Import files:
import java.util.Collection;
import java.util.HashMap;
import java.util.Iterator;
import java.util.Map;
import java.util.regex.Pattern;

import org.apache.spark.SparkConf;
import org.apache.spark.api.java.function.Function;
import org.apache.spark.streaming.Duration;
import org.apache.spark.streaming.api.java.JavaDStream;
import org.apache.spark.streaming.api.java.JavaPairReceiverInputDStream;
import org.apache.spark.streaming.api.java.JavaStreamingContext;
import org.apache.spark.streaming.kafka.KafkaUtils;
import org.codehaus.jackson.map.DeserializationConfig.Feature;
```

```
import org.codehaus.jackson.map.ObjectMapper;
import org.codehaus.jackson.type.TypeReference;

import scala.Tuple2;

Then main classes:
public class JavaKafkaWordCount {
private static final Pattern SPACE = Pattern.compile("");

private JavaKafkaWordCount() {
}

@SuppressWarnings("serial")
public static void main(String[] args) throws InterruptedException {
//    if (args.length < 4) {
//        System.err.println("Usage: JavaKafkaWordCount
<zkQuorum><group><topics><numThreads>");
//        System.exit(1);
//    }
```

Defining arrays:

```
args = new String[4];
    args[0]="localhost:2181";
    args[1]= "1";
    args[2]= "test";
    args[3]= "1";
```

We define the methods:

```
    SparkConf sparkConf = new
SparkConf().setAppName("JavaKafkaWordCount").setMaster("spark://Impetus-
NL163U:7077");
    // Create the context with a 1 second batch size
    JavaStreamingContext jssc = new JavaStreamingContext(sparkConf, new
Duration(20000));
```

The translation for the arguments:

```
    int numThreads = Integer.parseInt(args[3]);
    Map<String, Integer> topicMap = new HashMap<String, Integer>();
    String[] topics = args[2].split(",");
    for (String topic: topics) {
      topicMap.put(topic, numThreads);
    }
```

Receive the parameters:

```
JavaPairReceiverInputDStream<String, String> messages =
        KafkaUtils.createStream(jssc, args[0], args[1], topicMap);

    final JavaDStream<String> lines = messages.map(new
Function<Tuple2<String,String>, String>() {
@Override
public String call(Tuple2<String, String> v1) throws Exception {
ObjectMapper objectMapper = new ObjectMapper();
objectMapper.configure(Feature.USE_ANNOTATIONS, false);
Map<String,String> mapValue = objectMapper.readValue(v1._2(), new
TypeReference<Map<String,String>>() {
});
```

Adapt the types of variables:

```
Collection<String> values = mapValue.values();
String finalString = "";
for (Iterator<String> iterator = values.iterator(); iterator.hasNext();) {
String value = iterator.next();
if(finalString.length()==0){
finalString = finalString +value;
}else {
finalString = finalString+","+ value;
}
}
```

Return function with parameters:

```
return finalString;
}
});

    lines.print();
    new Thread(){
public void run() {
while(true){
try {
Thread.sleep(1000);
} catch (InterruptedException e) {
// TODO Auto-generated catch block
e.printStackTrace();
}
System.out.println("#############################################################
#####################"+lines.count());
}
};
```

```
    }.start();

    jssc.start();
    jssc.awaitTermination();
  }
}
```

Summary

In this chapter, we introduced the readers to Apache Spark Streaming, and to the concept of streams and their realization under Spark. We looked at the semantics and differences between Spark and other streaming platforms. We also got the users acquainted with situations where Spark is a better choice than Storm. We helped our users to understand the language semantics by getting to know the API and operations followed by a word count example using an integration with Kafka.

12
Working with Apache Flink

In this chapter, we get the readers acquainted with Apache Flink as a candidate for real-time processing. While most of the appendages in terms of data source tailing and sink remain the same, the compute methodology is changed to Flink and the integrations and topology wiring are very different for this technology. Here the reader will understand and implement end-to-end Flink processes to parse, transform, and converge compute on real-time streaming data.

In this chapter, we will look at the following topics:

- Flink architecture and execution engine
- Flink basic components and processes
- Integration of source stream to Flink
- Flink processing and computation
- Flink persistence
- FlinkCEP
- Gelly
- Examples and DIY
- Source to sink: Flink execution
- Executing storm topology on Flink

Flink architecture and execution engine

Flink is a platform for distributed stream and batch data processing. The core of Flink is a streaming dataflow engine. Flink is based on Kappa architecture. Kappa architecture was introduced in 2014 by *Jay Kreps* in `https://www.oreilly.com/ideas/questioning-the-lambda-architecture` which addresses the pitfalls of Lambda architecture. So before going into the details of Flink, let's figure out the base of Flink: Kappa architecture. Kappa architecture is designed to handle real-time data processing and continuous data reprocessing using a single data stream. There were two main concerns raised related to Lambda architecture: maintaining two different code bases for real-time analytics and batch analytics on the same source data and the reprocessing of events will require code changes which is not easy to maintain as seen in the following figure:

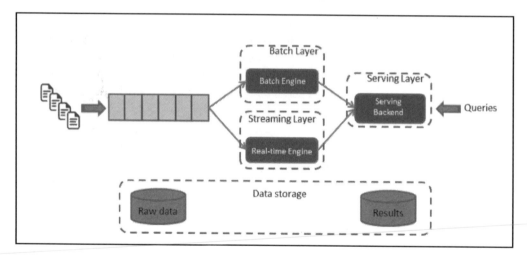

So in Kappa architecture, there is everything in streaming data. In case of the failure and reprocessing of events, a new process will be started from the ETL tool from the reprocessing event and fed to the serving layer using another flow. The batch of events has a defined start to end and the stream is infinite. In other terms, the batch is bounded and the stream is unbounded. So the batch is a subset of the stream and can be processed using stream processing, as seen in the following figure:

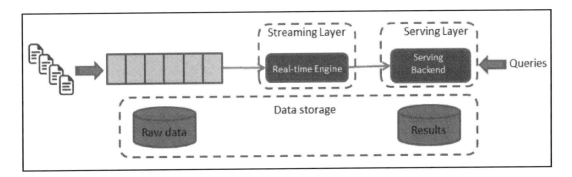

Flink is based on the same concept of Kappa architecture: it uses a single streaming layer for both real-time and batch processing. The Flink execution model has multiple aspects that are described as follows:

- **Exactly-once semantics**: Flink ensures exactly-once semantics by maintaining checkpoints at regular intervals without adding load on processing.
- **Event time processing**: Flink processes events based on event time, which helps in maintaining the order of events as well as identifying and taking appropriate action on late arriving data.
- **Flexible windowing**: There is windowing available on duration, count, and session based. Windows can be customized with flexible triggering conditions to support sophisticated streaming patterns.
- **High throughput and Low latency**: Flink gives high throughput and low latency by using checkpoints with barriers and maintaining states.
- **Fault tolerance**: Flink is a light weight fault tolerant framework. There is a concept of checkpoint and state snapshot in Flink that helps to achieve full fault tolerance. Also, the source should be like in which events can be rewind and reprocess for example Apache Kafka. Fink provides fault tolerance with other sources, which we will discuss in another section of this chapter. A fault tolerance mechanism ensures that in case of failure, no event is processed twice, that is exactly once processing.

A fault tolerance mechanism continuously takes a snapshot in the form of states of distributed streaming data flow. This state can be stored in the master node or HDFS as per the configuration. In case of failure, Flink stops processing events. The system restarts the operator and resets to the last checkpoint. The input streams are reset to the point of the state snapshot. Let's discuss what check pointing is and how states are maintained.

Taking a snapshot in distributed stream data flow is based on the *Chandy Lamport* algorithm. Check pointing in Flink is based on two concepts: Barriers and State. Barriers are a core element of Flink and are injected in distributed streaming data flow along with events. Barriers separate the records into a set of records. Each barrier has its own unique ID.

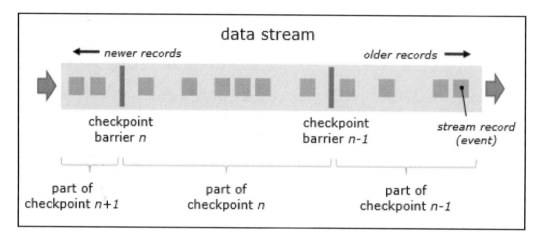

The point where the barriers for snapshot *n* are injected (let's call it *Sn*) is the position in the source stream up to which the snapshot covers the data. This position *Sn* is reported to the checkpoint coordinator (Flink's **JobManager**).

The barriers flow with downstream. When an intermediate operator has received a barrier for snapshot *n* from all of its input streams, it emits a barrier for snapshot *n* into all of its outgoing streams. Once a sink operator has received the barrier n from all of its input streams, it acknowledges that snapshot *n* to the checkpoint coordinator. After all sinks have acknowledged a snapshot, it is considered completed.

Once snapshot n has been completed, the job will never again ask the source for records from before Sn, since at that point these records will have passed through the entire data flow topology.

When operators contain any form of state, this state must be part of the snapshots as well. Operator state comes in different forms:

- **User-defined state**: This is the state that is created and modified directly by the transformation functions (such as `map()` or `filter()`).
- **System state**: This state refers to data buffers that are part of the operator's computation. A typical example for this state are the window buffers, inside which the system collects (and aggregates) records for windows until the window is evaluated and evicted.

Operators snapshot their state at the point in time when they have received all snapshot barriers from their input streams, and before emitting the barriers to their output streams. At that point, all updates to the state from records before the barriers will have been made, and no updates that depend on records from after the barriers have been applied. Because the state of a snapshot may be large, it is stored in a configurable state backend. By default, this is the JobManager memory, but for production use, a distributed reliable storage should be configured (such as HDFS). After the state, has been stored, the operator acknowledges the checkpoint, emits the snapshot barrier into the output streams, and proceeds.

Flink basic components and processes

As per the official documentation of Flink `https://ci.apache.org/projects/flink/flink-docs-release-1.3/concepts/runtime.html` and `https://ci.apache.org/projects/flink/flink-docs-release-1.3/internals/components.html`, the following are some of the processes and basic components of Flink.

Processes: There are two types of processes in Flink, as shown in the following figure:

- **JobManagers (Master)**: It is responsible for distributing the task among the **TaskManagers**, maintaining check points and for recovery in case of any failure. To achieve high availability, we need to set up more than one JobManager where one acts as a leader and the other as standby. The leader and standby JobManager are always in sync and in case of leader failure, the standby JobManager becomes the leader.
- **TaskManagers (workers)**: TaskManagers are responsible for executing the tasks, maintaining buffers for operators, and so on. TaskManager is a JVM process and subtasks are executed in multiple threads known as task slots. TaskManagers can have more than one slot. One slot can be shared by multiple subtasks of a job.

The client is not part of the program execution. It is just to submit the job and it may stay connected to get the status of the job regularly.

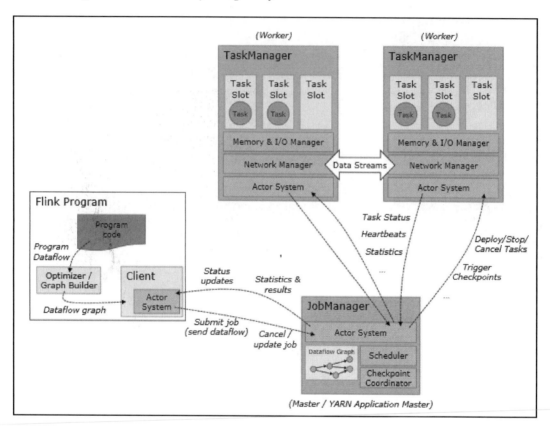

Components: Flink is a layered system with different layers of stack, as shown in the following figure:

- JobGraphs, which are in the form of a program generated by the **DataStream** and **Dataset** API through a separate compilation process. **DataStream API** is used for real-time processing on a distributed data flow and **Dataset API** is used for batch processing on distributed data flow.
- The **Runtime** layer receives a program in the form of a JobGraph which executes them on a variety of deployment options available, such as local, cluster, or cloud.

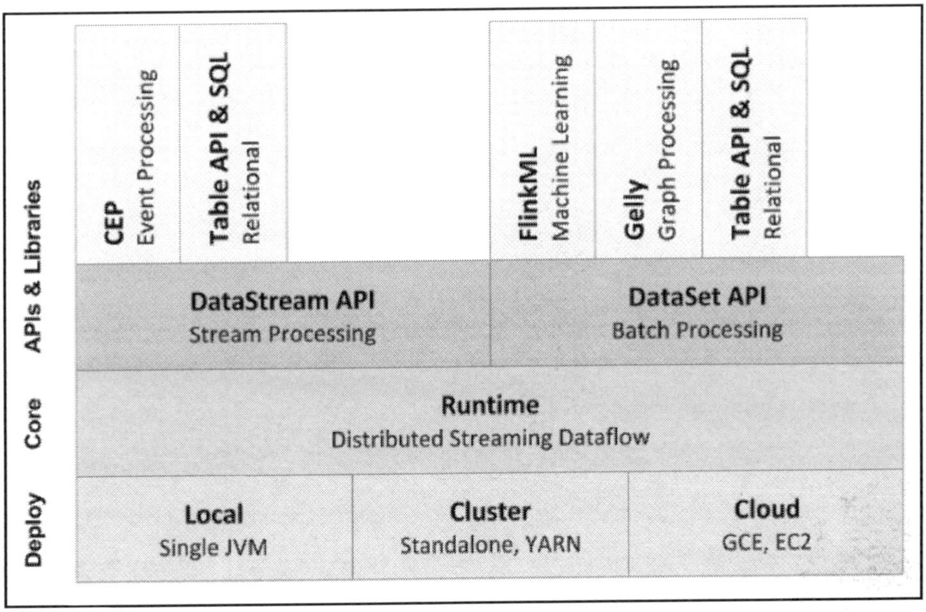

Integration of source stream to Flink

Multiple sources are available to integrate with, the following is a list:

- Apache Kafka
- Amazon Kinesis Streams
- RabbitMQ
- Apache NiFi
- Twitter Streaming API

We will now see a demonstration of integration with Apache Kafka and RabbitMQ.

Integration with Apache Kafka

We have discussed Apache Kafka setup in previous chapters, so we will focus on Java code to integrate Flink and Kafka.

Follow the given steps:

1. Add dependency in `pom.xml`:

```
<dependency>
    <groupId>org.apache.flink</groupId>
    <artifactId>flink-streaming-java_2.11</artifactId>
    <version>1.2.0</version>
</dependency>
```

The previous dependency is required for all type of the integration. The following dependencies are specific to Flink and Kafka integration:

```
<dependency>
    <groupId>org.apache.flink</groupId>
    <artifactId>flink-connector-kafka-0.8_2.11</artifactId>
    <version>1.2.0</version>
</dependency>
<dependency>
    <groupId>org.apache.kafka</groupId>
    <artifactId>kafka_2.11</artifactId>
    <version>0.8.2.2</version>
</dependency>
```

2. Set up the Kafka source:

```
Properties properties = new Properties();
properties.setProperty("bootstrap.servers", "localhost:9092");
properties.setProperty("zookeeper.connect", "localhost:2181");
properties.setProperty("group.id", "test");
properties.setProperty("auto.offset.reset", "latest");
FlinkKafkaConsumer08<String> flinkKafkaConsumer08 = new
FlinkKafkaConsumer08<>("flink-test", new SimpleStringSchema(),
properties);
```

Create properties that contain information related to Kafka such as Broker, Zookeeper, group id, offset. `FlinkKafkaConsumer08` is available for Kafka 0.8 in Flink package. Create an object of it with the parameter as the topic name and message serializer.

3. Create the Streaming environment:

```
StreamExecutionEnvironment env =
StreamExecutionEnvironment.getExecutionEnvironment();
```

Now, create an object of the streaming environment in Flink.

4. Add the Kafka source in the streaming environment:

```
DataStream<String> messageStream =
env.addSource(flinkKafkaConsumer08);
```

When the Kafka source is added in the Flink environment then it returns the `DataStream` object with the return data type.

5. Read from the source and print on the console:

```
messageStream.rebalance().map(new MapFunction<String, String>() {
    private static final long serialVersionUID =
-6867736771747690202L;
    @Override
    public String map(String value) throws Exception {
        return "Kafka and Flink says: " + value;
    }
}).print();
```

Apply the `map()` function on the message stream to read messages.

6. Execute the environment:

```
env.execute();
```

You have to execute the environment, otherwise the program will not execute on Flink. It would be like creating DAG, but not submitting it on JobManager.

Example

The following input is required for Kafka and the output will be displayed on the console.

Input:

Open the console and add the messages on the Kafka topic using the command line producer available. Refer to the following screenshot:

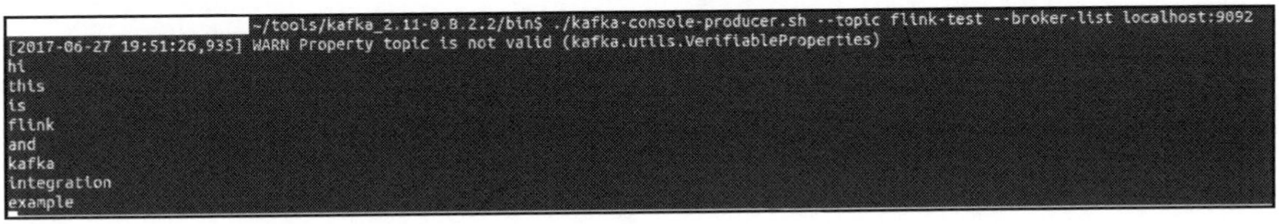

Output:

Go to `FlinkKafkaSourceExample` in the code bundle and execute the program with a right-click, selecting option **Run as Java Application**. The output will be shown on the console as seen in the following screenshot:

```
Connected to JobManager at Actor[akka://flink/user/jobmanager_1#-1479811007]
06/27/2017 19:51:35     Job execution switched to status RUNNING.
06/27/2017 19:51:35     Source: Custom Source(1/4) switched to SCHEDULED
06/27/2017 19:51:35     Source: Custom Source(1/4) switched to DEPLOYING
06/27/2017 19:51:35     Source: Custom Source(2/4) switched to SCHEDULED
06/27/2017 19:51:35     Source: Custom Source(2/4) switched to DEPLOYING
06/27/2017 19:51:35     Source: Custom Source(3/4) switched to SCHEDULED
06/27/2017 19:51:35     Source: Custom Source(3/4) switched to DEPLOYING
06/27/2017 19:51:35     Source: Custom Source(4/4) switched to SCHEDULED
06/27/2017 19:51:35     Source: Custom Source(4/4) switched to DEPLOYING
06/27/2017 19:51:35     Map -> Sink: Unnamed(1/4) switched to SCHEDULED
06/27/2017 19:51:35     Map -> Sink: Unnamed(1/4) switched to DEPLOYING
06/27/2017 19:51:35     Map -> Sink: Unnamed(2/4) switched to SCHEDULED
06/27/2017 19:51:35     Map -> Sink: Unnamed(2/4) switched to DEPLOYING
06/27/2017 19:51:35     Map -> Sink: Unnamed(3/4) switched to SCHEDULED
06/27/2017 19:51:35     Map -> Sink: Unnamed(3/4) switched to DEPLOYING
06/27/2017 19:51:35     Map -> Sink: Unnamed(4/4) switched to SCHEDULED
06/27/2017 19:51:35     Map -> Sink: Unnamed(4/4) switched to DEPLOYING
06/27/2017 19:51:36     Source: Custom Source(2/4) switched to RUNNING
06/27/2017 19:51:36     Source: Custom Source(4/4) switched to RUNNING
06/27/2017 19:51:36     Source: Custom Source(1/4) switched to RUNNING
06/27/2017 19:51:36     Source: Custom Source(3/4) switched to RUNNING
06/27/2017 19:51:36     Map -> Sink: Unnamed(1/4) switched to RUNNING
06/27/2017 19:51:36     Map -> Sink: Unnamed(2/4) switched to RUNNING
06/27/2017 19:51:36     Map -> Sink: Unnamed(3/4) switched to RUNNING
06/27/2017 19:51:36     Map -> Sink: Unnamed(4/4) switched to RUNNING
1> Kafka and Flink says: hi
2> Kafka and Flink says: this
3> Kafka and Flink says: is
1> Kafka and Flink says: and
4> Kafka and Flink says: flink
2> Kafka and Flink says: kafka
3> Kafka and Flink says: integration
4> Kafka and Flink says: example
```

Integration with RabbitMQ

Download RabbitMQ from `http://www.rabbitmq.com/download.html` and set up. The following steps are required to integrate Flink with RabbitMQ:

1. Add dependencies in `pom.xml`:

```
<dependency>
    <groupId>org.apache.flink</groupId>
    <artifactId>flink-connector-rabbitmq_2.11</artifactId>
    <version>1.2.0</version>
</dependency>
```

2. Set up RMQ publisher:

```
ConnectionFactory factory = new ConnectionFactory(); // line 1
factory.setUsername("guest");
factory.setPassword("guest");
factory.setVirtualHost("/");
factory.setHost("localhost");
factory.setPort(5672);
Connection newConnection = factory.newConnection(); // line 2
Channel channel = newConnection.createChannel(); // line 3
Scanner scanner = new Scanner(System.in); // line 5
String message = "";
while(!message.equals("exit")){ // line 6
    System.out.println("Enter your message");
    message = scanner.next();
    channel.queueDeclare("flink-test", true, false, false, null);
// line 7
    channel.basicPublish("", "flink-test", new
BasicProperties.Builder()
.correlationId(java.util.UUID.randomUUID().toString()).build();,
    message.getBytes()); // line 8
}
```

To make message processing as exactly once in Flink with RabbitMQ, we need to add a `correlationId` with every message. The `correlationId` should be unique. In the previous program, we created a connection factory with the RabbitMQ server in `line 1`. Get a new connection from the connection factory in `line 2`. Get the channel from the connection in `line 3`. Get the message from the user on the console and loop the request until the message has not exited in `line 5` and `line 6`. Declare the queue in the channel with the required information in `line 7`. Publish the message on the queue `flink-test` in `line 8` with the setting unique `correlationId` in basic properties.

3. Set up RabbitMQ source:

```
final RMQConnectionConfig connectionConfig = new
RMQConnectionConfig.Builder.setHost("localhost").setPort(5672).setV
irtualHost("/").setUserName("guest").setPassword("guest").build();
```

Now, the Flink program starts with the RMQ connection config with the required details of the RMQ server.

4. Create the Streaming environment:

```
final StreamExecutionEnvironment env =
StreamExecutionEnvironment.getExecutionEnvironment();
env.enableCheckpointing(30000, CheckpointingMode.EXACTLY_ONCE);
```

Create the streaming environment and enable the checkpoint with time and policy as EXACTLY_ONCE. This is mandatory if you want to exactly once semantic with RMQ and Flink. Otherwise it would be at least once.

5. Add the RabbitMQ source in the environment:

```
final DataStream<String> stream = env.addSource(new
RMQSource<String>(connectionConfig,"flink-test", true, new
SimpleStringSchema())).setParallelism(1);
```

Add the RabbitMQ source in the Streaming environment. RMQSource is taking the parameters as queue name, correlationId set or not, and message de-serializer.

6. Read from the source and print on the console:

```
messageStream.rebalance().map(new MapFunction<String, String>() {
    private static final long serialVersionUID =
-6867736771747690202L;
    @Override
    public String map(String value) throws Exception {
        return "RabbitMQ and Flink says: " + value;
    }
}).print();
```

7. Execute the environment:

```
env.execute();
```

Running example

The following input is required to give on RMQ using RMQ Publisher and the output will be displayed on console.

Input:

Run the RMQ publisher program in your eclipse. It will ask for the message to be keyed in RMQ on console.

```
Enter your message
hi
Enter your message
this
Enter your message
is
Enter your message
RMQ
Enter your message
and
Enter your message
Flink
Enter your message
integration
Enter your message
example
Enter your message
```

RMQ UI shows eight messages in the queue, as shown in the following screenshot:

Output:

Run the program `FlinkRabbitMQSourceExample` in Eclipse and the output will be displayed on the console after reading all messages from the RMQ queue. The sequence of the message is not guaranteed here. Output is as shown in the following screenshot:

```
Connected to JobManager at Actor[akka://flink/user/jobmanager_1#-1293803841]
06/28/2017 18:26:29     Job execution switched to status RUNNING.
06/28/2017 18:26:29     Source: Custom Source(1/1) switched to SCHEDULED
06/28/2017 18:26:29     Source: Custom Source(1/1) switched to DEPLOYING
06/28/2017 18:26:29     Map -> Sink: Unnamed(1/4) switched to SCHEDULED
06/28/2017 18:26:29     Map -> Sink: Unnamed(1/4) switched to DEPLOYING
06/28/2017 18:26:29     Map -> Sink: Unnamed(2/4) switched to SCHEDULED
06/28/2017 18:26:29     Map -> Sink: Unnamed(2/4) switched to DEPLOYING
06/28/2017 18:26:29     Map -> Sink: Unnamed(3/4) switched to SCHEDULED
06/28/2017 18:26:29     Map -> Sink: Unnamed(3/4) switched to DEPLOYING
06/28/2017 18:26:29     Map -> Sink: Unnamed(4/4) switched to SCHEDULED
06/28/2017 18:26:29     Map -> Sink: Unnamed(4/4) switched to DEPLOYING
06/28/2017 18:26:29     Source: Custom Source(1/1) switched to RUNNING
06/28/2017 18:26:29     Map -> Sink: Unnamed(1/4) switched to RUNNING
06/28/2017 18:26:29     Map -> Sink: Unnamed(2/4) switched to RUNNING
06/28/2017 18:26:29     Map -> Sink: Unnamed(3/4) switched to RUNNING
06/28/2017 18:26:29     Map -> Sink: Unnamed(4/4) switched to RUNNING
4> RabbitMQ and Flink says: RMQ
1> RabbitMQ and Flink says: hi
4> RabbitMQ and Flink says: example
2> RabbitMQ and Flink says: this
1> RabbitMQ and Flink says: and
2> RabbitMQ and Flink says: Flink
3> RabbitMQ and Flink says: is
3> RabbitMQ and Flink says: integration
```

Flink processing and computation

As we have discussed different sources for Flink, now we will discuss the processing of source data. Depending upon the type of data sources, that is bounded or unbounded, processing API's are available in Flink. DataStream API is available for unbounded data source and DataSet API is available for bounded data sources.

DataStream API

Before moving to transformation functions, let's have a look at an example of DataStream. The following code snippet is a word count example implemented using DataStream API:

```
StreamExecutionEnvironment env =
StreamExecutionEnvironment.getExecutionEnvironment();
DataStream<Tuple2<String, Integer>> dataStream = env
.socketTextStream("localhost", 9999)
.flatMap(new Splitter())
.keyBy(0)
.timeWindow(Time.seconds(5))
.sum(1);
```

`StreamExecutionEnviornment` is used to create a DataStream Object. In the previous example, the environment first connects with the source of data using a socket. Then we apply `flatMap` function which splits the sentence into a tuple of words and count it as 1. `KeyBy` is used to group the stream on the basis of key which is word. We apply a `timeWindow` function of five seconds to perform the word count. In the end, we apply the aggregate function that is sum, to add all the count of words.

The following are the different transformations available with DataStream API:

- map: The map is the simplest transformation. There is no change in the number of input/output parameters, it just changes/modifies the value or changes the type of value. For example:

```
dataStream.map(new MapFunction<Integer, Integer>() {
    @Override
    public Integer map(Integer value) throws Exception {
        return value + 2;
    }
});
```

- FlatMap: FlatMap returns the value in collection. It might return one or more or no value. For example:

```
dataStream.flatMap(new FlatMapFunction<String, String>() {
@Override
    public void flatMap(String value, Collector<String> out)
    throws Exception {
      for(String word: value.split(" ")){
        out.collect(word);
      }
    }
});
```

- Filter: Filter transformation is used to filter events in the data stream. For example:

```
dataStream.filter(new FilterFunction<Integer>() {
    @Override
    public boolean filter(Integer value) throws Exception {
        return value != 0;
    }
});
```

- KeyBy: It partitions the stream and each partition has events of the same key. It returns keyed Stream. The key can't be an array and class object without the hashCode method overridden. For example:

```
dataStream.keyBy(0)
```

- reduce: It performs the specified action on the current value and the last record value and emits a new value. The difference between KeyBy and reduce is that KeyBy works on a partition, so shuffling is less, but reduce is performing a function on each and every event in the stream that requires shuffling. For example:

```
keyedStream.reduce(new ReduceFunction<Integer>() {
@Override
    public Integer reduce(Integer value1, Integer value2)
    throws Exception {
        return value1 * value2;
    }
});
```

- Fold: Fold is the same as Reduce, with the only difference being that Fold specifies a seeding value before executing the specified function. For example:

```
DataStream<String> result =
keyedStream.fold(1, new FoldFunction<Integer, Integer>() {
@Override
    public Integer fold(Integer current, Integer value) {
        return current * value;
    }
});
```

- **Aggregations**: There are multiple aggregate functions available such as:

```
keyedStream.sum(0);
keyedStream.sum("key");
keyedStream.min(0);
keyedStream.min("key");
keyedStream.max(0);
keyedStream.max("key");
keyedStream.minBy(0);
keyedStream.minBy("key");
keyedStream.maxBy(0);
keyedStream.maxBy("key");
```

- **Window**: Window can be defined on already partitioned KeyedStreams. Windows groups the data in each key according to a time specified by the user. For example:

```
dataStream.keyBy(0).timeWindow(Time.seconds(5))
```

DataSet API

DataSet API is used for batch processing. It has almost the same type of transformations as DataStream API provides. The following code snippet is a small example of word count using DataSet API:

```
final ExecutionEnvironment env =
ExecutionEnvironment.getExecutionEnvironment();
DataSet<String> text = env.fromElements(
"Who's there?",
"I think I hear them. Stand, ho! Who's there?");
DataSet<Tuple2<String, Integer>> wordCounts = text
.flatMap(new LineSplitter())
.groupBy(0)
.sum(1);
```

Here the execution environment is different compared to DataStream, that is ExecutionEnviornment. The previous program is doing the same task, but using a different method on bounded data.

The following are the transformations available with DataSet API and they are different from DataStream API:

- `distinct()`: Returns distinct elements of the data set. For example:

  ```
  data.distinct();
  ```

- `join()`: `join()` transformation joins two datasets based on the key. For example:

  ```
  result = input1.join(input2)
  .where(0) // key of the first input (tuple field 0)
  .equalTo(1); // key of the second input (tuple field 1)
  ```

- Union: Union of two data sets. For example:

  ```
  DataSet<String> result = data1.union(data2);
  ```

- First-n: Returns the first n elements from a data set. For example:

  ```
  DataSet<Tuple2<String,Integer>> result1 = in.first(3);
  ```

We have discussed sources, processing and computation, now let's discuss the sinks that are supported by Flink.

Flink persistence

Flink provides a connector with the sinks or persistences, such as:

- Apache Kafka
- Elasticsearch
- Hadoop Filesystem
- RabbitMQ
- Amazon Kinesis Streams
- Apache NiFi
- Apache Casssandra

In this book, we will discuss the Flink and Cassandra connection as it is the most popular.

Integration with Cassandra

We have discussed and explained the setup of Cassandra in previous chapters so we will directly go to the program required to make a connection between Flink and Cassandra:

- Add dependencies in `pom.xml`:

```
<dependency>
    <groupId>org.apache.flink</groupId>
    <artifactId>flink-connector-cassandra_2.11</artifactId>
    <version>1.2.0</version>
</dependency>
<dependency>
    <groupId>com.codahale.metrics</groupId>
    <artifactId>metrics-json</artifactId>
    <version>3.0.2</version>
</dependency>
```

- Create the data stream:

```
DataStream<Tuple4<Long,Integer,Integer,Long>> messageStream =
env.addSource(flinkKafkaConsumer08).map(new MapFunction<String,
Tuple4<Long,Integer,Integer,Long>>() {
    private static final long serialVersionUID =
47232145703728872O8L;
    @Override
        public Tuple4<Long,Integer,Integer,Long> map(String input)
throws        Exception
        {
            String[] inputSplits = input.split(",");
            return Tuple4.of(Long.parseLong(inputSplits[0]),
            Integer.parseInt(inputSplits[1]),
            Integer.parseInt(inputSplits[2]),
            Long.parseLong(inputSplits[3]));
        }
});
```

To integrate with Cassandra sink, we have to convert the data stream of the string into `Tuples`. We have 4 columns that we need to persist in Cassandra so we used `Tuple4` with the required data types. We apply the `map` function to transform the value from one format to another format.

- Creating the `CassandraSink`:

```
CassandraSink.addSink(messageStream).setQuery("INSERT INTO
tdr.packet_tdr (phone_number, bin, bout, timestamp) values (?, ?, ?
,?);").setClusterBuilder(new ClusterBuilder() {
    private static final long serialVersionUID = 1L;
    @Override
        public Cluster buildCluster(Cluster.Builder builder) {
            return builder.addContactPoint("127.0.0.1").build();
        }
}).build();
```

`CassandraSink` has static methods to add input data stream `addSink`. You can add a query using the `setQuery` method. `setClusterBuilder` is used to define the Cassandra cluster details.

Running example

To run the example, you have to run the data generator; `DataGenerator`, which pushes the data into the Kafka topic and then the Flink program that is `FlinkCassandraConnector` reads it from the Kafka topic and pushes it into Cassandra.

Input:

Run the program in Eclipse and it will show the following screenshot on the console. The data set will be different as it is random.

```
9999999983,7086759,8629334,1499350308660
9999999953,3927537,5309044,1499350308926
9999999993,2433812,7203793,1499350308926
9999999976,7046874,7056789,1499350308927
9999999997,9897191,4827991,1499350308928
9999999975,6247369,6145325,1499350308933
9999999961,1320813,4681550,1499350308934
9999999973,6989620,7262999,1499350308934
9999999971,2767230,8894962,1499350308934
9999999984,6499812,4954905,1499350308934
9999999968,5716208,6606575,1499350308934
9999999990,7270925,9005006,1499350308935
9999999995,3363460,1700805,1499350308935
9999999986,5162460,9524685,1499350308935
9999999951,3616511,3256483,1499350308935
```

Output:

After running `FlinkCassandraConnector`, nothing will be printed on the console but you have to check whether data is present in Cassandra or not. So run the following query shown in the screenshot:

```
cqlsh> select * from tdr.packet_tdr;

 phone_number | bin     | bout    | timestamp
--------------+---------+---------+----------------
   9999999961 | 1320813 | 4681550 | 1499350308934
   9999999997 | 2569390 | 5402894 | 1499350308936
   9999999980 | 7408468 | 5847162 | 1499350308941
   9999999966 | 1411547 |  437142 | 1499350308938
   9999999973 | 9236533 | 1126944 | 1499350308939
   9999999963 | 7331779 | 9856425 | 1499350308938
   9999999990 | 7270925 | 9005006 | 1499350308935
   9999999975 | 6247369 | 6145325 | 1499350308933
   9999999989 | 9972201 | 6324716 | 1499350308938
   9999999971 | 7340551 | 9944114 | 1499350308939
   9999999962 | 6044840 | 2620601 | 1499350308938
   9999999957 | 4361881 |  260005 | 1499350308935
   9999999951 | 3616511 | 3256483 | 1499350308935
   9999999995 | 3363460 | 1700805 | 1499350308935
```

FlinkCEP

CEP stands for **Complex Event Processing**. Flink provides API's for implementing CEP on the data stream with high throughput and low latency. CEP is kind of a processing data stream, that applies rules or conditions and whatever event satisfies the condition will be saved in the database as well as send notifications to the user as shown in the following figure. Flink matches a complex pattern against each event in the stream. This process filters out the events that are useful and discards the irrelevant ones. This gives us the opportunity to quickly get hold of what's really important in the data. Let's take an example. Let's say we have smart gensets which send the status of electricity produced and temperature of the system. Suppose if the temperature of the genset goes above 40 degrees then the user should get a notification to shut it down for a period of time or take immediate action to avoid an accident.

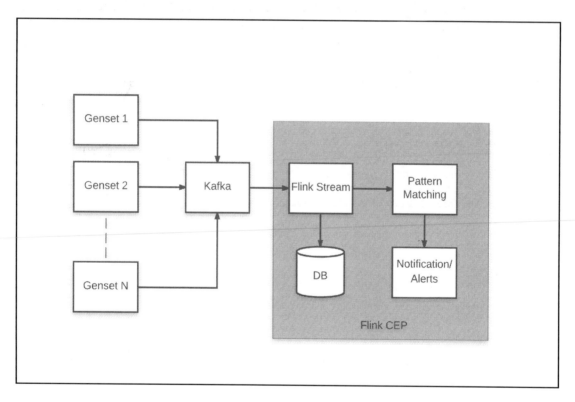

Pattern API

Apache Flink provides a pattern API to apply complex event processing on the data stream. Some important methods are:

- `begin`: This defines the pattern starting state and can be written as follows:

  ```
  Pattern<Event, ?> start = Pattern.<Event>begin("start");
  ```

- `followedBy`: This appends a new pattern state but here other events can occur between two matching events as follows:

  ```
  Pattern<Event, ?> followedBy = start.followedBy("next");
  ```

- `where`: This defines a filter condition for the current pattern state and, if the event passes the filter, it can match the state as follows:

  ```
  patternState.where(new FilterFunction <Event>() {
  @Override
      public boolean filter(Event value) throws Exception {
          return ... // some condition
      }
  });
  ```

- `within`: This defines the maximum time interval for an event sequence to match the pattern post that is discarded. It's written as follows:

  ```
  patternState.within(Time.seconds(10));
  ```

- `subtype(subClass)`: This defines a subtype condition for the current pattern. An event can only match the pattern if it is of this subtype:

  ```
  pattern.subtype(SubEvent.class);
  ```

Detecting pattern

Once you have created a pattern then you have to apply the pattern on the data stream to match the pattern. The following is the way to do this by code:

```
DataStream<Event> input = ...
Pattern<Event, ?> pattern = ...
PatternStream<Event> patternStream = CEP.pattern(input, pattern);
```

Here you have to create the `PatternStream` using the input data stream and pattern that you have created. Now the `PatternStream` will have the events that will match the pattern defined.

Selecting from patterns

We have created the pattern, and applied it on the data stream - now how do we get the matched events? This can be done by using the following code snippet:

```
class MyPatternSelectFunction<IN, OUT> implements PatternSelectFunction<IN,
OUT> {
@Override
    public OUT select(Map<String, List<IN>> pattern) {
        IN startEvent = pattern.get("start").get(0);
        IN endEvent = pattern.get("end").get(0);
        return new OUT(startEvent, endEvent);
    }
}
```

In is the class on which the event pattern is applied. The `Out` class is the form of output as an action on matched events.

Example

Let's take one more example with the following code, which explains the available pattern API and their use. Here in this example we are generating an alert in case a mobile/IOT device generates data of more than 15 MB within 10 seconds:

```
Pattern<DeviceEvent, ?> alertPattern =
Pattern.<DeviceEvent>begin("first").subtype(DeviceEvent.class).where(new
DeviceFilterFunction()).followedBy("second").subtype(DeviceEvent.class).whe
re(new DeviceFilterFunction()).within(Time.seconds(TXN_TIMESPAN_SEC));
```

In the preceding snippet, we defined the pattern to be matched with each event of the data stream:

```
PatternStream<DeviceEvent> tempPatternStream =
CEP.pattern(messageStream.rebalance().keyBy("phoneNumber"), alertPattern);
```

In the preceding snippet, we applied the pattern on the data stream and got the pattern stream which contains matched events only.

```
DataStream<DeviceAlert> alert = tempPatternStream.select(new
PatternSelectFunction<DeviceEvent, DeviceAlert>() {
    private static final long serialVersionUID = 1L;
    @Override
        public DeviceAlert select(Map<String, DeviceEvent> pattern) {
            DeviceEvent first = (DeviceEvent) pattern.get("first");
            DeviceEvent second = (DeviceEvent) pattern.get("second");
            allTxn.clear();
            allTxn.add(first.getPhoneNumber() + " used " + ((first.getBin()
            + first.getBout())/1024/1024) +" MB at " + new
            Date(first.getTimestamp()));
            allTxn.add(second.getPhoneNumber() + " used " +
            ((second.getBin() + second.getBout())/1024/1024) +" MB at " +
            new Date(second.getTimestamp()));
            return new DeviceAlert(first.getPhoneNumber(), allTxn);
        }
});
```

Previously we applied the `select` function to take action on the matched event. The full code is available in the code bundle. To run the example, first start `DataGenerator` which pushes data on Kafka, and then start `DeviceUsageMonitoring`.

Gelly

Gelly is a graph API for Flink. In Gelly, graphs can be created, transformed, and modified. Gelly API provides all the basic and advanced functions of graph analytics. You can also select the different graph algorithms.

Gelly API

Gelly provides the API with the ability to take actions on graphs. We will discuss the API's in the follwing section.

Graph representation

A graph is represented by a DataSet of Vertices and Edges. Graph nodes are represented by `Vertex` type. A vertex is defined by unique ID and value. A `NullValue` can be defined for a `Vertex` with no value. The following are the methods used for creating vertex in a graph:

```
Vertex<String, Long> v = new Vertex<String, Long>("vertex 1", 8L);
Vertex<String, NullValue> v = new Vertex<String, NullValue>("vertex 1",
NullValue.getInstance());
```

Graph edges are represented by edge type. An edge is defined by source ID (ID of source vertex), target ID (ID of target vertex), and optional value. The source and target IDs should be of the same type as the Vertex IDs. The following is the way to create an `Edge` in a graph:

```
Edge<String, Double> e = new Edge<String, Double>("vertex 1", "vertex 2",
0.5);
```

Graph creation

A graph can be created as per the following statements in `ExecutionEnvironment`:

- Graph creation from text files:

```
ExecutionEnvironment env =
ExecutionEnvironment.getExecutionEnvironment();
DataSet<Tuple2<String, Long>> vertexTuples =
env.readCsvFile("path/to/vertex/input").types(String.class,
Long.class);
DataSet<Tuple3<String, String, Double>> edgeTuples =
env.readCsvFile("path/to/edge/input").types(String.class,
String.class, Double.class);
Graph<String, Long, Double> graph =
Graph.fromTupleDataSet(vertexTuples, edgeTuples, env);
```

- Graph creation from collections:

```
ExecutionEnvironment env =
ExecutionEnvironment.getExecutionEnvironment();
List<Vertex<Long, Long>> vertexList = new ArrayList...
List<Edge<Long, String>> edgeList = new ArrayList...
Graph<Long, Long, String> graph = Graph.fromCollection(vertexList,
edgeList, env);
```

Graph transformations

The following are some important graph transformations:

- map: map transformation can be applied on the vertex or edge. The ID's of the vertex and edge remain unchanged and you can change the value as per the user-defined function:

```
Graph<Long, Long, Long> updatedGraph = graph.mapVertices(new
MapFunction<Vertex<Long, Long>, Long>() {
public Long map(Vertex<Long, Long> value) {
return value.getValue() + 1;
}
});
```

- filter: By using filter, you can filter the vertices or edges from the graph. If filter is applied on the edges, then the filtered edges will remain in the graph but the vertices will not be removed. If filter is applied on the vertices, then the filtered vertices will remain in the graph:

```
graph.subgraph(new FilterFunction<Vertex<Long, Long>>() {
public boolean filter(Vertex<Long, Long> vertex) {
return (vertex.getValue() > 0);
}
},
new FilterFunction<Edge<Long, Long>>() {
public boolean filter(Edge<Long, Long> edge) {
return (edge.getValue() < 0);
}
})
```

- reverse: The reverse() method returns a new Graph where the direction of all the edges has been reversed.

- **Union**: In union operation, duplicate vertices are removed, but duplicate edges are preserved.

This is it for the Gelly graph library as per the scope of this book. If you want to explore more on this then go to https://ci.apache.org/projects/flink/flink-docs-release-1. 3/dev/libs/gelly/index.html.

DIY

Lot of examples are shown in the previous sections. Now, let's get ready to do some hands-on. Code will be available in the code bundle for reference. Read README.MD in the code bundle for the execution of the program.

Source to sink – Flink execution:

We have already seen examples where we integrated Apache Kafka or RabbitMQ as source to Cassandra as sink. Now, here we will integrate Apache Kafka as source and ElasticSearch 2.x as sink. The connector will be changed. Instead of using Cassandra, we will use ElasticSearch.

Here we have the import files:

```
package com.boof.flink.diy;
import java.net.InetAddress;
import java.net.InetSocketAddress;
import java.util.ArrayList;import java.util.HashMap;
import java.util.List;
import java.util.Map;
import java.util.Properties;
import org.apache.flink.api.common.functions.RuntimeContext;
import org.apache.flink.streaming.api.datastream.DataStream;
import
org.apache.flink.streaming.api.environment.StreamExecutionEnvironment;
import
org.apache.flink.streaming.connectors.elasticsearch2.ElasticsearchSink;
import
org.apache.flink.streaming.connectors.elasticsearch2.ElasticsearchSinkFunct
ion;
import org.apache.flink.streaming.connectors.elasticsearch2.RequestIndexer;
import org.apache.flink.streaming.connectors.kafka.FlinkKafkaConsumer08;
import org.elasticsearch.action.index.IndexRequest;
import org.elasticsearch.client.Requests;
import com.book.flinkcep.example.DeviceEvent;
import com.book.flinkcep.example.DeviceSchema;
```

Flink Elasticsearch integration main class

In the following part the main classes:

```java
public class FlinkESConnector {
    public static void main(String[] args) throws Exception {
        Properties properties = new Properties();
        properties.setProperty("bootstrap.servers", "localhost:9092");
        properties.setProperty("zookeeper.connect", "localhost:2181");
        properties.setProperty("group.id", "test");
        properties.setProperty("auto.offset.reset", "latest");
        FlinkKafkaConsumer08<DeviceEvent> flinkKafkaConsumer08 = new
        FlinkKafkaConsumer08<>("device-data",
                new DeviceSchema(), properties);
        StreamExecutionEnvironment env =
        StreamExecutionEnvironment.getExecutionEnvironment();
        DataStream<DeviceEvent> messageStream =
        env.addSource(flinkKafkaConsumer08);
```

Next, we have the methods that we call:

```java
Map<String, String> config = new HashMap<>();
config.put("cluster.name", "my-application");
// This instructs the sink to emit after every element, otherwise they
would be buffered
config.put("bulk.flush.max.actions", "1");
        List<InetSocketAddress> transportAddresses = new ArrayList<>();
        transportAddresses.add(new
        InetSocketAddress(InetAddress.getByName("127.0.0.1"), 9300));
        messageStream.addSink(new
ElasticsearchSink<DeviceEvent>(config,
        transportAddresses, new ESSink()));
        env.execute();        }}
```

Eleasticsearch sink as Flnk operator

Next, we show the code for JSON objects:

```java
class ESSink implements ElasticsearchSinkFunction<DeviceEvent> {
    private static final long serialVersionUID = -4286031843082751966L;
    @Override
    public void process(DeviceEvent element, RuntimeContext ctx,
RequestIndexer indexer) {
    Map<String, Object> json = new HashMap<>();
        json.put("phoneNumber", element.getPhoneNumber());
        json.put("bin", element.getBin());
        json.put("bout", element.getBout());
        json.put("timestamp", element.getTimestamp());
```

```
                System.out.println(json);
            IndexRequest source = Requests.indexRequest()
                    .index("flink-test")
                    .type("flink-log")
                    .source(json);
            indexer.add(source);
        }
    }
```

Domain class to hold event data

In the next code snippet, we have `public` methods that are called:

```
    package com.book.flinkcep.example;

public class DeviceEvent {

        private long phoneNumber;
        private int bin;
        private int bout;
        private long timestamp;

        public long getPhoneNumber() {
                return phoneNumber;
        }

        public void setPhoneNumber(long phoneNumber) {
                this.phoneNumber = phoneNumber;
        }

        public int getBin() {
                return bin;
        }

        public void setBin(int bin) {
                this.bin = bin;
        }

        public int getBout() {
                return bout;
        }

        public void setBout(int bout) {
                this.bout = bout;
        }

        public long getTimestamp() {
                return timestamp;
```

```
        }

    public void setTimestamp(long timestamp) {
            this.timestamp = timestamp;
    }
  public static DeviceEvent fromString(String line) {

            String[] tokens = line.split(",");

            if (tokens.length != 4) {
                    throw new RuntimeException("Invalid record: " + line);
            }

            DeviceEvent deviceEvent = new DeviceEvent();

            deviceEvent.phoneNumber = Long.parseLong(tokens[0]);
            deviceEvent.bin = Integer.parseInt(tokens[1]);
            deviceEvent.bout = Integer.parseInt(tokens[2]);
            deviceEvent.timestamp = Long.parseLong(tokens[3]);

            return deviceEvent;
    }
     @Override
    public int hashCode() {
            final int prime = 31;
            int result = 1;
            result = prime * result + bin;
            result = prime * result + bout;
            result = prime * result + (int) (phoneNumber ^ (phoneNumber >>>
32));
            result = prime * result + (int) (timestamp ^ (timestamp >>>
32));
            return result;
    }

    @Override
    public boolean equals(Object obj) {
            if (this == obj)
                    return true;
            if (obj == null)
                    return false;
            if (getClass() != obj.getClass())
                    return false;
            DeviceEvent other = (DeviceEvent) obj;
            if (bin != other.bin)
                    return false;
            if (bout != other.bout)
                    return false;
```

```
                if (phoneNumber != other.phoneNumber)
                        return false;
                if (timestamp != other.timestamp)
                        return false;
                return true;
        }
    @Override
        public String toString() {
                return "DeviceEvent [phoneNumber=" + phoneNumber + ", bin=" +
bin + ", bout=" + bout + ", timestamp="
                                + timestamp + "]";
        }
}
```

Device schema serializer and de-serializer

```
package com.book.flinkcep.example;

import java.io.IOException;

import org.apache.flink.api.common.typeinfo.TypeInformation;
import org.apache.flink.api.java.typeutils.TypeExtractor;
import org.apache.flink.streaming.util.serialization.DeserializationSchema;
import org.apache.flink.streaming.util.serialization.SerializationSchema;

public class DeviceSchema implements DeserializationSchema<DeviceEvent>,
SerializationSchema<DeviceEvent>{

        private static final long serialVersionUID = 1051444497161899607L;

        @Override
        public TypeInformation<DeviceEvent> getProducedType() {
                return TypeExtractor.getForClass(DeviceEvent.class);
        }

        @Override
        public byte[] serialize(DeviceEvent element) {
                return element.toString().getBytes();
        }

        @Override
        public DeviceEvent deserialize(byte[] message) throws IOException {
                return DeviceEvent.fromString(new String(message));
        }

        @Override
        public boolean isEndOfStream(DeviceEvent nextElement) {
                return false;
```

```
        }

    }
```

Data generate in form of device object:

Finally, we have the rest of the code that allows us to translate the variables of the data to real numbers:

```
    package com.book.flinkcep.example;

import java.util.Properties;
import java.util.concurrent.ThreadLocalRandom;

import org.apache.kafka.clients.producer.KafkaProducer;
import org.apache.kafka.clients.producer.ProducerRecord;

public class DataGenerator {
    public static void main(String args[]) {
            Properties properties = new Properties();
            properties.put("bootstrap.servers", "localhost:9092");
            properties.put("key.serializer",
"org.apache.kafka.common.serialization.StringSerializer");
            properties.put("value.serializer",
"org.apache.kafka.common.serialization.StringSerializer");
            properties.put("acks", "1");
            KafkaProducer<Integer, String> producer = new
KafkaProducer<Integer, String>(properties);
            int counter =0;
            int nbrOfEventsRequired = Integer.parseInt(args[0]);
            while (counter<nbrOfEventsRequired) {
                StringBuffer stream = new StringBuffer();
                long phoneNumber =
ThreadLocalRandom.current().nextLong(99999999501,
                        99999999991);
                int bin = ThreadLocalRandom.current().nextInt(100000,
9999999);
                int bout = ThreadLocalRandom.current().nextInt(100000,
9999999);
                stream.append(phoneNumber);
                stream.append(",");
                stream.append(bin);
                stream.append(",");
                stream.append(bout);
                stream.append(",");
                stream.append(System.currentTimeMillis());

                System.out.println(stream.toString());
```

```
                    ProducerRecord<Integer, String> data = new
        ProducerRecord<Integer, String>(
                                "device-data", stream.toString());
                    producer.send(data);
                    counter++;
            }
            producer.close();
        }
    }
```

Executing Storm topology on Flink:

Storm topology can run in a Flink environment without modification. Just keep the following points in mind while making changes:

- `StormSubmitter` replaced by `FlinkSubmitter`
- `NimbusClient` and Client replaced by `FlinkClient`
- `LocalCluster` replaced by `FlinkLocalCluster`

In the following lines we can show the code for that function.

Main class for Flink and Storm integration

```
package com.book.flink.diy;

import org.apache.flink.storm.api.FlinkTopology;

import backtype.storm.topology.TopologyBuilder;

public class FlinkStormExample {
    public static void main(String[] args) throws Exception {
        TopologyBuilder topologyBuilder = new TopologyBuilder();
        topologyBuilder.setSpout("spout", new FileSpout("/tmp/device-
data.txt"), 1);
        topologyBuilder.setBolt("parser", new ParserBolt(),
1).shuffleGrouping("spout");
        topologyBuilder.setBolt("tdrCassandra", new
TDRCassandraBolt("localhost", "tdr"), 1).shuffleGrouping("parser",
"tdrstream");
        FlinkTopology.createTopology(topologyBuilder).execute();
    }
}
```

File spout in Storm:

```java
package com.book.flink.diy;

import java.io.BufferedReader;
import java.io.FileReader;
import java.io.IOException;
import java.util.Map;

import backtype.storm.spout.SpoutOutputCollector;
import backtype.storm.task.TopologyContext;
import backtype.storm.topology.OutputFieldsDeclarer;
import backtype.storm.topology.base.BaseRichSpout;
import backtype.storm.tuple.Fields;
import backtype.storm.tuple.Values;

public class FileSpout extends BaseRichSpout {
    private static final long serialVersionUID = -6167039596158642349L;
    private SpoutOutputCollector collector;
    private String fileName;
    private BufferedReader reader;

    public FileSpout(String fileName) {
        this.fileName = fileName;
    }
    @Override
    public void open(Map conf, TopologyContext context, SpoutOutputCollector
collector) {
        //fileName = (String) conf.get("file");
        this.collector = collector;

        try {
            reader = new BufferedReader(new FileReader(fileName));
        } catch (Exception e) {
            throw new RuntimeException(e);
        }
    }

    @Override
    public void nextTuple() {
        try {
            String line = reader.readLine();
            if (line != null) {
                collector.emit(new Values(line));
            }
        } catch (IOException e) {
            e.printStackTrace();
        }
```

```
        }

        @Override
        public void close() {
                try {
                        reader.close();
                } catch (IOException e) {
                        e.printStackTrace();
                }
        }

        @Override
        public void declareOutputFields(OutputFieldsDeclarer declarer) {
                Fields schema = new Fields("line");
                declarer.declare(schema);
        }
}
```

Cassandra persistence bolt:

```
package com.book.flink.diy;

import java.util.Map;

import com.datastax.driver.core.Cluster;
import com.datastax.driver.core.Session;

import backtype.storm.task.TopologyContext;
import backtype.storm.topology.BasicOutputCollector;
import backtype.storm.topology.OutputFieldsDeclarer;
import backtype.storm.topology.base.BaseBasicBolt;
import backtype.storm.tuple.Tuple;

public class TDRCassandraBolt extends BaseBasicBolt {
    private static final long serialVersionUID = 1L;
    private Cluster cluster;
    private Session session;
    private String hostname;
    private String keyspace;

    public TDRCassandraBolt(String hostname, String keyspace) {
            this.hostname = hostname;
            this.keyspace = keyspace;
    }

    @Override
    public void prepare(Map stormConf, TopologyContext context) {
            cluster = Cluster.builder().addContactPoint(hostname).build();
```

```
            session = cluster.connect(keyspace);
    }

    public void execute(Tuple input, BasicOutputCollector arg1) {
            PacketDetailDTO packetDetailDTO = (PacketDetailDTO)
input.getValueByField("tdrstream");
            System.out.println("field value "+ packetDetailDTO);
            session.execute("INSERT INTO packet_tdr (phone_number, bin, bout,
timestamp) VALUES ("
                            + packetDetailDTO.getPhoneNumber()
                            + ", "
                            + packetDetailDTO.getBin()
                            + ","
                            + packetDetailDTO.getBout()
                            + "," + packetDetailDTO.getTimestamp() + ")");
    }

    public void declareOutputFields(OutputFieldsDeclarer arg0) {

    }

    @Override
    public void cleanup() {
            session.close();
            cluster.close();
    }
}
```

Parsing event in bolt:

```
package com.book.flink.diy;

import java.util.Map;

import backtype.storm.task.TopologyContext;
import backtype.storm.topology.BasicOutputCollector;
import backtype.storm.topology.OutputFieldsDeclarer;
import backtype.storm.topology.base.BaseBasicBolt;
import backtype.storm.tuple.Fields;
import backtype.storm.tuple.Tuple;
import backtype.storm.tuple.Values;

public class ParserBolt extends BaseBasicBolt {

    private static final long serialVersionUID = 1271439619204966337L;

    @Override
    public void prepare(Map stormConf, TopologyContext context) {
```

```
        }

        @Override
        public void execute(Tuple input, BasicOutputCollector collector) {
                String valueByField = input.getString(0);
                System.out.println("field value "+ valueByField);
                String[] split = valueByField.split(",");
                PacketDetailDTO tdrPacketDetailDTO = new PacketDetailDTO();
                tdrPacketDetailDTO.setPhoneNumber(Long.parseLong(split[0]));
                tdrPacketDetailDTO.setBin(Integer.parseInt(split[1]));
                tdrPacketDetailDTO.setBout(Integer.parseInt(split[2]));
                tdrPacketDetailDTO.setTimestamp(Long.parseLong(split[3]));

                collector.emit("tdrstream", new Values(tdrPacketDetailDTO));
        }

        @Override
        public void cleanup() {
        }

        @Override
        public void declareOutputFields(OutputFieldsDeclarer declarer) {
                declarer.declareStream("tdrstream", new Fields("tdrstream"));
        }

}
```

Data transfer object between bolts:

```
package com.book.flink.diy;

import java.io.Serializable;

public class PacketDetailDTO implements Serializable {

    private static final long serialVersionUID = 9148607866335518739L;
    private long phoneNumber;
    private int bin;
    private int bout;
    private int totalBytes;
    private long timestamp;

    public long getPhoneNumber() {
            return phoneNumber;
    }

    public void setPhoneNumber(long phoneNumber) {
            this.phoneNumber = phoneNumber;
```

```
    }

    public int getBin() {
        return bin;
    }

    public void setBin(int bin) {
        this.bin = bin;
    }

    public int getBout() {
        return bout;
    }

    public void setBout(int bout) {
        this.bout = bout;
    }

    public int getTotalBytes() {
        return totalBytes;
    }

    public void setTotalBytes(int totalBytes) {
        this.totalBytes = totalBytes;
    }

    public long getTimestamp() {
        return timestamp;
    }

    public void setTimestamp(long timestamp) {
        this.timestamp = timestamp;
    }
}
```

Summary

In this chapter, we acquainted the reader with Flink architecture. We discussed KAPPA architecture and how Flink works. There are different sources and sinks available with Flink. Examples of sources such as Kafka and RabbitMQ were explained. Examples of sinks such as Cassandra were explained with Kafka as a source. Flink gives us DataSet and DataFrame API for stream and batch processing respectively. We explained the different transformations available with each API. There are two advanced level libraries provided by Flink: CEP and Gelly. CEP is used for real-time processing with pattern implementations. Gelly is a graph API over Flink. In the end, we have given the reader problems to solve for themselves.

In the next chapter, we will see how to develop a real example using the applications of all this book's scenarios.

13

Case Study

After reading all previous chapters, you have been acquainted with different frameworks available for real-time as well batch streaming. In this chapter, we will discuss a case study which uses frameworks we discussed in previous chapters.

We will cover the following components:

- Case study introduction
- Data modeling
- Tools and frameworks
- Setting up the infrastructure
- Implementing the case study
- Running a case study

Introduction

We will discuss and implement a Geofencing use case as a case study. Geofencing is the use of the **Global Positioning System (GPS)** satellite network and/or local radio-frequency identifiers (such as WiFi nodes or Bluetooth beacons) to create virtual boundaries around a location. Geofencing is paired with software/hardware to detect the virtual boundary and take the appropriate action defined by the user. Most of the Geofencing use cases are solved with IOT. Real-time use cases based on Geofencing are:

- Suppose your children took your car to buy goods from the market and you don't want them to go beyond 5 KM/Miles from your home or you want to know your kids/other family member's location on a map to track them
- When you have put your car in for servicing and you want it not to go beyond 1 KM/Miles from the car service center

- When you are approaching home, the garage gate opens automatically without having to get out of the car and manually open it by pushing/pulling it
- When you are leaving home, wondering whether you have locked the door or not
- Suppose you have a cattle farm and you want your cattle not to stray beyond a certain distance
- A beacons-based use case can be implemented in stores or malls to find out about the customer and recommend what he/she probably likes

As well as the previous mentioned use cases, there are many more. We have picked the use case mentioned first: Vehicle Geofencing. The user will get an alert if the vehicle goes beyond the virtual boundary defined by the user. An example is illustrated in the following image:

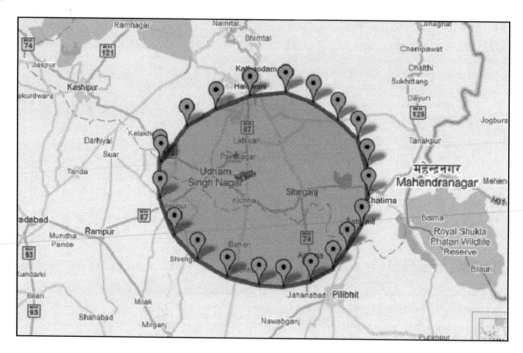

In this use case, we push real-time vehicle location data into Kafka. We will keep the static data of the vehicle which contains the starting point of the vehicle and the threshold distance in Kafka and push it into Hazelcast. Real-time vehicle data will be read by Storm, which starts processing every vehicle event. It checks the distance of the current location and the location defined by the user. If the vehicle goes beyond the threshold distance, then an alert is generated.

Data modeling

The real-time vehicle sensor data model is:

Field name	Vehicle Id	Latitude	Longitude	Speed	Timestamp
Data type	String	Double	Double	Integer	Long

The `Vehicle Id` is the unique identifier of any vehicle. Generally, it is the chassis number shown in different locations for different types of vehicle. `Latitude` and `Longitude` are detected by GPS which tells us the current location. `Speed` is the speed of the vehicle. `Timestamp` is the time when this event was generated.

The static vehicle data model is:

Field name	Vehicle Id	Latitude	Longitude	Distance	Phone number
Data type	String	Double	Double	Double	String

This static data is provided by the owner of the vehicle while setting up the alert for his/her vehicle. The `Vehicle Id` is the unique identifier of any vehicle. `Latitude` and `Longitude` are the starting location of the vehicle or the location from where distance is calculated to check the alert. `Distance` is the threshold distance in meters. The `Phone number` is used to send a notification in case of an alert ID being generated.

Output is pushed into Elasticsearch. There will be two types of data models used. One for saving real-time vehicle sensor data and the other for alert information generated by the system.

Real-time sensor data model:

Field name	Coords	Speed	Timestamp	Vehicle_id
Data type	Geo_point	Integer	Date	Text

`Coords` contains latitude and longitude in JSON format which is converted into `geo_point` type by Elasticsearch. `Speed` is the speed of the vehicle. `Timestamp` is the time the event occurred. `Vehicle_id` is the unique identifier of the vehicle.

Alert Information data model:

Field name	Actual_coords	Expected_distance	Actual_distance	Expected_coords	Timestamp	Vehicle_id
Data type	Geo_point	Double	Double	Geo_point	Date	Text

Actual_coords contains the real-time current latitude and longitude of the vehicle as location. Expected_distance is the threshold value of distance configured by the user for their vehicle. Actual_distance is the current distance between the actual_coords and the expected_coords. Expected_coords is the starting point or location configured by the user while setting up the vehicle alert. Timestamp is the time of the alert generated by the system. Vehicle_id is the unique identifier of the vehicle.

Two types of Maps will be created by Hazelcast to process events in real-time: VehicleAlertInfo and GeneratedAlerts. In VehicleAlertInfo, the Map key is the vehicle id and the value is a java object which contains the vehicleId, latitude, longitude, distance, and phoneNumber. The GeneratedAlerts Map key is the vehicle id and the value is thresholdDistance, actualDistance, startingLatitude, startingLongitude, actualLatitude, actualLongitude, vehicleId, timestamp, and phoneNumber.

Tools and frameworks

The following tools and frameworks are used to implement a complete use case:

Name	Version
Java	1.8
Zookeeper	3.4.6
Kafka	2.11-0.8.2.2
Hazelcast	3.8
Storm	1.1.1
Elasticsearch	5.2.2
Kibana	5.2.2

Setting up the infrastructure

To implement the use case, the following tools must be setup:

- **Hazelcast**: We have discussed the setup of Hazelcast in previous chapters using java code and running it in eclipse. Here, we will discuss running Hazelcast using scripts. First download the setup of Hazelcast from: `https://download.hazelcast.com/download.jsp?version=hazelcast-3.8amp;type=taramp;p=`

    This will download the 3.8 version of Hazelcast. Extract it and you will get the following folders and files shown in the following screenshot:

    Make changes in `hazelcast.xml` to enable Hazelcast UI that is `mancenter` as:

    ```
    <management-center enabled="true">
    http://localhost:8080/mancenter</management-center >
    ```

    Now, execute the following script to start Hazelcast:

    ```
    /bin/start.sh
    ```

    This will start Hazelcast on the localhost and bind to port 5701. If we want to create a cluster for Hazelcast then copy the Hazelcast setup directory to a different location and execute the start.sh script again. It will start Hazelcast in cluster mode on the localhost and bond the second instance with port 5702.

    To start the mancenter UI, execute the the following script:

    ```
    /mancenter/startMancenter.sh
    ```

    It will start the mancenter UI on the localhost on port 8080. The URL is `http://localhost:8080/mancenter/`. It automatically creates a work directory at the `mancenter` directory. If you want to start the UI at a different port and another work directory location, then execute the following command:

    ```
    /mancenter/startMancenter.sh <PORT> <PATH>
    ```

The following screenshot shows the mancenter UI:

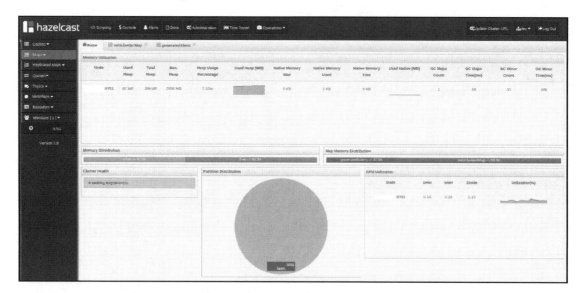

- **Notification using WhatsApp**: For sending notifications on WhatsApp, we need a library such as Yowsup which can send and receive messages. Following are the steps to set up Yowsup on your system:

    1. Clone git repository `Yowsup` using the following command:

        git clone git://github.com/tgalal/yowsup.git

    2. Change the following properties in `yowsup/env/env_android.py`:

        ```
        _MD5_CLASSES = "ox998VW0nBTueMVfjuZkmQ=="
        _VERSION = "2.17.212"
        ```

    3. **Register your number with WhatsApp**: Use an unused number which is not on WhatsApp to register, as you can't register the same number again. Use the following command to register:

        ```
        yowsup-cli registration -d -r sms -C <Country Code> -p
        <Phone number with country code and without '+'> -m <MCC> -
        n <MNC> -E android
        ```

After executing the previous steps, you will get a 6 digit code on your number and the following response on the console:

```
INFO:yowsup.common.http.warequest:{"login":"          ","status":"sent","length":6,"method":"sms","retry_after":65,"sms_wait":65,"voice_wait":
5}
status: sent
retry_after: 65
length: 6
login:
method: sms
```

Use the following command to register your number with a verification code:

```
yowsup-cli registration -d -R 705-933 -p 917988141683 -C 91
-E android
```

You will get the following response on the console:

```
INFO:yowsup.common.http.warequest:{"status":"ok","login":"          ","type":"new","pw":"                    ","expiration":4444444444
0,"kind":"free","price":"\u20b9 55","cost":"55.00","currency":"INR","price_expiration":1507271117]
status: ok
kind: free
pw:
price: ₹ 55
price_expiration: 1507271117
currency: INR
cost: 55.00
expiration: 4444444444.0
login:
type: new
```

4. Now, create a config file with the following properties:

```
cc=<Country Code>
phone=<Phone number with country code and without '+'>
password=<Password that you received in previous step>
```

Save it as `whatsapp_config.txt`. (You can name it whatever you like. Update the file name in the next step accordingly).

5. After registration, you can test by sending a message using the following command:

```
yowsup-cli demos --config whatsapp_config.txt --send
<Receiver Phone number with country code and without '+'>
"<Your message>"
```

Check your mobile and you should already have received the message.

- **Zookeeper**: Zookeeper is required for Kafka and Storm. Zookeeper can be started from Kafka setup. We have discussed Kafka setup in detail in Chapter 3, *Understanding and Tailing Data Streams*. So, let's just start it using the following command:

```
/bin/zookeeper-server-start.sh ../config/zookeeper.properties
```

- **Kafka**: Let's just start Kafka using the following command:

```
/bin/kafka-server-start.sh ../config/server.properties
```

Create two topics on Kafka: vehicle-data and vehicle-static-data by using the following commands:

```
/bin/kafka-topics.sh --create --topic vehicle--data --zookeeper
localhost:2181 --partitions 1 --replication-factor 1
/bin/kafka-topics.sh --create --topic vehicle-static-data --
zookeeper localhost:2181 --partitions 1 --replication-factor 1
```

- **Elasticsearch**: We have discussed Elasticsearch set up in Chapter 3, *Understanding and Tailing Data Streams, DIY* section. So, let's just start it using the following command:

```
/bin/elasticsearch
```

Create two indexes in Elasticsearch: tdr and alert. The following commands are used to create them:

```
curl -XPUT 'localhost:9200/vehicle-tdr?pretty&amp;pretty'
curl -XPUT 'localhost:9200/vehicle-tdr/_mapping/tdr' -d '{
        "properties": {
            "coords": {
                "type": "geo_point"
            },
            "speed": {
                "type": "integer"
            },
            "timestamp": {
                "type": "date"
            },
            "vehicle_id" : {
                "type" : "text",
                "fields" : {
                    "keyword" : {
                        "type" : "keyword",
                        "ignore_above" : 256
                    }
```

```
                }
              }
            }
          }'
curl -XPUT 'localhost:9200/vehicle-alert?pretty&amp;pretty'
curl -XPUT 'localhost:9200/vehicle-alert/_mapping/alert' -d
'{
        "properties": {
          "actual_coords": {
            "type": "geo_point"
          },
          "expected_distance": {
            "type": "double"
          },
          "actual_distance": {
            "type": "double"
          },
          "expected_coords": {
            "type": "geo_point"
          },
          "timestamp": {
            "type": "date"
          },
          "vehicle_id" : {
              "type" : "text",
              "fields" : {
                "keyword" : {
                  "type" : "keyword",
                  "ignore_above" : 256
                }
              }
          }
        }
      }'
```

- **Kibana**: Download Kibana from: https://artifacts.elastic.co/downloads/
  kibana/kibana-5.5.2-linux-x86_64.tar.gz. This will download the 5.2.2
  version of Kibana, the same as Elasticsearch. Extract it and you will get the
  following folders and files:

```
:~/demo/kibana-5.2.2-linux-x86_64$ ls
bin  config  data  LICENSE.txt  node  node_modules  NOTICE.txt  optimize  package.json  plugins  README.txt  src  ui_framework  webpackShims
```

To start Kibana, execute the following command:

```
/bin/ kibana
```

Kibana UI can be accessed using the URL `http://localhost:5601`.

- **Storm**: We discussed the setup and configuration of Storm in `Chapter 4`, *Setting up the Infrastructure for Storm* in detail. So let's start `nimbus`, `supervisor`, `ui`, and `logviewer` service. As the Hazelcast mancenter UI is running on 8080, we need to change the port for Storm UI to run on port 8081. So add the following line in `storm.yaml`:

```
ui.port: 8081
```

Start Storm services by executing the following commands:

- **Nimbus**: First of all, we need to start the Nimbus service in Storm. Execute the following command to start:

```
/bin/storm nimbus
```

- **Supervisor**: Next we need to start supervisor nodes to connect with the nimbus node. Execute the following command to start:

```
/bin/storm supervisor
```

- **UI**: To start Storm UI, execute the following command:

```
/bin/storm ui
```

You can access UI on `http://nimbus-host:8081`.

- **Logviewer**: The log viewer service helps to see the worker logs on Storm UI. Execute the following command to start:

```
/bin/storm logviewer
```

Implementing the case study

To implement the `geofencing` use case, we use the following components to build and develop it.

Building the data simulator

Before generating the real-time data of the vehicle, we need to have the starting point of the vehicle. Following is the code snippet to the generate data:

```java
package com.book.simulator;
import java.util.HashMap;
import java.util.Map;
import java.util.Properties;
import java.util.Random;
import org.apache.kafka.clients.producer.KafkaProducer;
import org.apache.kafka.clients.producer.ProducerRecord;
import org.apache.kafka.common.serialization.StringSerializer;
import com.book.domain.Location;
import com.fasterxml.jackson.core.JsonProcessingException;
import com.fasterxml.jackson.databind.ObjectMapper;
/**
* This class is used to generate vehicle start point for number of vehicle
* specified by user.
*
* @author SGupta
*
*/
public class VehicleStartPointGenerator {
  static private ObjectMapper objectMapper = new ObjectMapper();
  static private Random r = new Random();
  static private String BROKER_1_CONNECTION_STRING = "localhost:9092";
  static private String KAFKA_TOPIC_STATIC_DATA = "vehicle-static-data";
  public static void main(String[] args) {
    if (args.length < 1) {
      System.out.println("Provide number of vehicle");
      System.exit(1);
    }
  // Number of vehicles for which data needs to be generated.
  int numberOfvehicle = Integer.parseInt(args[0]);
  // Get producer to push data into Kafka
  KafkaProducer<Integer, String> producer = configureKafka();
  // Get vehicle start point.
  Map<String, Location> vehicleStartPoint =
getVehicleStartPoints(numberOfvehicle);
```

```
    // Push data into Kafka
    pushVehicleStartPointToKafka(vehicleStartPoint, producer);
    producer.close();
  }

  private static KafkaProducer<Integer, String> configureKafka() {
    Properties properties = new Properties();
    properties.put("bootstrap.servers", BROKER_1_CONNECTION_STRING);
    properties.put("key.serializer", StringSerializer.class.getName());
    properties.put("value.serializer", StringSerializer.class.getName());
    properties.put("acks", "1");
    KafkaProducer<Integer, String> producer = new KafkaProducer<Integer,
String>(properties);
    return producer;
  }
  private static Map<String, Location> getVehicleStartPoints(int
numberOfvehicle) {
    Map<String, Location> vehicleStartPoint = new HashMap<String,
Location>();
    for (int i = 1; i <= numberOfvehicle; i++) {
      vehicleStartPoint.put("v" + i,
      new Location((r.nextDouble() * -180.0) + 90.0, (r.nextDouble() *
-360.0) + 180.0));
    }
    System.out.println(vehicleStartPoint);
    return vehicleStartPoint;
  }
  private static void pushVehicleStartPointToKafka(Map<String, Location>
vehicleStartPoint,
  KafkaProducer<Integer, String> producer) {
    ProducerRecord<Integer, String> data = null;
    try {
      data = new ProducerRecord<Integer, String>(KAFKA_TOPIC_STATIC_DATA,
      objectMapper.writeValueAsString(vehicleStartPoint));
      } catch (JsonProcessingException e) {
      e.printStackTrace();
    }
    producer.send(data);
  }
}
```

We need to build a real-time data simulator which generates vehicle data within a radius of the user specified value:

```java
package com.book.simulator;

import java.io.IOException;
import java.util.HashMap;
import java.util.Map;
import java.util.Properties;
import java.util.Random;

import org.apache.kafka.clients.producer.KafkaProducer;
import org.apache.kafka.clients.producer.ProducerRecord;
import org.apache.kafka.common.serialization.StringDeserializer;
import org.apache.kafka.common.serialization.StringSerializer;

import com.book.domain.Location;
import com.book.domain.VehicleSensor;
import com.fasterxml.jackson.core.JsonProcessingException;
import com.fasterxml.jackson.core.type.TypeReference;
import com.fasterxml.jackson.databind.ObjectMapper;

import kafka.consumer.Consumer;
import kafka.consumer.ConsumerConfig;
import kafka.consumer.ConsumerIterator;
import kafka.consumer.KafkaStream;
import kafka.javaapi.consumer.ConsumerConnector;

/**
 * This class is used to generate real-time vehicle data with updated
location
 * within distance in radius of user specified value. Messages are pushed
into Kafka topic.
 *
 * @author SGupta
 *
 */
public class VehicleDataGeneration {

    static private ObjectMapper objectMapper = new ObjectMapper();
    static private Random r = new Random();
    static private String BROKER_1_CONNECTION_STRING = "localhost:9092";
    static private String ZOOKEEPER_CONNECTION_STRING = "localhost:2181";
    static private String KAFKA_TOPIC_STATIC_DATA = "vehicle-static-data";
    static private String KAFKA_TOPIC_REAL_TIME_DATA = "vehicle-data";

    public static void main(String[] args) {
```

```
        if (args.length < 2) {
            System.out.println("Provide total number of records and
range of distance from start point");
            System.exit(1);
        }

        //Total number of records this simulator will generate
        int totalNumberOfRecords = Integer.parseInt(args[0]);
        //Distance in meters as Radius
        int distanceFromVehicleStartPoint = Integer.parseInt(args[1]);

        // Get Kafka producer
        KafkaProducer<Integer, String> producer = configureKafka();

        // Get Vehicle Start Points
        Map<String, Location> vehicleStartPoint = getVehicleStartPoints();
        // Generate data within distance and push to Kafka
        generateDataAndPushToKafka(producer, vehicleStartPoint.size(),
totalNumberOfRecords,
                distanceFromVehicleStartPoint, vehicleStartPoint);
        producer.close();
    }

    private static KafkaProducer<Integer, String> configureKafka() {
        Properties properties = new Properties();

        properties.put("bootstrap.servers", BROKER_1_CONNECTION_STRING);
        properties.put("key.serializer",
StringSerializer.class.getName());
        properties.put("value.serializer",
StringSerializer.class.getName());
        properties.put("acks", "1");

        KafkaProducer<Integer, String> producer = new
KafkaProducer<Integer, String>(properties);
        return producer;
    }

    private static void generateDataAndPushToKafka(KafkaProducer<Integer,
String> producer, int numberOfvehicle,
                int totalNumberOfRecords, int distanceFromVehicleStartPoint,
Map<String, Location> vehicleStartPoint) {
        for (int i = 0; i < totalNumberOfRecords; i++) {
            int vehicleNumber = r.nextInt(numberOfvehicle);
            String vehicleId = "v" + (vehicleNumber + 1);
            Location currentLocation = vehicleStartPoint.get(vehicleId);
            Location locationInLatLngRad =
getLocationInLatLngRad(distanceFromVehicleStartPoint, currentLocation);
```

```
                    System.out.println(
                              "Vehicle number is " + vehicleId + " and
location is " + locationInLatLngRad + " with distance of "
                                          +
(getDistanceFromLatLonInKm(currentLocation.getLatitude(),
currentLocation.getLongitude(),
locationInLatLngRad.getLatitude(), locationInLatLngRad.getLongitude()) *
1000));

                    VehicleSensor vehicleSensor = new VehicleSensor(vehicleId,
locationInLatLngRad.getLatitude(),
                              locationInLatLngRad.getLongitude(),
r.nextInt(100), System.currentTimeMillis());

                    ProducerRecord<Integer, String> data = null;
                    try {
                         data = new ProducerRecord<Integer,
String>(KAFKA_TOPIC_REAL_TIME_DATA,
objectMapper.writeValueAsString(vehicleSensor));
                    } catch (JsonProcessingException e) {
                         e.printStackTrace();
                    }

                    try {
                         Thread.sleep(1000);
                    } catch (InterruptedException e) {
                         e.printStackTrace();
                    }

                    producer.send(data);
               }
     }

     private static Map<String, Location> getVehicleStartPoints() {
          Map<String, Location> vehicleStartPoint = new HashMap<String,
Location>();
          Properties props = new Properties();
          props.put("zookeeper.connect", ZOOKEEPER_CONNECTION_STRING);
          props.put("group.id", "DataLoader" + r.nextInt(100));
          props.put("key.deserializer", StringDeserializer.class.getName());
          props.put("value.deserializer",
StringDeserializer.class.getName());

          ConsumerConnector consumer =
Consumer.createJavaConsumerConnector(new ConsumerConfig(props));

          Map<String, Integer> topicCountMap = new HashMap<String,
Integer>();
```

```
            topicCountMap.put(KAFKA_TOPIC_STATIC_DATA, new Integer(1));

            KafkaStream<byte[], byte[]> stream =
    consumer.createMessageStreams(topicCountMap).get(KAFKA_TOPIC_STATIC_DATA)
                        .get(0);

            ConsumerIterator<byte[], byte[]> it = stream.iterator();

            while (it.hasNext()) {
                String message = new String(it.next().message());
                try {
                    vehicleStartPoint = objectMapper.readValue(message,
    new TypeReference<Map<String, Location>>() {
                        });
                } catch (IOException e) {
                    e.printStackTrace();
                }
                break;
            }
            consumer.shutdown();
            return vehicleStartPoint;
    }

    public static double getDistanceFromLatLonInKm(double lat1, double lon1,
    double lat2, double lon2) {
            int R = 6371; // Radius of the earth in km
            double dLat = deg2rad(lat2 - lat1); // deg2rad below
            double dLon = deg2rad(lon2 - lon1);
            double a = Math.sin(dLat / 2) * Math.sin(dLat / 2)
                        + Math.cos(deg2rad(lat1)) * Math.cos(deg2rad(lat2)) *
    Math.sin(dLon / 2) * Math.sin(dLon / 2);
            double c = 2 * Math.atan2(Math.sqrt(a), Math.sqrt(1 - a));
            double d = R * c; // Distance in km
            return d;
    }

    private static double deg2rad(double deg) {
            return deg * (Math.PI / 180);
    }

    protected static Location getLocationInLatLngRad(double radiusInMeters,
    Location currentLocation) {
            double x0 = currentLocation.getLongitude();
            double y0 = currentLocation.getLatitude();

            Random random = new Random();

            // Convert radius from meters to degrees.
```

```
        double radiusInDegrees = radiusInMeters / 111320f;

        // Get a random distance and a random angle.
        double u = random.nextDouble();
        double v = random.nextDouble();
        double w = radiusInDegrees * Math.sqrt(u);
        double t = 2 * Math.PI * v;
        // Get the x and y delta values.
        double x = w * Math.cos(t);
        double y = w * Math.sin(t);

        // Compensate the x value.
        double new_x = x / Math.cos(Math.toRadians(y0));

        double foundLatitude;
        double foundLongitude;

        foundLatitude = y0 + y;
        foundLongitude = x0 + new_x;

        Location copy = new Location(currentLocation);
        copy.setLatitude(foundLatitude);
        copy.setLongitude(foundLongitude);
        return copy;
    }
}
```

Hazelcast loader

We need to add the static value of the vehicle along with the user's phone number into
Hazelcast so that, while processing the event, Storm will be able to calculate the distance
between the starting point of the vehicle and the current location:

```
package com.book.simulator;
import java.io.IOException;
import java.util.HashMap;
import java.util.Map;
import java.util.Properties;
import java.util.Random;
import org.apache.kafka.common.serialization.StringDeserializer;
import com.book.domain.Location;
import com.book.domain.VehicleAlertInfo;
import com.fasterxml.jackson.core.JsonParseException;
import com.fasterxml.jackson.core.type.TypeReference;
import com.fasterxml.jackson.databind.JsonMappingException;
import com.fasterxml.jackson.databind.ObjectMapper;
```

```java
import com.hazelcast.client.HazelcastClient;
import com.hazelcast.client.config.ClientConfig;
import com.hazelcast.core.HazelcastInstance;
import kafka.consumer.Consumer;
import kafka.consumer.ConsumerConfig;
import kafka.consumer.ConsumerIterator;
import kafka.consumer.KafkaStream;
import kafka.javaapi.consumer.ConsumerConnector;
/**
 * This class is used to load static information in to Hazelcast like 1. Map
1
 * contains information of vehicle and its owner. 2. Map 2 contains
information
 * of geo fencing range configured for each vehicle by user
 *
 * @author Sgupta
 *
 */
  public class HazelCastLoader {
    static private Random r = new Random();
    static private ObjectMapper objectMapper = new ObjectMapper();
    public static void main(String[] args) {
      if (args.length < 3) {
        System.out.println("Provide phonenumber, topic and threshold
distance for each vehicle");
        System.exit(1);
      }
    // Phone number on which user will get alert.
    String phoneNUmber = args[0];
    // Topic Name from which static data will be read and feed into
Hazelcast
    String topic = args[1];
  // Threshold distance in meters.
    int distanceFromVehicleStartPoint = Integer.parseInt(args[2]);
    // Get vehicle alert info map from Hazelcast
    Map<String, VehicleAlertInfo> vehicleAlertMap = getHCAlertInfoMap();
    // Get message from Kafka and push into Hazelcast
    getAndLoadHCMap(phoneNUmber, topic, distanceFromVehicleStartPoint,
vehicleAlertMap);
  }
  private static void getAndLoadHCMap(String phoneNUmber, String topic, int
distanceFromVehicleStartPoint,
  Map<String, VehicleAlertInfo> vehicleAlertMap) {
    Properties props = new Properties();
    props.put("zookeeper.connect", "localhost:2181");
    props.put("group.id", "myGroup"+r.nextInt(100));
    props.put("key.deserializer", StringDeserializer.class.getName());
    props.put("value.deserializer", StringDeserializer.class.getName());
```

```
          ConsumerConnector consumer = Consumer.createJavaConsumerConnector(new
    ConsumerConfig(props));
          Map<String, Integer> topicCountMap = new HashMap<String, Integer>();
          topicCountMap.put(topic, new Integer(1)); // number of consumer threads
          KafkaStream<byte[], byte[]> stream =
    consumer.createMessageStreams(topicCountMap).get(topic).get(0);
          ConsumerIterator<byte[], byte[]> it = stream.iterator();
          while(it.hasNext()) {
            try {
              String message = new String(it.next().message());
              System.out.println("Message: "+ message);
              Map<String, Location> readValue = objectMapper.readValue(message,
              new TypeReference<Map<String, Location>>() {
              });
              for (String vehicleId : readValue.keySet()) {
              VehicleAlertInfo vehicleAlertInfo = new VehicleAlertInfo();
              vehicleAlertInfo.setVehicleId(vehicleId);
    vehicleAlertInfo.setLatitude(readValue.get(vehicleId).getLatitude());
    vehicleAlertInfo.setLongitude(readValue.get(vehicleId).getLongitude());
              vehicleAlertInfo.setDistance(distanceFromVehicleStartPoint);
               vehicleAlertInfo.setPhoneNumber(phoneNUmber);
              vehicleAlertMap.put(vehicleId, vehicleAlertInfo);}
            } catch (JsonParseException e) {
              e.printStackTrace();
            } catch (JsonMappingException e) {
              e.printStackTrace();
            } catch (IOException e) {
              e.printStackTrace();\
            } catch (Exception e1) {
             e1.printStackTrace();
            }
          }
          consumer.shutdown();
      }
      private static Map<String, VehicleAlertInfo> getHCAlertInfoMap() {
        HazelcastInstance client = getHazelcastClient();
        Map<String, VehicleAlertInfo> vehicleAlertMap =
    client.getMap("vehicleAlertMap");
        vehicleAlertMap.clear();
        return vehicleAlertMap;
      }
      private static HazelcastInstance getHazelcastClient() {
        ClientConfig clientConfig = new ClientConfig();
        return HazelcastClient.newHazelcastClient(clientConfig);
      }
    }
```

Building Storm topology

We need a different unit of work to build a complete topology. As a starting point for the topology we need a spout, which is `KafkaSpout` in this case. We used the Storm-Kafka prebuild API available with Storm. After spout, following are the components required for this use case.

Parser bolt

This bolt is used to read messages from Kafka spout and complete it into Java POJO class.

```
package com.book.processing;
import java.io.IOException;
import java.util.Map;
import org.apache.storm.task.TopologyContext;
import org.apache.storm.topology.BasicOutputCollector;
import org.apache.storm.topology.OutputFieldsDeclarer;
import org.apache.storm.topology.base.BaseBasicBolt;
import org.apache.storm.tuple.Fields;
import org.apache.storm.tuple.Tuple;
import org.apache.storm.tuple.Values;
import com.book.domain.VehicleSensor;
import com.fasterxml.jackson.core.JsonParseException;
import com.fasterxml.jackson.databind.JsonMappingException;
import com.fasterxml.jackson.databind.ObjectMapper;
/**
* This bolt is used to parse Vehicle real-time data from Kafka and convert it
* into {@link VehicleSensor} POJO object
*
* @author SGupta
*
*/
public class ParseBolt extends BaseBasicBolt {
  private static final long serialVersionUID = -2557041273635037199L;
  ObjectMapper objectMapper;
  @Override
  public void prepare(Map stormConf, TopologyContext context) {
    objectMapper = new ObjectMapper();
  }
  @Override
  public void execute(Tuple input, BasicOutputCollector collector) {
    // Take default message from KafkaSpout
    String valueByField = input.getString(0);
    VehicleSensor vehicleSensor = null;
    try {
```

```
      //Covert JSON value into VehicleSensor object
      vehicleSensor = objectMapper.readValue(valueByField,
VehicleSensor.class);
    } catch (JsonParseException e) {
      e.printStackTrace();
    } catch (JsonMappingException e) {
      e.printStackTrace();
    } catch (IOException e) {
     e.printStackTrace();
    }
    // Emit tuple to next bolt with steamId as parsedstream\
    collector.emit("parsedstream", new Values(vehicleSensor));
  }
  @Override
  public void declareOutputFields(OutputFieldsDeclarer declarer) {
    // Declare Stream with streamId as parsedstream with fields
parsedstream
    declarer.declareStream("parsedstream", new Fields("parsedstream"));
  }
}
```

Check distance and alert bolt

This bolt checks the distance between the starting location of the vehicle read from
Hazelcast and the current location received from parser bolt. If the current distance is
greater than the threshold distance, then emit the tuple to the next bolt to process the alert:

```
package com.book.processing;
import java.util.Map;
import org.apache.storm.task.TopologyContext;
import org.apache.storm.topology.BasicOutputCollector;
import org.apache.storm.topology.OutputFieldsDeclarer;
import org.apache.storm.topology.base.BaseBasicBolt;
import org.apache.storm.tuple.Fields;
import org.apache.storm.tuple.Tuple;
import org.apache.storm.tuple.Values;
import com.book.domain.AlertEvent;
import com.book.domain.VehicleAlertInfo;
import com.book.domain.VehicleSensor;
import com.hazelcast.client.HazelcastClient;
import com.hazelcast.client.config.ClientConfig;
import com.hazelcast.core.HazelcastInstance;
/**
* This bolt is used to first check distance between start point of vehicle
and
* current location of vehicle. Only those tuples are emitted which are
related
```

```
 * to alerts.
 *
 * @author SGupta
 *
 */
public class CheckDistanceAndAlertBolt extends BaseBasicBolt {
  private static final long serialVersionUID = -8873075873347212209L;
  private Map<String, VehicleAlertInfo> vehicleAlertMap;
  private HazelcastInstance hazelcastClient;
  private String host;
  private String port;
  public CheckDistanceAndAlertBolt(String host, String port) {
    this.host = host;
    this.port = port;
  }
  @Override
  public void prepare(Map stormConf, TopologyContext context) {
    ClientConfig clientConfig = new ClientConfig();
    clientConfig.getNetworkConfig().addAddress(host + ":" + port);
    hazelcastClient = HazelcastClient.newHazelcastClient(clientConfig);
    vehicleAlertMap = hazelcastClient.getMap("vehicleAlertMap");
  }
  @Override
  public void execute(Tuple input, BasicOutputCollector collector) {
    // Read input with field name as parsedstream
    VehicleSensor vehicleSensor = (VehicleSensor)
input.getValueByField("parsedstream");
    String vehicleId = vehicleSensor.getVehicleId();
    // Get vehicle alert information from Hazelcast
    VehicleAlertInfo vehicleAlertInfo = vehicleAlertMap.get(vehicleId);
    // Get the distance between starting location and current location.
    double actualDistance =
getDistanceFromLatLonInKm(vehicleAlertInfo.getLatitude(),
    vehicleAlertInfo.getLongitude(), vehicleSensor.getLatitude(),
vehicleSensor.getLongitude()) * 1000;
    long thresholdDistance = vehicleAlertInfo.getDistance();
    // If current distance is more than threshold distance then emit tuple
    // to next bolt
    if (actualDistance > thresholdDistance) {
      AlertEvent alertEvent = new AlertEvent();
      alertEvent.setActualDistance(actualDistance);
      alertEvent.setThresholdDistance(thresholdDistance);
      alertEvent.setStartingLatitude(vehicleAlertInfo.getLatitude());
      alertEvent.setStartingLongitude(vehicleAlertInfo.getLongitude());
      alertEvent.setActualLatitude(vehicleSensor.getLatitude());
      alertEvent.setActualLongitude(vehicleSensor.getLongitude());
      alertEvent.setVehicleId(vehicleId);
      alertEvent.setTimeStamp(System.currentTimeMillis());
```

```
        alertEvent.setPhoneNumber(vehicleAlertInfo.getPhoneNumber());
        collector.emit("alertInfo", new Values(alertEvent));}
  }
  @Override
  public void declareOutputFields(OutputFieldsDeclarer declarer) {
     declarer.declareStream("alertInfo", new Fields("alertInfo"));
  }
  @Override
  public void cleanup() {
     hazelcastClient.shutdown();
  }
  public static double getDistanceFromLatLonInKm(double lat1, double lon1,
double lat2, double lon2) {
     int R = 6371; // Radius of the earth in km
     double dLat = deg2rad(lat2 - lat1); // deg2rad below
     double dLon = deg2rad(lon2 - lon1);
     double a = Math.sin(dLat / 2) * Math.sin(dLat / 2)
     + Math.cos(deg2rad(lat1)) * Math.cos(deg2rad(lat2)) * Math.sin(dLon /
2) * Math.sin(dLon / 2);
     double c = 2 * Math.atan2(Math.sqrt(a), Math.sqrt(1 - a));
     double d = R * c; // Distance in km
     return d;
  }
  private static double deg2rad(double deg) {
     return deg * (Math.PI / 180);
  }
}
```

Generate alert Bolt

This bolt is used to generate an alert in the form of an SMS using the **Twilio** application. Also, emit tuples so that it can be saved into Elasticsearch:

```
package com.book.processing;
import java.io.BufferedReader;
import java.io.InputStreamReader;
import java.math.BigDecimal;
import java.math.RoundingMode;
import java.util.Map;
import org.apache.storm.task.TopologyContext;
import org.apache.storm.topology.BasicOutputCollector;
import org.apache.storm.topology.OutputFieldsDeclarer;
import org.apache.storm.topology.base.BaseBasicBolt;
import org.apache.storm.tuple.Fields;
import org.apache.storm.tuple.Tuple;
import org.apache.storm.tuple.Values;
import com.book.domain.AlertEvent;
```

```java
import com.hazelcast.client.HazelcastClient;
import com.hazelcast.client.config.ClientConfig;
import com.hazelcast.core.HazelcastInstance;
/**
* This bolt is used to generate alert in form of SMS using Twilio
application.
* Also emit tuples so that it can be saved into Elasticsearch.
*
* @author SGupta
*
*/
public class GenerateAlertBolt extends BaseBasicBolt {
   private static final long serialVersionUID = -6802250427993673417L;
   private Map<String, AlertEvent> vehicleAlertMap;
   private HazelcastInstance hazelcastClient;
   private String host;
   private String port;
   public GenerateAlertBolt(String host, String port) {
      this.host = host;
      this.port = port;
   }
   @Override
   public void prepare(@SuppressWarnings("rawtypes") Map stormConf,
TopologyContext context) {
      ClientConfig clientConfig = new ClientConfig();
      clientConfig.getNetworkConfig().addAddress(host + ":" + port);
      hazelcastClient = HazelcastClient.newHazelcastClient(clientConfig);
      vehicleAlertMap = hazelcastClient.getMap("generatedAlerts");
   }
   public void execute(Tuple input, BasicOutputCollector collector) {
      // Get alert event from checkDistanceAndAlert bolt.
      AlertEvent alertEvent = (AlertEvent)
input.getValueByField("alertInfo");
      // Reading map containing alerts from Hazelcast
      AlertEvent previousAlertEvent =
vehicleAlertMap.get(alertEvent.getVehicleId());
      // Check whether alert is already generated for this vehicle or not.
      if (previousAlertEvent == null) {
         // Add entry in Hazelcast Map
         vehicleAlertMap.put(alertEvent.getVehicleId(), alertEvent);
         System.out.println(alertEvent.toString());
         String message = "ALERT!! Hi, your vehicle id " +
alertEvent.getVehicleId()
            + " is moving out of start location i.e. ("
            + BigDecimal.valueOf(alertEvent.getActualLatitude()).setScale(2,
RoundingMode.HALF_DOWN)
         .doubleValue()
         + ","
```

```
            + BigDecimal.valueOf(alertEvent.getActualLongitude()).setScale(2,
RoundingMode.HALF_DOWN)
          .doubleValue()
          + ") with distance " +
BigDecimal.valueOf(alertEvent.getActualDistance())
          .setScale(2, RoundingMode.HALF_DOWN).doubleValue();
      System.out.println(" GenerateAlertBOLT: >>>>> " + message);
      // Generate SMS.
      sendMessage(alertEvent.getPhoneNumber(), message);
      // Emit tuple for next bolt.
      collector.emit("generatedAlertInfo", new Values(alertEvent));
      } else {
        System.out.println(" GenerateAlertBOLT: >>>>> Alert is already
generated for " +
        alertEvent.getVehicleId());
      }
    }
  public void declareOutputFields(OutputFieldsDeclarer declarer) {
    declarer.declareStream("generatedAlertInfo", new
Fields("generatedAlertInfo"));
  }
  public void sendMessage(String phoneNumber, String message) {
    String s;
    Process p;
    try {
      String[] sendCommand = { "python", "yowsup-cli", "demos", "-c",
      "whatsapp_config.txt", "-s", phoneNumber, message };
      p = Runtime.getRuntime().exec(sendCommand);
      BufferedReader br = new BufferedReader(new
InputStreamReader(p.getInputStream()));
      while ((s = br.readLine()) != null)
      System.out.println("line: " + s);
      BufferedReader errBr = new BufferedReader(new
InputStreamReader(p.getErrorStream()));
      while ((s = errBr.readLine()) != null)
      System.out.println("line: " + s);
      p.waitFor();
      System.out.println("exit: " + p.exitValue());
      p.destroy();
    } catch (Exception e) {
      }
  }
}
```

Elasticsearch Bolt

This bolt is a persistence bolt. real-time sensor data or generated alerts are persisted into Elasticsearch for further analysis in Kibana:

```
package com.book.processing;
import java.net.InetSocketAddress;
import java.util.Date;
import java.util.HashMap;
import java.util.Map;
import org.apache.storm.task.TopologyContext;
import org.apache.storm.topology.BasicOutputCollector;
import org.apache.storm.topology.OutputFieldsDeclarer;
import org.apache.storm.topology.base.BaseBasicBolt;
import org.apache.storm.tuple.Tuple;
import org.elasticsearch.action.index.IndexResponse;
import org.elasticsearch.client.Client;
import org.elasticsearch.common.settings.Settings;
import org.elasticsearch.common.transport.InetSocketTransportAddress;
import org.elasticsearch.transport.client.PreBuiltTransportClient;
import com.book.domain.AlertEvent;
import com.book.domain.VehicleSensor;
import com.fasterxml.jackson.databind.ObjectMapper;
/**
 * This bolt is used to create index in Elasticsearch.
 *
 * @author SGupta
 *
 */
public class ElasticSearchBolt extends BaseBasicBolt {
  private static final long serialVersionUID = -9123903091990273369L;
  Client client;
  PreBuiltTransportClient preBuiltTransportClient;
  ObjectMapper mapper;String index;
  String type;
  String clusterName;
  String applicationName;
  String host;
  int port;
  public ElasticSearchBolt(String index, String type, String clusterName,
String applicationName, String host,
    int port) {
    this.index = index;
    this.type = type;
    this.clusterName = clusterName;
    this.applicationName = applicationName;
    this.host = host;
    this.port = port;
```

```
  }
  @Override
  public void prepare(@SuppressWarnings("rawtypes") Map stormConf,
TopologyContext context) {
    mapper = new ObjectMapper();
    Settings settings = Settings.builder().put("cluster.name", "my-
application").build();
    preBuiltTransportClient = new PreBuiltTransportClient(settings);
    client = preBuiltTransportClient
    .addTransportAddress(new InetSocketTransportAddress(new
InetSocketAddress("localhost", 9300)));
  }
  @Override
  public void cleanup() {
    preBuiltTransportClient.close();
    client.close();
  }
  public void declareOutputFields(OutputFieldsDeclarer declarer) {
  // No further processing is required so no emit from this bolt.
  }
  public void execute(Tuple input, BasicOutputCollector collector) {
    Map<String, Object> value = null;
    // Check type and based on it processing the value
    if (type.equalsIgnoreCase("tdr")) {
      VehicleSensor vehicleSensor = (VehicleSensor)
input.getValueByField("parsedstream");
      // Converting POJO object into Map
      value = convertVehicleSensortoMap(vehicleSensor);
    } else if (type.equalsIgnoreCase("alert")) {
    AlertEvent alertEvent = (AlertEvent)
input.getValueByField("generatedAlertInfo");
    //Converting POJO object into Map
    value = convertVehicleAlerttoMap(alertEvent);
  }
  // Inserting into Elasticsearch
  IndexResponse response = client.prepareIndex(index,
type).setSource(value).get();
  System.out.println(response.status());
  }
  public Map<String, Object> convertVehicleSensortoMap(VehicleSensor
vehicleSensor) {
    System.out.println("Orignal value " + vehicleSensor);
    Map<String, Object> convertedValue = new HashMap<String, Object>();
    Map<String, Object> coords = new HashMap<>();
    convertedValue.put("vehicle_id", vehicleSensor.getVehicleId());
    coords.put("lat", vehicleSensor.getLatitude());
    coords.put("lon", vehicleSensor.getLongitude());
    convertedValue.put("coords", coords);
```

```
        convertedValue.put("speed", vehicleSensor.getSpeed());
        convertedValue.put("timestamp", new
Date(vehicleSensor.getTimeStamp()));
        System.out.println("Converted value " + convertedValue);
        return convertedValue;]
    }
    public Map<String, Object> convertVehicleAlerttoMap(AlertEvent
alertEvent) {
        System.out.println("Orignal value " + alertEvent);
        Map<String, Object> convertedValue = new HashMap<String, Object>();
        Map<String, Object> expected_coords = new HashMap<>();
        Map<String, Object> actual_coords = new HashMap<>();
        convertedValue.put("vehicle_id", alertEvent.getVehicleId());
        expected_coords.put("lat", alertEvent.getStartingLatitude());
        expected_coords.put("lon", alertEvent.getStartingLongitude());
        convertedValue.put("expected_coords", expected_coords);
        actual_coords.put("lat", alertEvent.getActualLatitude());
        actual_coords.put("lon", alertEvent.getActualLongitude());
        convertedValue.put("actual_coords", actual_coords);
        convertedValue.put("expected_distance",
alertEvent.getThresholdDistance());
        convertedValue.put("actual_distance", alertEvent.getActualDistance());
        convertedValue.put("timestamp", new Date(alertEvent.getTimeStamp()));
        System.out.println("Converted value " + convertedValue);
        return convertedValue;
    }
}
```

Complete Topology

Topology contains the binding of all bolts with spout:

```
package com.book.processing;
import java.util.UUID;
import org.apache.storm.Config;
import org.apache.storm.LocalCluster;
import org.apache.storm.StormSubmitter;
import org.apache.storm.generated.AlreadyAliveException;
import org.apache.storm.generated.AuthorizationException;
import org.apache.storm.generated.InvalidTopologyException;
import org.apache.storm.kafka.BrokerHosts;
import org.apache.storm.kafka.KafkaSpout;
import org.apache.storm.kafka.SpoutConfig;import
org.apache.storm.kafka.StringScheme;
import org.apache.storm.kafka.ZkHosts;
import org.apache.storm.spout.SchemeAsMultiScheme;
import org.apache.storm.topology.TopologyBuilder;
```

```
/**
* This is complete topology to bind spout and all bolts.
*
* @author SGupta
*
*/
public class GeoFencingProcessorTopology {
  public static void main(String[] args) {
    if(args.length <1){
      System.out.println("Please mention deployment mode either local or
cluster");
      System.exit(1);
    }
    String deploymentMode = args[0];
    Config config = new Config();
    config.setNumWorkers(3);
    TopologyBuilder topologyBuilder = new TopologyBuilder();
    String zkConnString = "localhost:2181";
    String topicName = "vehicle-data";
    String hcHostName = "localhost";
    String hcPort = "5701";
    String esClusterName = "cluster.name";
    String esApplicationName = "my-application";
    String esHostName = "localhost";
    int esPort = 9300;
    BrokerHosts hosts = new ZkHosts(zkConnString);
    SpoutConfig spoutConfig = new SpoutConfig(hosts, topicName , "/" +
topicName, UUID.randomUUID().toString());
    spoutConfig.scheme = new SchemeAsMultiScheme(new StringScheme());
    KafkaSpout kafkaSpout = new KafkaSpout(spoutConfig);
    topologyBuilder.setSpout("spout", kafkaSpout, 1);
    topologyBuilder.setBolt("parser", new ParseBolt(),
1).shuffleGrouping("spout");
    topologyBuilder.setBolt("checkAndAlert", new
CheckDistanceAndAlertBolt(hcHostName, hcPort),
    1).shuffleGrouping("parser","parsedstream");
    topologyBuilder.setBolt("saveTDR", new ElasticSearchBolt("vehicle-tdr",
"tdr",esClusterName,
    esApplicationName,esHostName,
esPort),1).shuffleGrouping("parser","parsedstream");
    topologyBuilder.setBolt("generateAlert", new
GenerateAlertBolt(hcHostName, hcPort),
    1).shuffleGrouping("checkAndAlert", "alertInfo");
    topologyBuilder.setBolt("saveAlert", new ElasticSearchBolt("vehicle-
alert", "alert",esClusterName,
    esApplicationName,esHostName, esPort),
1).shuffleGrouping("generateAlert", "generatedAlertInfo");
    LocalCluster cluster = new LocalCluster();
```

```
    if (deploymentMode.equalsIgnoreCase("local")) {
        System.out.println("Submitting topology on local");
        cluster.submitTopology(topicName, config,
topologyBuilder.createTopology());
    } else {
        try {
            System.out.println("Submitting topology on cluster");
            StormSubmitter.submitTopology(topicName, config,
topologyBuilder.createTopology());
        } catch (AlreadyAliveException | InvalidTopologyException |
AuthorizationException e) {
            e.printStackTrace();
        }
    }
  }
}
```

Running the case study

Before running the code, let's build it using the following command:

```
mvn clean install
```

This will create a JAR file with the name as `chapter13-0.0.1-SNAPSHOT-jar-with-dependencies.jar` in `chapter13/target` directory.

Load Hazelcast

Execute the following command to load static values into Hazelcast:

```
java -cp target/chapter12-0.0.1-SNAPSHOT-jar-with-dependencies.jar
com.book.simulator.HazelCastLoader <phone_number> vehicle-static-data 10000
```

The output will be as the following screenshot. Wait for the next step to be executed as the program reads only the latest entries from the Kafka topic:

```
Aug 28, 2017 10:22:11 AM com.hazelcast.core.LifecycleService
INFO: hz.client_0 [dev] [3.8] HazelcastClient 3.8 (20170217 - d7998b4) is STARTING
Aug 28, 2017 10:22:11 AM com.hazelcast.core.LifecycleService
INFO: hz.client_0 [dev] [3.8] HazelcastClient 3.8 (20170217 - d7998b4) is STARTED
Aug 28, 2017 10:22:11 AM com.hazelcast.client.spi.impl.ClusterListenerSupport
INFO: hz.client_0 [dev] [3.8] Trying to connect to [127.0.0.1]:5702 as owner member
Aug 28, 2017 10:22:11 AM com.hazelcast.client.spi.impl.ClusterListenerSupport
INFO: hz.client_0 [dev] [3.8] Trying to connect to [127.0.0.1]:5703 as owner member
Aug 28, 2017 10:22:11 AM com.hazelcast.client.spi.impl.ClusterListenerSupport
INFO: hz.client_0 [dev] [3.8] Trying to connect to [127.0.0.1]:5701 as owner member
Aug 28, 2017 10:22:11 AM com.hazelcast.client.connection.ClientConnectionManager
INFO: hz.client_0 [dev] [3.8] Setting ClientConnection{alive=true, connectionId=1, socketChannel=DefaultSocketChannelWrapper{socketChannel=java.
nio.channels.SocketChannel[connected local=/127.0.0.1:46344 remote=/127.0.0.1:5701]}, remoteEndpoint=[           ]:5701, lastReadTime=2017-08-28
 10:22:11.730, lastWriteTime=2017-08-28 10:22:11.637, closedTime=never, lastHeartbeatRequested=never, lastHeartbeatReceived=never, connected ser
ver version=3.8} as owner  with principal ClientPrincipal{uuid='09fdc53c-78f3-43e1-97f2-bacdb27fb83e', ownerUuid='33d4bd78-3972-48e9-b4bb-4c1367
c1ad42'}
Aug 28, 2017 10:22:11 AM com.hazelcast.client.connection.ClientConnectionManager
INFO: hz.client_0 [dev] [3.8] Authenticated with server [           ]:5701, server version:3.8 Local address: /127.0.0.1:46344
Aug 28, 2017 10:22:11 AM com.hazelcast.client.spi.impl.ClientMembershipListener
INFO: hz.client_0 [dev] [3.8]

Members [1] {
        Member [           ]:5701 - 33d4bd78-3972-48e9-b4bb-4c1367c1ad42
}

Aug 28, 2017 10:22:11 AM com.hazelcast.core.LifecycleService
INFO: hz.client_0 [dev] [3.8] HazelcastClient 3.8 (20170217 - d7998b4) is CLIENT_CONNECTED
log4j:WARN No appenders could be found for logger (kafka.utils.VerifiableProperties).
log4j:WARN Please initialize the log4j system properly.
Message: {"v90":{"latitude":-76.91581286438987,"longitude":-172.79525570657302},"v92":{"latitude":-23.28653879793636,"longitude":-107.9764994612
5799},"v91":{"latitude":77.07205793229375,"longitude":85.37973753112556},"v94":{"latitude":24.709464276216437,"longitude":101.24511566642433},"v
93":{"latitude":-44.131840621340785,"longitude":72.93272965215431},"v96":{"latitude":-17.80104847284892,"longitude":-163.93501881051913},"v95":
"latitude":47.16475087490206,"longitude":-155.37744902489345},"v10":{"latitude":12.715023937026473,"longitude":-65.21205163917398},"v98":{"lati
ude":0.19835909750455616,"longitude":-93.78479206636905},"v97":{"latitude":5.874924999977111,"longitude":101.6634669483074},"v12":{"latitude":-
```

Hazelcast UI will display one map: `vehicleAlertInfo`, as shown in the following screenshot:

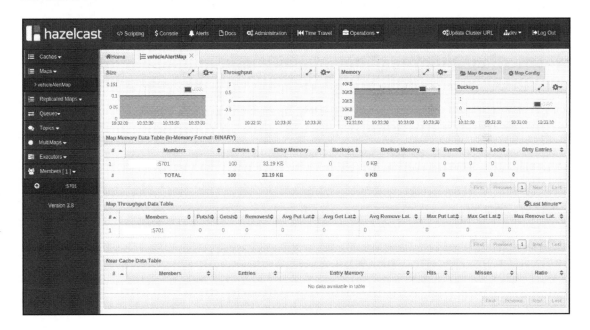

Generate Vehicle static value

Execute the following command to generate vehicle static values which contains the vehicle and its starting location as latitude and longitude. It pushes into Kafka:

```
java -cp target/chapter12-0.0.1-SNAPSHOT-jar-with-dependencies.jar
com.book.simulator.VehicleStartPointGenerator 100
```

The output will be as the following screenshot:

Deploy topology

Execute the following command to deploy the topology on Storm:

```
/bin/storm jar chapter12-0.0.1-SNAPSHOT-jar-with-dependencies.jar
com.book.processing.GeoFencingProcessorTopology cluster
```

Once the topology is deployed, Storm UI starts showing the **Topology summary**, as displayed in the following screenshot:

Topology Summary

Search:

Name	Owner	Status	Uptime	Num workers	Num executors	Num tasks	Replication count	Assigned Mem (MB)	Scheduler Info
vehicle-data		ACTIVE	53s	3	9	9	1	2496	

Showing 1 to 1 of 1 entries

When you click on the topology name then details of the spout and bolts are shown along with other details, as shown in the following screenshot:

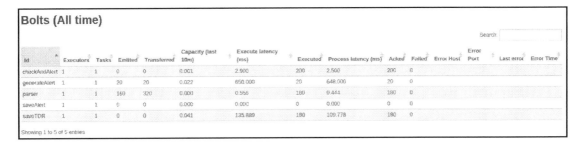

You can visualize the complete topology in DAG form, by clicking on the **visualization** button, as shown in the following screenshot:

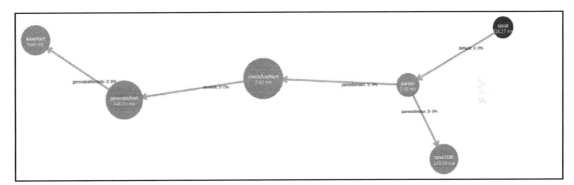

Start simulator

Finally, we are done with all the set ups and starting them. Now, by executing the following command, messages will start pushing in the Kafka topic `vehicle-data`:

```
java -cp chapter12-0.0.1-SNAPSHOT-jar-with-dependencies.jar
com.book.simulator.VehicleDataGeneration 10000 10000
```

Sample output is as shown in the following screenshot:

```
Vehicle number is v49 and location is Location [latitude=-7.6698612125606305, longitude=-138.54867104671214] with distance of 9849.950429749624
Vehicle number is v82 and location is Location [latitude=31.900635029381203, longitude=162.31161428761396] with distance of 8474.416541049288
Vehicle number is v85 and location is Location [latitude=38.844019413615125, longitude=-145.19956111097568] with distance of 6294.098258447987
Vehicle number is v47 and location is Location [latitude=-5.821601351897914, longitude=19.250734584110756] with distance of 2888.6768884874405
Vehicle number is v74 and location is Location [latitude=-36.92991384395876, longitude=70.75061178262486] with distance of 2780.9056322562074
Vehicle number is v48 and location is Location [latitude=-59.27509524726495, longitude=-45.47201540057545] with distance of 4045.9218649679897
Vehicle number is v92 and location is Location [latitude=31.73486140660741, longitude=-32.842234152757335] with distance of 8638.489914409496
Vehicle number is v46 and location is Location [latitude=78.52030520115879, longitude=-136.06803487522743] with distance of 4893.841703322136
Vehicle number is v63 and location is Location [latitude=-21.71852360954859, longitude=-1.188225293344341] with distance of 5905.072235359277
Vehicle number is v22 and location is Location [latitude=-25.353264481461704, longitude=156.01621452583572] with distance of 4830.399442856724
Vehicle number is v99 and location is Location [latitude=45.520452620116856, longitude=84.49384273492409] with distance of 7910.100321410494
```

Visualization using Kibana

Build a dashboard with different visualizations available. First you have to add the indexes by clicking on **Management** and then index patterns. Add `vehicle-alert` and `vehicle-tdr` as indexes in Kibana for visualization. Once you click on **Visualize** the available options are displayed, as shown in the following screenshot:

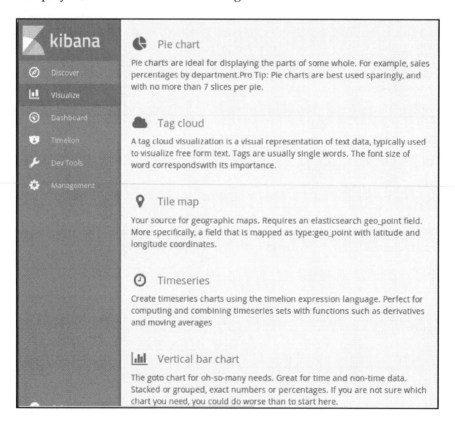

When you select any type of visualization then Kibana asks you to select the index name first, as shown in the following screenshot:

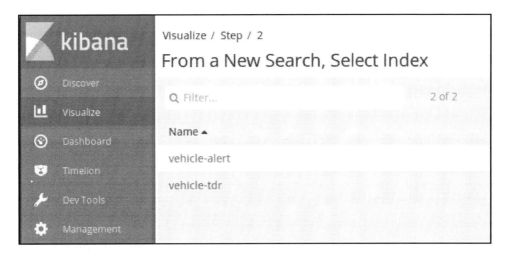

Now, add visualizations as per your need. A few of the examples:

- **Tile Map**: By selecting the following options for `vehicle-alert` index, Geo points start showing on the map as shown in the following screenshot (As data points are random so they can be anywhere on the map):

- **Vertical Bar Chart**: This chart shows vertical bars of any selected aggregation versus selected *x*-axis value, as shown in the following screenshot:

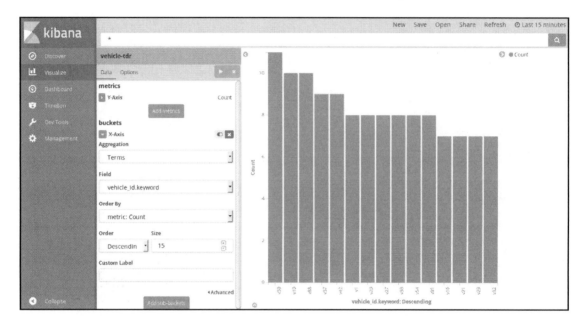

- **Data Table**: Get the actual values and perform an aggregation operation. Configure your visualization as seen in the preceeding figures to use it. Figure 18 shows the total number of events for each vehicle and another one is the top 10 vehicles for alerts.

Now, you must build your dashboard by adding all the visualizations previously configured by selecting the add option. After adding all visualizations, the dashboard looks like the following screenshots:

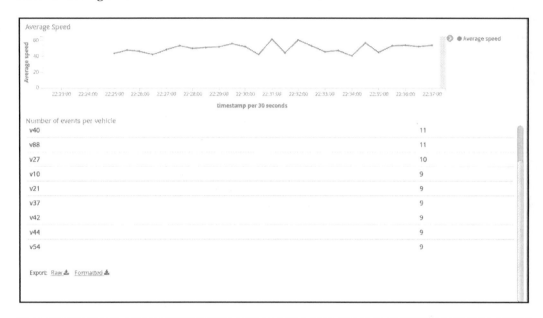

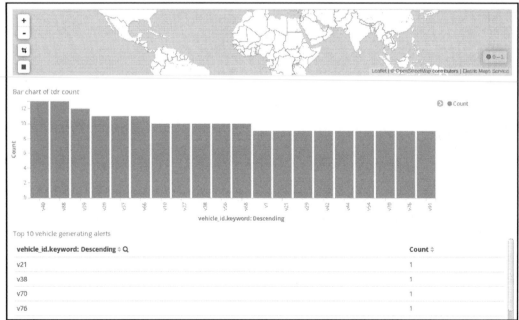

The following is a screenshot of messages received on mobile WhatsApp:

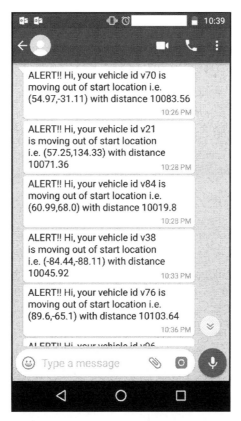

Summary

In this chapter, we discussed the case study; we selected a GeoFencing use case as a case study and explained the different use cases around GeoFencing. We explained the data model used in use case implementation: input data set, output data set, and elastic search indexes. We explained different types of tools used for implementing the use case. We had a detailed discussion on how to set up a complete environment with the different tools available and we completed implementation of the case study along with code.

In the end, we looked at how to run the use case and visualize it.

Index

joins 194

K

Kafka
  connecting, to Spark Streaming 253
  download link 52
Kappa architecture 258
key aspects, for evaluating NRT tools
  capacity 40
  management 40
  performance 40
  scalability 41
  total cost of ownership (TCO) 41
Keyspace 145

L

Lambda architecture
  analytics possibilities 20, 21
local mode
  job, running on 87
Logstash
  about 43, 59
  download link 59
  features 43
  reference 43
logviewer service 74

M

map function
  characteristics 182
MapR 93
Master Batch Coordinator (MBC) 181
merge operation 194
Messaging Queue Telemetry Transport (MQTT) 25
methods, bolt
  execute 76
  prepare 76
methods, Spout
  Ack 76
  Fail 76
  nextTuple 76
  Open 76
MinimalWordCount example 108, 109, 110, 111

N

narrow transformations
  versus wide transformations 226
near real-time (NRT) processing 40
near realspan class= 15, 16, 17, 18, 19
NiFi Version 1.1.1
  download link 52
Nimbus node 73
NRT event partitioned processing 40
NRT system
  about 31
  building blocks 32, 33
  high-level system view 38
  technology view 40

O

opaque transactional spout 177
org.apache.spark package 221
org.apache.spark.broadcast package
  about 222
  HttpBroadcast 222
  TorrentBroadcast 222
org.apache.spark.io package 222
org.apache.spark.rdd.RDD.scala package
  about 221
  DoubleRDDFunctions 221
  PairRDDFunctions 221
  SequenceFileRDDFunctions 221
org.apache.spark.scheduler package 222
org.apache.spark.SparkContext package 221
org.apache.spark.storage package 223
org.apache.spark.util package 223
output operations, DStreams
  foreachRDD(func) 253
  print() 252
  saveAsHadoopFiles(prefix, suffix) 252
  saveAsObjectFiles(prefix, suffix) 252
  saveAsTextFiles(prefix, suffix) 252

P

partition aggregate 189
pattern API
  example 280
peek operation 183